AF522100

LIBRARY AND MULTIMEDIA RESOURCES

LIBRARY AND MULTIMEDIA RESOURCES

By

Dr. Pankaj Kumar Singh

Librarian & H.O.D.

Dept. of Library & Information Science

D.S.N. (P.G.) College

Unnao - 209 801 (U.P.)

(India)

DISCOVERY PUBLISHING HOUSE PVT. LTD.

NEW DELHI-110 002

Published by:
Tilak Wasan
DISCOVERY PUBLISHING HOUSE PVT. LTD.
4383/4B, Ansari Road, Darya Ganj
New Delhi-110 002 (India)
Phone : +91-11-23279245, 43596064-65
Fax : +91-11-23253475
E-mail : discoverypublishinghouse@gmail.com
sales@discoverypublishinggroup.com
parul.wasan@gmail.com
web : www.discoverypublishinggroup.com

Reprinted: **2019**
First Edition: **2014**

ISBN: 978-93-5056-426-4

Library and Multimedia Resources

Printed at:
Dynamic Printers
Delhi

Preface

The fame of the World Wide Web and the hard to believe rapid growth of the web technology could not be anticipated a decade ago. Web is an internationally hyperlinked electronic environment on which a lot of newest information is available in almost all subject areas. Keeping this in mind, a comprehensive information search was conducted on Internet to amass a list-of different web sites providing information on the use of multimedia systems for library applications. With multimedia, learning can happen anytime, anywhere. Students can listen to a pod cast or view a vodcast at home, in the car or on a field trip. These tools are great ways to reinforce concepts and enable students to learn in context. Multimedia resources can help you meet the needs of many different types of learners Visual learners can watch an online video, while auditory learners listen to streaming audio and hands-on learners play an interactive game. Students who need extra practice can use these tools again and again. Libraries, articles, blogs, social networking sites and wikis allow students to interact with and teach each other, not only within their own school, but with learners across the country and the world as well.

— ***Author***

Contents

1

Educating the Net Generation

INTRODUCTION

The remarkable visitors logged on library illustrate how much a library can become part of campus life if it is designed with genuine understanding of the needs of Net Generation students. This understanding relates not just to the physical facility of the library but to all of the things that a library encompasses: content, access, enduring collections, and services. Libraries have been adjusting their collections, services, and environments to the digital world for at least 20 years. Even prior to ubiquitous use of the Internet, libraries were using technology for access to scholarly databases, for circulation systems, and for online catalogs.

With the explosion of Internet technology, libraries incorporated a wide array of digital content resources into their offerings; updated the network, wiring, and wireless infrastructures of their buildings; and designed new virtual and in-person services. However, technology has resulted in more modernisation than transformation. There is an apparent disconnect between the culture of library organisations and that of Net Gen students. This chapter will explore how libraries might better adapt to the needs of Net Gen students in a number of specific areas. Libraries and digital information resources can play a critical role in the education of today's students. Libraries license access to electronic journals, which provide key readings in many courses, and set up electronic reserve systems to facilitate easy use of materials. Libraries are an important resource for assignments that encourage students to go beyond the course syllabus. They provide access to the marketplace of ideas that is a hallmark of American higher education. Since, much of the learning in higher education institutions takes place outside the classroom, libraries can be one important venue for such learning.

The library can play a critical role in learning directly related to courses and processes related to lifelong learning, such as gathering information on political candidates in order to make informed choices in an upcoming election. Libraries provide collections, organised information, systems that promote access, and in-person and virtual assistance to encourage students to pursue their education beyond the classroom. It is difficult to generalise, but this chapter will use some characteristics of the Net Gen student that have been described by a number of researchers. Given that this generation of college students has grown up with computers and video games, the students have become accustomed to multimedia environments: figuring things out for themselves without consulting manuals; working in groups; and multi tasking.

These qualities differ from those found in traditional library environments, which, by and large, are text-based, require learning the system from experts (librarians), were constructed for individual use, and assume that work progresses in a logical, linear fashion. What are some of the major disconnects between many of today's academic libraries and Net Gen students? The most common one is students' dependence on Google or similar search engines for discovery of information resources rather than consultation of library Web pages, catalogs, and databases as the main source of access. Since, students often find library-sponsored resources difficult to figure out on their own, and they are seldom exposed to or interested in formal instruction in information literacy, they prefer to use the simplistic but responsive Google. Another disconnect is that digital library resources often reside outside the environment that is frequently the digital home of students' coursework, namely, the course management system, or CMS. Library services are often presented in the library organisation context rather than in a user-centered mode. Libraries emphasise access to information but generally do not have facilities, software, or support for student creation of new information products. All of these disconnects can be remedied if appropriate attention is paid to the style of Net Gen students.

ACCESS TO AND USE OF INFORMATION RESOURCES

When students use a wide array of information resources that they seek out on their own, they can enrich their learning through exploration of topics of interest. However, with the vast resources of the Web available, students must first make choices about how to access information and then which information resources to use in their explorations and assignments. Increasingly, students use Web search engines such as Google to locate information resources rather than seek out library online catalogs or databases of scholarly journal articles. Many faculty express concern that students do not know how to adequately evaluate the quality of information resources found on the Web, and librarians share this concern.

Libraries need to find ways to make their information access systems more approachable by students, integrate guides to quality resources into course pages, and find ways to increase their presence in general Web search engines. Newly emerging services such as Google Scholar are providing access to more library resources in the general Internet environment. Libraries also need to be more cognizant of Net Gen students' reliance on visual cues in using the Internet and build Web pages that are more visually oriented.

THE LIBRARY VERSUS THE WEB

Net Gen students clearly perceive the open space of the World Wide Web as their information universe. This is in opposition to the worldview of librarians and many faculty, who perceive the library as the locus of information relevant to academic work. Students usually approach their research without regard to the library's structure or the way that the library segments different resources into different areas of its Web site. Library Web sites often reflect an organisational view of the library (for example, how to access the reference department or online catalog); they do not do a particularly good job of aggregating content on a particular subject area. Students usually prefer the global searching of Google to more sophisticated but more time-consuming searching provided by the library, where students must make separate searches of the online catalog and every database of potential interest, after first identifying which databases might be relevant.

In addition, not all searches of library catalogs or databases yield full-text materials, and Net Gen students want not just speedy answers, but full gratification of their information requests on the spot, if possible. Recent surveys exploring college student use of the Web versus the library confirm the commonly held perception of faculty and librarians that students' pri-mary sources of information for coursework are resources found on the Web and that most students use a search engine such as Google as their first point of entry to information rather than searching the library Web site or catalog. Several campus studies also examined where students gather information for a paper or an assignment. One study at Colorado State University yielded information that 58 per cent of freshmen used Google or a comparable search engine first, while only 23 per cent started with a database or index.

The world of information is large and complex. There are no easy answers to providing simplified searching to the wealth of electronic information resources produced by a wide range of publishers using different structures and vocabu-laries. Students may perceive that librarians have developed systems that are complex and make sense to information professionals but are too difficult to use without being an expert. However, as new generations of information products are developed, producers and system developers should try to address the information seeking habits of Net Gen students. Libraries and the global service provider OCLC are working with Google so that information from peer-reviewed journals, books, theses, and other academic resources can be accessed through the Google Scholar search service. This is a step in the right direction, taking library resources to where students want to find them.

Libraries also need to integrate more multimedia resources into their searchable content; this type of digital content is becoming increasingly important to Net Gen students, who may wish to study an audio recording of political speeches and incorporate segments into a term project as well as access books and journals on the topic. However, libraries typically incorporate information objects into their catalogs only when those resources are owned or licensed by the library. Is this still a relevant strategy in a world of global access to information via the Internet?

LOCATING QUALITY DIGITAL INFORMATION

Providing mechanisms for information seekers from academe to locate quality information resources in a particular subject area is also a challenge for libraries—a very important one. Many academic libraries provide "library guides" or pathfinders to quality information resources, available through the library Web site, but typically they are not heavily used. A limited number of subject disciplines have developed coordinated Web guides to information resources; a notable example is AgNIC, serving the field of agriculture.

Some libraries are developing mechanisms to link subject pathfinders into course management systems for every course at the institution. This useful strategy brings the information to the place where students will be actively engaged in academic work. Librarians at the University of Rochester looked for new ways to bring quality subject resources to the attention of students.

They recognised that "undergraduate students' mental model is one focused on courses and coursework, rather than disciplines." Therefore, they developed a mechanism to incorporate pathfinders into every course at the institution using the course management system. Both students and faculty believe that the library is doing a poor job with helping them discern which Web resources are suitable for academic work. Libraries are addressing this concern by developing portals to catalogs, licensed databases, and Web sites that would meet the kinds of criteria used in building academic library collections and by working with such projects as Google Scholar.

INCORPORATING VISUAL CUES

Designing Web pages that are responsive to Net Gen students' style would also help guide students to appropriate content or help them when they have problems with searches. A study of high school students' Web searching revealed that students relied heavily on information displayed in graphic form on Web pages and often relied on graphics and visual cues to interpret the relevance of such pages.

Libraries and information service providers generally do not design their resources with such criteria in mind. Incorporating students on design teams and giving them the go-ahead to re-envision the way the library displays its resources would be a useful method of developing information that resonates better with Net Gen students.

To summarise, Net Gen access services will:

* Continue to integrate library information into Google or other popular access mechanisms
* Offer simplified and graphic ways for students to approach subject searches
* Integrate subject guides or pathfinders into CMS or other locations conducive to use
* Integrate searching of "open" Web resources and materials owned or licensed by the library

LIBRARY AND INFORMATION SERVICES

Librarians often take great pride in the personalised information services they offer to their constituencies and the classes they teach to incorporate information literacy into the academic curriculum. While many of today's Net Gen students have grown up with technology, they do not necessarily have the requisite knowledge or skills to use technology and digital information in ways appropriate to the academy. Librarians should persist in their efforts to find ways to help students learn about digital information, including important policy issues in this arena, such as privacy and intellectual property. They should consider updating some of their methods for teaching students, incorporating gaming technology, or developing more visually oriented instruction aids, for example. One-on-one services offered electronically should be tailored to students' characteristics, such as their propensity to work late hours and use a variety of technologies, including laptops and cell phones.

FLUENCY WITH TECHNOLOGY AND INFORMATION LITERACY

Are Net Gen students already so technology literate and information savvy that they have no need for instruction or personal assistance in using technology and library and information resources? We know that Net Gen students come to campus having played hours of video games, having spent much of their spare time surfing the Net and instant messaging their friends, and having used multiple electronic devices simultaneously. On the other hand, we hear complaints from faculty that students use inappropriate sources from the Web to support their ideas in term papers instead of peer-reviewed academic resources; that they submit multimedia projects that are superficial and full of glitz, not substance —and that they no longer read, period.

When students graduate, their faculty in graduate degree programmes and their employers expect that they will have a facility with technology and with digital information that the older generations do not have. New office recruits are often hired because of their Internet skill and are given projects that exploit their technology and information skills, developed during their college years.

In addition, today's college graduates live in a world where it is important to understand key information policy issues. Intellectual property, privacy, and First Amendment issues are fundamental to operating as an informed citisen in today's information society and directly affect the work of individuals who create, as well as use, networked information. While Net Gen students generally can multitask, learn systems without consulting manuals, and surf the Web, they lack technology and information skills appropriate for academic work. Higher education institutions do not integrate or package technology and digital information skills instruction into the mainstream curriculum.

A National Academies report described a model set of skills for "fluency in information technology," which incorporates both information technology and literacy skills. The report's authors divided skills into three categories: foundational concepts, contemporary skills, and intellectual capabilities. They recommended that each university's subject area curriculum develop ways to incorporate instruction in these topics; however, they lamented that this is not currently the case.

The Association of College and Research Libraries (ACRL), a division of the American Library Association, has also developed guidelines for information literacy, but they have not been widely implemented by universities. Technology and information literacy are generally perceived to be "library" or "IT" problems, not overall curricular issues.

At Southwestern University, a team of IT professionals, librarians, and faculty developed a student survey based on both the National Academies' fluency with information technology principles and the ACRL Information Literacy Competency Standards. Their findings revealed that while students rated themselves highly in their ability to find information on the Internet, they recognised that they floundered when they attempted to find materials appropriate for their research and wasted much time in the process.

The students also expressed a desire for more technology applications to be integrated into their courses. This model is being explored through a Mellon Foundation–sponsored project at the University of California, Berkeley, where selected faculty and librarians are working in partnership to incorporate information literacy skills and undergraduate research into large-enrollment courses with the goal of assisting students in developing skills that will serve them throughout their coursework at the institution.

DELIVERING SERVICE WITH STYLE

Information and technology literacy represents a content area in Net Gen students' education that has not been fully addressed. Separate but related is the "style" issue of how best to deliver this educational content and provide information and technology services to Net Gen students. Net Gen students work in information environments, and a very important one in college is the course management system. Libraries should develop tutorials, exercises, and guides that can readily be embedded in course materials within course management systems, and some are already doing this. They can develop games to teach these skills; TILT, the Texas Information Literacy Tutorial developed by The University of Texas at Austin libraries, is an early example. Simulations such as Environmental Detectives can incorporate information-seeking skills into the game, reinforcing Net Gen students' interest in figuring things out and working in groups. Libraries should explore blogs as a mechanism for students to exchange information on valuable information resources they find for particular course assignments.

Blogs sponsored by the library might be particularly effective for graduate students beginning their dissertations and needing advice from peers and information professionals on locating materials for their literature reviews. An emerging area of literacy is the need for students to increase their fluency with representing their knowledge in the digital, multimedia world. George Lucas stated that students need to learn a "language of screens" in order to be effective communicators today. The Visible Knowledge Project, in which university faculty are working with multimedia content and developing assessment mechanisms to measure the effectiveness of their instruction, is also working on guidelines to assist faculty in evaluating student multimedia projects. While Net Gen students often prefer creating a multimedia project rather than a term paper that is entirely text, they need assistance in understanding how to represent their knowledge in a form that is appropriate for academic work, just as they need to learn to write in a way that meets the standards of the academy.

REFERENCE SERVICES

Although libraries have offered e-mail reference services for a number of years, they were slow to adopt chat and sometimes developed sophisticated but complex chat software rather than the simpler systems typically used by Net Gen students. Librarians might need to change their mindset of employing the most sophisticated software that enables features they believe could provide improved service, such as permitting the librarian to demonstrate a search or review an information resource in one window while chatting with the student in another, in preference for software that students are more likely to use. In one study where a library did use standard AOL Instant Messenger software, other roadblocks to student adoption were put into place.

The librarians noted in their report on the service that they did not staff it during late-night hours when students were most likely to use the service and that they did not market the service in information literacy class sessions for fear that the response might overwhelm their capabilities.

Instead, the service was not heavily used. They did collect some responses as to why students took advantage of the service, and convenience was the main reason. One student reinforced why this type of service has appeal to the multitasking Net Gen students by replying that he had used the service instead of phoning the library so that he could continue working and browsing while waiting for an answer from the librarian.

VISUAL, INTERACTIVE SERVICES

Students also like self-service, interactive Web sites, and it is surprising that libraries haven't developed visual representations of their services that students could explore. A survey by OCLC found that one of students' top suggestions for libraries was to offer interactive maps, study tips, and guides. An example of that type of environment is a Web site developed by the British Museum as a "student's room" for an exhibit of Mughal, India, an ancient civilisation. Students see an office-style room that they can explore by clicking on components such as a globe, file cabinets, book shelves, and so forth. They are then led to museum resources including an atlas and primary resources from the museum's collections on the Mughal period. This type of model could be used for a library reference room and its resources.

Libraries could add value to key pages of their Web sites by including interactive tutorials on how to find information or how to judge quality information resources. Libraries could use part of their home page to highlight a "resource of the week," to better publicise information content that could likely assist students in their assignments. They could use customised mouse pads to advertise URLs for selected information resources. Libraries also need to think about new services using mobile technology such as cell phones.

They might allow students to reserve group study rooms and be alerted to availability via their cell phones, send simple text-message queries to library catalogs or databases, or check library hours via text messaging. Such services might be particularly valuable for students who live off campus. How will we conceive and design these new services? Librarians should consult with students in the design phase of services and incorporate students on teams that make decisions about the implementation of those services.

Making use of the imagination, creativity, technical skills, and perspectives of Net Gen students is the best way to ensure that new services will be responsive to both their needs and their style.

To summarise, Net Gen information services will:

* Use students on teams that design new services and environments
* Integrate services into course management systems
* Explore services for mobile devices
* Represent services and instruction visually and in multimedia modes
* Focus on partnership models
* Emphasise how to evaluate information resources
* Emphasise information policy issues

ENVIRONMENTS

Although technology has transformed many campuses, physical spaces remain important in most higher education institutions. The library offers a venue where academic work can be carried out in a social context. As libraries renovate facilities to incorporate technology, they are also making them more suitable for student group work, informal socialising, and ubiquitous computing.

Information Commons often provide space, workstations, and software that encourage both access to information and the capability to create new information products. Some Information Commons offer joint support to users from both the library and IT units. It is less common for libraries to rethink their virtual services to provide a better complement to their physically based services. Libraries have opportunities to alter their marketing strategies and their use of visual representations of information to encourage more and new creative uses of digital information resources.

LIBRARY PHYSICAL SPACES

As the Leavey Library at USC demonstrates, students will flock to library facilities that offer environments conducive to Net Gen learners. What Leavey offers are hundreds of workstations in configurations that support both individuals and small groups, group study rooms where students can work together on projects, workstations equipped with a wide array of software that can be used for creation of new information products, and staff with both library and information technology expertise who can address subject-information requests and technology hardware or software issues. Many academic libraries are following the Leavey Library model and are transforming part of their physical space into information commons, multimedia production areas, classrooms, or all three. For example, the University of Arizona's Learning Center has components that include a library information commons where students can work on workstations configured for individual or group work, develop multimedia projects, and get advice from reference librarians. Adjacent to the information commons are multimedia classrooms and a computer lab with support by Information Technology staff. The Indiana University information commons, developed jointly by the library and IT and situated on the first floor of the library, incorporates single and multiuser workstation areas, group study rooms, and classrooms and offers a wide range of services supported from a circular central desk staffed by library and IT staff.

While there is no one widely accepted definition of an information commons, generally it is a physical space, not always in the library, that incorporates many workstations equipped with software supporting a variety of uses, offers work-space for individuals and groups, provides comfortable furniture, and has staff that can support activities related to access to information and use of technology to develop new products. While information commons are usually developed for student use, some incorporate centers for teaching excellence or instructional technology support services for faculty.These new types of library spaces communicate a welcoming attitude to Net Gen students. They are the opposite of old-style formal reference rooms where students were expected to sit on straight wooden chairs and work individually and silently, without access to technology. Instead, these spaces project a comfortable, relaxed environment, a celebration of technology, and an invitation to communicate.

Library physical spaces continue to be valued places for building community in colleges and universities. Importantly, they also provide an atmosphere in which social and academic interests can easily intersect.

When students were asked what they desired in an upcoming renovation of Teachers College at Columbia University Library, they replied that they wanted "a social academic experience." Libraries can promote community by providing comfortable spaces for informal gatherings of students. Many libraries are adding coffee bars to their lobby areas or a building adjacent to the library; such spaces encourage students to continue conversations on topics of academic interest. Libraries might develop new ways of promoting community among students, related to course activity. For example, they may develop a message board or online mechanism for students to identify who else in the library building might be working on an assignment for a particular course if they need help from a peer or wish to study as a group.

INTEGRATING PHYSICAL AND VIRTUAL ENVIRONMENTS

Most libraries have not yet learned how to effectively integrate physical spaces with virtual spaces and services. For example, the introductory screen on work-stations in an information commons may have no description of the services or digital information products offered there. Vassar College has remedied this in their Media Cloisters, where entering visitors are confronted with a brightly colored set of screens introducing student members of the multimedia team and advertising their areas of expertise.

How might libraries market services to Net Gen students, who are often visual learners? One possibility is to literally project information onto the walls of the information commons. In a changing display, libraries could develop programmes to project pages of electronic journals, guides to subject fields or topics that many students are working on during a specific week, quality Web sites with good visual displays (for example, museum Web sites), and student or faculty multimedia information products. Such displays would alert students to the broad array of electronic information resources accessible through the library and could prompt student interaction with a reference librarian to pursue similar sources for their projects.

To summarise, Net Gen information environments will:

* Provide individual and group learning spaces
* Support access to and creation of information resources
* Offer staff and faculty development and training
* Provide staff with a range of technology and information skills
* Effectively market services to all groups of potential users
* Integrate physical spaces and services with virtual spaces and services
* Build community

CONCLUSION

Developing library content, services, and environments that are responsive to Net Gen students can be achieved by examining the characteristics of those students and making a conscious effort to address deficiencies and transform the current situation in libraries. Why should libraries and librarians adapt their well-structured organisations and systems to the needs of students rather than insist that students learn about and adapt to existing library systems? The answer is that students have grown up in and will live in a society rich in technology and digital information. By blending the technology skills and mindset that students have developed all their lives with the fruits of the academy, libraries can offer environments that resonate with Net Gen students while enriching their college education and lifelong learning capabilities.

2

Library Networks

INTRODUCTION

Libraries are at the forefront of providing no-fee Internet access to the public. In 1994, just 8.2 percent of public libraries provided this service; as of 2009, 100 percent of libraries do so. While this is a vital role in every community, the library is the only source of no-fee public Internet access in 71 percent of communities. The core mission of libraries is to connect people with ideas and information. Internet access makes it possible for libraries to fulfill this mission through online resources that can, for example, help people find jobs, improve their skills, access government services, create small businesses, complete school homework, and conduct research. Libraries have reported high demand for Internet access; indeed, in the majority of libraries, the demand for publicaccess computers far outweighs the supply. As demand for public access to the Internet grows, so, too, does the need for higher bandwidth in the library.

In some communities, libraries play the important role of broadband anchor institution; in other words, by obtaining high-bandwidth connections, they drive the deployment of advanced technologies to communities that might be unable to obtain that level of service through residential demand alone.

In short, libraries that are able to meet the demand for no-fee public Internet access play a vital role in serving both their users and their communities. To help libraries achieve this capability, the Bill and Melinda Gates Foundation initiated the

Opportunity Online Broadband Grant Programme. This programme provides funding and support to help State Library agencies in seven states—Massachusetts, New York, Virginia, Arkansas, Kansas, California, and Texas—develop leadership and improve library connectivity to the Internet.

The American Library Association's Office for Information Technology Policy (OITP) is participating in this programme, providing research and consulting services to state libraries, as well as developing publications that address key issues salient to the program's goals. The purpose of this publication is to provide a snapshot of five different library networks that provide users with no-fee Internet access.

LEADERSHIP, COOPERATION, AND THE ABILITY TO LEARN FROM PAST SUCCESSES

Strong leadership was an essential element in the development of each of the five networks. At the same time, leadership was distributed among different players at the state, regional, and local levels and was not the exclusive domain of one person or organisation. Moreover, cooperation among these players was a hallmark of the effort. The case studies also illustrate how the various organisations involved often drew on the experiences of other successful cooperative projects to help in the development of their network.

In the formative stage of the Ohio Public Library and Information Network (OPLIN), public libraries that wanted to emulate successful school and academic networks broached the idea of a public library network with the state library association. This association, later called the Ohio Library Council (OLC), assumed a leadership role, and two OLC staff members organised planning and advocacy efforts that led to OPLIN's development.

The West Virginia Network was the first network to centralise the state's computing and data needs. Statewide Library Network (SLN) leadership acknowledged learning from this first statewide network during the project development. Taking a cooperative approach similar to that applied in the development of OPLIN, Wisconsin's local and regional libraries and State Library officials worked together to define the libraries' role in BadgerNet. A past collaborative project to establish a distance learning video network was a key factor in the creation of a 1993 Governor's Blue Ribbon Telecommunications Infrastructure Task Force, which in turn recommended the creation of BadgerNet.

The Maine School and Library Network (MSLN) was also the result of cooperation between statewide library associations and the State Library agency. Finally, the member libraries of California's Peninsula Library System (PLS) developed the Peninsula Libraries Automated Network (PLAN) based on their past success with a common circulation and catalog system. Perhaps the most important factor contributing to the success of PLAN is the spirit and habit of cooperation among PLS members. Since, 1982, member libraries have been cooperating to operate a joint circulation system.

Such collaborations require that libraries engage in significant give-and-take to modify longstanding local policies and procedures so as to accommodate a centralised system. This habit of collaboration led to the success of other collective endeavors, including PLAN.

AGGREGATION OF DEMAND AND SERVICES

Aggregation of demand is an acknowledged successful approach to network management. Among its benefits are:

* Improved planning
* Support for a business case for providers to deploy broadband
* More affordable pricing
* Sharing of costs

Aggregation of demand allowed the establishment of each of the five successful networks profiled here, and its benefits have contributed to the networks' continued success. For example, MSLN aggregates library traffic to two nodes, which results in lower recurring expenses for Internet access. Aggregation offers other, less obvious benefits. An example is streamlining and standardisation of members' E-rate participation. All of the statewide networks profiled here regularly file for E-rate discounts on behalf of their members or offer assistance to members in doing so.

A centralised application relieves the burden on individual libraries. MSLN files an aggregated application for federal E-rate discounts and an application for Maine's state universal service fund. Wisconsin files one aggregated E-rate application that includes every K-12 school district and public library on BadgerNet (about 910 sites), and also completes all the required follow-up.

Considering that the most frequently cited reason for libraries' non-participation in the E-rate programme is the complexity of the process, this is a very real benefit with tangible results. Standardisation is a key requirement for aggregation. OPLIN, MSLN, PLS, and BadgerNet require the same router configuration for every library site; SLN requires that all members have the same network equipment; and every school and library on BadgerNet has the same standard Ethernet interface.

Standardisation avoids the logistical challenges associated with customisation. It also allows for aggregation of technical support services. The benefits of aggregating technical support are readily apparent in West Virginia, where these services are typically beyond the means of individual public libraries with limited budgets and staff expertise. MSLN employs a shared project manager to provide planning guidance to individual libraries, a service that would otherwise be too costly for individual libraries.

USE OF DEMONSTRATIONS

OITP's past research suggests that technology demonstrations are necessary to convince a library's community to support a major new effort such as a regional or statewide network. Such demonstrations, while providing essential training to library staff, also serve a critical outreach and public relations function. For example, during the initial phase of network development, OPLIN staff members visited libraries around the state to demonstrate how access to the Internet would help their users. While demonstrations can be very helpful in growing network membership, their usefulness does not end with the network's establishment.

OPLIN and SLN representatives continue to provide information on network services and their use at annual conferences and meetings. Other library systems offer ongoing training on new resources provided via the network and on how library staff can use these resources to improve library services and ultimately benefit the library's patrons. Demonstrations can also help achieve the network's sustainability when used as an advocacy tool for continued funding and support of network projects.

PROVISION OF TECHNICAL SUPPORT AND TRAINING FOR LIBRARY STAFF

Library networks are complex technical entities that support many users and applications; it is unreasonable to expect local library staff, especially those in smaller or rural libraries, to provide comprehensive technical support for the network. All the networks profiled here provide members with some level of technical support and training in how to solve technical problems. The level of support ranges from handling all network problems to training local librarians in problem solving. Two of the networks—PLAN and Badger Net—continuously monitor network traffic and respond with solutions when they are needed. The case studies demonstrate several innovative approaches to supporting large networks:

* In a centralised model, OPLIN manages a support center that offers members a first line of defence for network troubleshooting.
* MSLN employs one circuit rider whose responsibilities include focusing on resource poor libraries with the most serious problems and developing technical skills among local library staff.
* SLN has network support staff in offices throughout the state and, like MSLN, works to develop the technical skills of library staff.
* In Wisconsin, regional library systems serve as the first point of contact to assist with troubleshooting and the installation of new equipment and software.
* In California, PLS meets the need for network-level support only; its member libraries all have technical support staff on site.

MULTIPLE FUNDING SOURCES

The networks profiled here rely on various revenue streams, such as grant funds, telecommunications settlement funds, universal service funds, state general funds, and local library funding. The five networks were established in economically favorable times, when state and other funds were more readily available for large capital projects than is the case today.

Nevertheless, all the networks face the challenge of securing ongoing funding. Even Maine, which has the most stable source of funding (state and federal universal service funds), struggles with balancing the need for increased network services with limited funding resources. The major sources of funding for the statewide networks have historically been state tax funds and universal service funds (both the federal E-rate programme and state-based programmes).

During the last year, however, tax revenues have decreased sharply in almost every state, and both OPLIN and SLN were in danger of losing significant state funding. California's PLS, funded primarily by member fees derived from local property taxes, has yet to see any significant reductions as assessments of property lag at least one year behind tax collections. Federal universal service funds are relatively stable. However, the total of applications for discounts is approaching fund availability, absent any policy intervention. Additionally, some organisations find the requirements for obtaining such funds to be onerous or contrary to their policies.

ROLE FOR LIBRARY REPRESENTATIVES IN NETWORK GOVERNANCE

The case study networks have widely varying governance and management structures.

For example:

* The Maine Public Utilities Commission (MPUC) governs MSLN.
* Wisconsin's Department of Administration manages BadgerNet.
* The West Virginia Library Commission administers SLN.

All of these networks are dependent on the network's information technology (IT) staff for ensuring the day-to-day management of network operations. But just as there are differences in network management (*e.g.*, some may be outsourced), there are also differences in overall network governance and how much input the library community has to make decisions or to set network policy. For example, the OPLIN governing board in Ohio consists solely of member library representatives. Wisconsin's BadgerNet Advisory Council includes representatives of all network users including libraries, K-12 schools, higher education and state government. The Advisory Council advises the state Administration Department in areas like member bandwidth needs and planning for the next generation network. California's PLS allows the technical staff of member libraries to be involved with network issues through a committee structure.

INVOLVEMENT OF THE STATE LIBRARY

One common characteristic of the statewide networks is the active involvement of the State Library:

* The State Library of Ohio has strong influence over OPLIN operations and development as a result of its authority to appoint all of the network's board members.
* The State Library in West Virginia operates SLN.
* In Wisconsin, the State Library influences BadgerNet planning and operations through its seat on the BadgerNet Council.

Although MSLN's governing board is the Maine Public Utilities Commission (MPUC), the state librarian is responsible for suggesting policy and for representing the interests of libraries before the MPUC. Furthermore, the Maine State Library has staff members responsible for assessing the needs of MSLN members and for preparing an annual report that outlines the network's needs and presents an annual budget request.

OHIO PUBLIC LIBRARY INFORMATION NETWORK

HISTORY

The Ohio Public Library Information Network (OPLIN) began to take shape in 1994 when a small group of librarians from a suburban library system discussed the need for a statewide public library network similar to the networks used by academic libraries (OhioLink) and K-12 libraries (INFOhio). This group of librarians reached out to the Ohio Library Council (OLC, then known as the Ohio Library Association), which helped to develop a plan to create the network and lobbied state legislators for the funding to build it.

Fran Haley, who had recently joined the OLC, was instrumental in bringing together experienced individuals to develop the network plan and in inviting the entire library community to participate in the process. Greg Byerly, was hired by the OLC to draft the initial plan for OPLIN.

He also worked to allow the state's public libraries to purchase telecommunications services from the statewide SOMACS (State of Ohio Multi-Agency Communications System) contract. The SOMACS contract provides postalised rates for its telecommunications circuits, so that the monthly price remains the same regardless of the length of the circuit or the location of the library.

OPLIN was created by state law in 1995. With the persistence of the OLC and the support of the legislature and then-Governor Voinovich, OPLIN was initially allocated $4.85 million. Before the state budget was passed in 1995, an additional $8 million was added to fund startup costs to network public libraries. The OPLIN board decided to provide funds for the initial installation connecting branch libraries to the network, but not to support recurring costs for these connections. The board also decided to provide a telecommunications line for one library site (usually the main library) and to support its recurring costs in addition to purchasing computers so that each library would have two public workstations with which to access OPLIN. All but one of the 251 main library systems in Ohio joined OPLIN immediately.

Local boards passed a resolution for each library system to join, and each established its own Internet access policy for the network. The library system pursued funding for the project at the right time, as the state budget was flush, and the overall economic situation in the state was favorable. Funds remained even after OPLIN had been built, allowing the libraries to purchase subscriptions to databases and other electronic materials.

SERVICES

OPLIN provides both broadband Internet connections and information services to Ohio public libraries. Its mission is to ensure that all Ohio residents have fast, free public Internet access through the state's local public library systems, as well as the use of highquality research and reference databases not available free of charge on the World Wide Web.

OPLIN provides these services at no cost to the libraries. Unlike the situation in many other states, OPLIN coordinates the acquisition and installation of the physical telecommunications circuits that connect the main libraries to the network's hub in Columbus. (Most other library networks deliver content and services primarily via a physical network provided by some other organisation.) OPLIN leases circuits for the main libraries under two contracts the state has with telecommunications service providers.

Branch libraries, however, must obtain their own local broadband telecommunications connection to their main library. OPLIN also serves as the Internet service provider (ISP) for all public libraries in Ohio. It manages mail servers and provides the libraries with e-mail services. In addition, OPLIN provides web hosting services for those libraries with their own web site.

User Support and Communications

The OPLIN Support Center serves as the first line of defence for database problems and network troubleshooting. The center received 2,304 library technical service requests in fiscal year 2008, the majority of which related to e-mail issues. The OPLIN Support Center is open only during the workweek; after-hours and weekend calls are directed to the State of Ohio's Network Operations Center. OPLIN communicates with its members in a number of ways. It operates three e-mail lists: one for non-technical topics, one for the OPLIN office to announce new services and important changes to existing services, and one for technical topics.

OPLIN also publishes a quarterly newsletter, participates on social networking web sites, publishes three blogs, and has a web site.

Telecommunications and Broadband Services

OPLIN obtains the local telecommunications circuits for all but one of the main libraries in the State of Ohio. These circuits connect the main library to the OPLIN hub in Columbus. As part of a state agency, OPLIN is authorised to lease these circuits under two state contracts: the SOMACS contract, serviced largely by AT&T and used to lease traditional T1 circuits that provide a capacity of 1.5 megabits per second (Mbps), and a separate contract for fibre-based Ethernet services.

OPLIN often transitions main libraries that need upgraded capacity to an Ethernet connection, but these Ethernet services are not available statewide. OPLIN also provides its members with continuous monitoring of broadband traffic. Every quarter, traffic statistics for each main library are reviewed to see whether traffic patterns warrant an upgrade to a fiberbased Ethernet circuit (or DS1 or DS3 if Ethernet is not available). The additional bandwidth and coordination for implementation are handled by OPLIN at no charge to the main library.

NETWORK STRUCTURE

In addition to the local circuits that connect the main libraries to the OPLIN hub, OPLIN maintains a high-capacity connection from its hub to the Internet over a shared, channelised DS3 connection that is managed by the Ohio Office of Information Technology (OIT). The OIT router manages traffic to OPLIN-provided resources, to the Internet, or back to other OPLIN member libraries.

The bandwidth charge for this connection to the Internet is the fastest-growing expense for OPLIN. As figure indicates, each main library receives a router provided by OPLIN to connect its circuit to the OPLIN hub. Management of this router is carried out collaboratively between OPLIN staff and the engineering group within OIT. The router represents the demarcation point between OPLIN services and the main library's local area network (LAN).

Each main library is responsible for its own LAN management services. OPLIN offers each main library a subnet of 32 publicly routable Internet Protocol (IP) addresses. Each main library administers these addresses following its own policies.

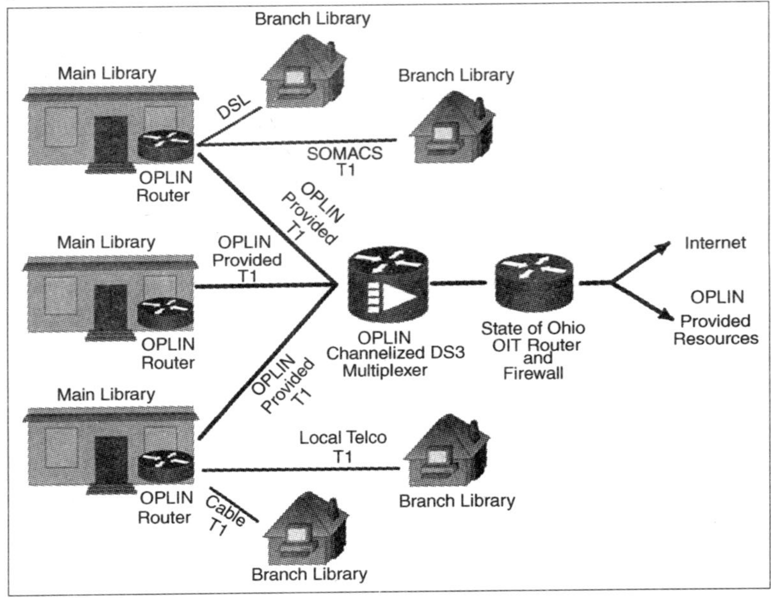

Fig. 2.1 Structure of OPLIN.

As noted, OPLIN does not provide the local broadband connections for branch libraries. The branch libraries associated with each main library system can use a variety of options for connecting to the main library. In many cases, the SOMACS contract allows libraries to pay for a postalised T1, which is available statewide for only $400 per month. Figure shows this option in green.

While the SOMACS contract is available to any branch library, occasionally less expensive options exist. Some branches choose to purchase a digital subscriber line (DSL) circuit to connect virtually to the main library through a virtual private network (VPN). On other occasions, the branch library is located close enough to the main library that a local telephone company can connect both locations with a DS1 for less than the $400 per month under the SOMACS contract.

The line in figure highlights this option. Finally, in some communities, cable TV companies offering telecommunications services can provide a branch library with either a DS1 or an Ethernet connection. Fibre is another option that is gaining popularity among libraries in Ohio. The State of Ohio has signed a separate contract that includes AT&T's Optical Ethernet Metropolitan Area Network (OPT-E-MAN). OPT-E-MAN is typically provisioned via a fibre connection with bandwidth increments as low as 5 Mbps and scalable to 100 Mbps.

Libraries that can purchase fibre-based service are ideally positioned to add bandwidth quickly and less expensively than is the case with traditional telephone company services (*e.g.*, T1/DS1, T3/DS3). Pricing for Ethernet services can vary significantly from location to location. The price for a 10 Mbps circuit can range from $600 per month to about $1,000 per month, not including router management fees and Internet access bandwidth.

GOVERNANCE

OPLIN is an independent state agency within the State Library of Ohio. It is governed by a board of eleven members selected by the State Library Board from the staffs of member public libraries and current or past trustees. The OPLIN Executive Director and the State Librarian or his/her designees serve as ex officio board members. Stephen Hedges has served as OPLIN's Executive Director since, 2006 and supervises four staff members.

OPLIN receives fiscal and logistical support services from the State Library of Ohio and contracts with OIT for assistance with network management. OPLIN is now defined in the Ohio Revised Code. Until recently, it was a line item in the State Library budget, meaning that it technically ceased to exist every 2 years. OPLIN is now part of the permanent law, which allows it to take advantage of longer service contracts.

FINANCE

The majority of OPLIN's budget—58 per cent—is spent on purchasing Internet connections to public libraries, which it regards as its most important role. Another 30 percent is spent on databases, which make up about a third of the total cost of the Ohio Web Library database collection. About 2 per cent of OPLIN's budget is allocated by the legislature for grant subsidies to local libraries to help defray the cost of filtering Internet content; another 1 per cent funds conferences and other training for public librarians.

The remaining 9 per cent of the budget is used for all other costs—rent, salaries and benefits (for five staff), supplies, postage, office equipment, etc. Thus more than 90 percent of the OPLIN budget is spent on direct services to public libraries, and less than 10 per cent on administrative costs. From the network's inception in the fiscal year (FY) 1995 budget bill through FY 2007, annual funding for OPLIN varied between $5 million and $8 million each year. Because of the state's recent fiscal problems, OPLIN's budget was reduced in 2008 and 2009, and additional reductions may occur in 2010.

To make up for the loss of state revenue, OPLIN has entered into an agreement with eTech Ohio to manage its E-rate applications this year. OPLIN expects that eTech Ohio's E-rate expertise will lead to more federal E-rate discounts than in the past. Libraries can call on eTech Ohio for E-rate consulting, and eTech Ohio will also be conducting E-rate workshops.

WEST VIRGINIA'S STATEWIDE LIBRARY NETWORK

HISTORY

Many West Virginians depend on their public libraries for Internet access. The West Virginia Library Commission (WVLC) established the centralised Statewide Library Network (SLN) to meet this need. Beginning in the 1990s, the WVLC received a federal grant for a project to connect West Virginia public libraries with 56 kilobits per second (Kbps) frame relay lines leased from Bell Atlantic (now Verizon) and other providers. By 1999, all but 3 of West Virginia's 177 public libraries were connected. The West Virginia Network (WVNET), the state's Internet service provider, was also instrumental in developing SLN. WVNET was established in 1975 to centralise the state's computing and data needs. It originally connected the colleges and universities in West Virginia to its central hub, and later grew to serve government offices, K-12 schools, and libraries. WVNET established a statewide intranet in 1994 and continues to provide Internet connectivity to libraries today. WVNET reports to the West Virginia Higher Education Policy Commission and is aided by a Computer Advisory Board, with representatives from higher education and other users of WVNET.

Internet access spurred demand at libraries across the state for such resources as electronic journals, shared library resources, e-mail, and learning programmes. Meeting this demand required more robust connections, so the Library Network 2000 plan was developed to upgrade and standardise the libraries' hardware and software.

Technicians visited every library in the network and installed suitable cabling, reprogrammed equipment, issued new Internet Protocol (IP) addresses, and provided standardised Internet connections. The network staff received a Governor's Award and a National Association of State Information Resource Executives nomination for the planning and implementation of the Network 2000 project. In September 2002, Verizon provided a $1.6 million grant (over 2 years) for the Digital Bridge Project, designed to upgrade the 56 Kbps connections with DS1 (1.5 megabits per second) lines. As of summer 2009, all 177 libraries had been connected with a DS1 line.

Today, the success of this upgraded network is evident in libraries across West Virginia. At a March 2009 WVLC meeting, the Director of Weirton's Mary H. Weir Library, Rik Rekowski, reported that the library's Internet center had 16,000 visitors every year in a town with a population of only 18,748.

Sandy Bumgardner, Director of the Upshur County Library, a service center for several libraries in very rural areas, said that many community residents lack access to highspeed Internet in their homes because dialup access is their only affordable choice. Furthermore, a number of residents who live in areas with affordable Internet access have cancelled their home subscriptions to save money.

These residents use the libraries' public-access computers to search the Internet, write résumés, and complete job applications. Further upgrades are planned for SLN. By 2012, the network will offer Ethernet connections that will operate approximately 10 times faster than T1.

SERVICES

SLN provides all the state's public libraries with Internet access, e-mail communication, data lines, hubs and switches, and technical support. Libraries may also receive funding and support for a shared integrated library system (ILS). In many other states, technical support for network services is the responsibility of the individual library.

West Virginia is different in that the libraries receive, at no charge, the following services:

* Wide area networking, local area networking, and wireless access support
* Help desk services
* Router installation and maintenance
* PC software/hardware replacement and maintenance
* UNIX hardware/software maintenance
* ILS (if shared with other libraries)
* Hubs, switches, and associated cabling (both installation and maintenance)
* Equipment contract support
* Data circuit installation and maintenance
* Network monitoring
* E-rate support

West Virginia made the strategic decision to centralise technology support for its libraries at the state level. As a result, it achieves excellent statewide coverage with just 11 technicians. Each of the technicians directly supports libraries within an assigned region of the state, but he or she also provides support to neighboring regions when the need arises. Most of West Virginia's public libraries had limited access to technical support before the WVLC filled this role.

Libraries now have access to technology assistance for simple problems, such as printer jams, and more complex problems, such as router maintenance. Network technicians also visit libraries to offer library staff members training on various topics, including using the Internet, e-mail, and online databases; establishing remote computer repair options; and completing E-rate applications. Network personnel also provide training sessions during annual library functions and offer classes throughout the year.

For example, one SLN technician teaches simple troubleshooting measures to library staff so they can solve technical problems independently instead of calling a technician. SLN's technical support takes a variety of other forms. A series of public service announcements provides basic information about computer viruses, how to perform software updates, and other troubleshooting tips. In addition, SLN maintains four regional desktop computer labs that allow library staff in those regions to access training without driving long distances or staying overnight. Two mobile laptop labs are available for on-site training in more remote libraries. Significant to this centralisation of technical support is the standardisation of the network equipment and configuration and deployment processes.

Any member of the SLN staff, regardless of the region of assignment, can walk into any library and know what equipment and network configuration to expect. In addition, technicians can implement upgrades to the network without having to customise each library's infrastructure. Director of the Wayne County Libraries, "The main benefit of having a statewide network is that it eliminates the need for duplication of service if every county had to run its own network.

The state is able to provide more qualified support than a county could. In the long run, it saves money. If there is a problem, there is one number the local library has to call for assistance. The state office always has somebody on staff qualified to assist with networking issues. Some of the counties may not have access to qualified technicians due to the rural nature of some areas of the state."

NETWORK STRUCTURE

The West Virginia Department of Administration manages a statewide contract for telecommunications services. All public libraries are connected to SLN by purchasing a DS1 from this contract; all of the state's 177 libraries now have a DS1 connection.

Ordering and installation of the circuit are coordinated by the WVLC. Depending on the location of a library, the DS1 connects to either the northern data center in Morgantown or the state capital of Charleston in the south. Traffic destined for the Internet is handed off to WVNET, and the rest remains within SLN. To comply with the Children's Internet Protection Act (CIPA), the WVLC provides Internet filtering using Netsweeper software hosted on the state backbone network.

The WVLC shares this service with other state agencies that must filter Internet traffic, allowing the expense to be spread across a larger pool of members. An advantage of the design of SLN is that only Internet traffic is filtered through Netsweeper. Centralising the filtering tools has eliminated the need for individual libraries or systems to purchase their own filtering software.

This large network requires careful bandwidth monitoring. The WVLC monitors the bandwidth use of individual libraries as well as the statewide network via a monitoring network operations center in Charleston. The monitoring software provides hourly/daily/monthly bandwidth charts for each library, audible/visual outage reports, and battery temperatures.

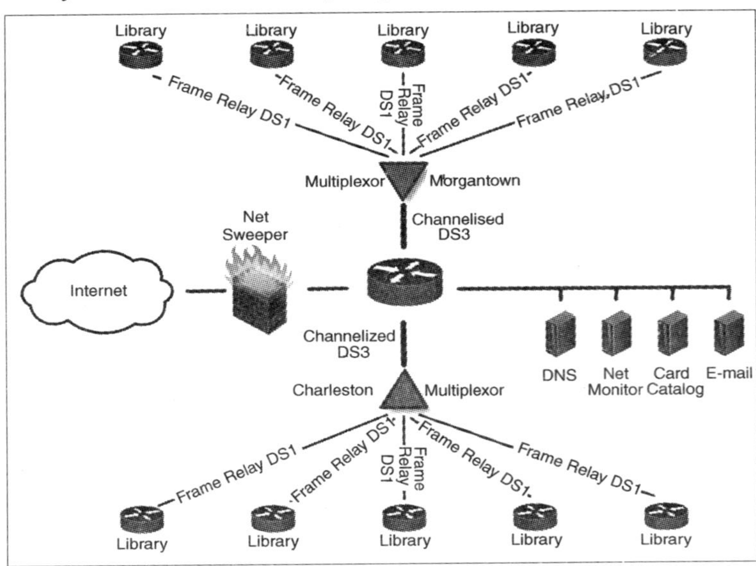

Fig. 2.2. Configuration of West Virginia's State Library Network.

GOVERNANCE

The WVLC, which established SLN, consists of seven members, all of whom are appointed by the governor and confirmed by the state senate. The WVLC appoints a secretary who serves as State Librarian and manages the WVLC Network Services department, one of the four departments within the commission's office.

As noted earlier, the WVLC centralises support for libraries at the state level and achieves statewide coverage with only 11 staff members. A key to SLN's success is the uniform approach to network design and service, which lends itself to economies of scale. The WVLC has encouraged all libraries to join the network, giving it more power to aggregate demand and further upgrade connections. The WVLC takes a similar approach to technology and E-rate support, centralising these services at the state level to derive benefits from the aggregation of service provision. The WVLC developed and expanded SLN through a combination of advocacy and strong leadership.

It directly recruited public libraries, which were added to the network as funds became available. At its inception, the network also included four academic libraries. As of 2009, there are two. One left the network as a result of a change in administration, and the other joined a private college consortium. The network includes other non-public library participants as well.

The Archives and History Library, a department of the state's Division of Culture and History, shares a catalog server with the WVLC. A few K-12 schools have also been added to SLN. Under state law, the WVLC cannot make direct grants to school libraries, so it pays for the cost of adding them as users of the integrated catalog software.

FINANCE

SLN has enjoyed strong support from the West Virginia legislature and has tapped other funding sources as well. In 1996, the WVLC, WVNET, and the West Virginia Department of Education successfully implemented a $2.5 million grant from the U.S. Department of Education. The first libraries received Internet access under this grant. Additional funding through federal and state grants expanded the number of libraries in SLN. The final public libraries added to the network benefited from federal Library Services and Technology Act (LSTA) funds.

Also in 1996, the legislature provided a onetime allocation of $1 million for upgrades and allocated $1 million for ongoing support. In March 1998, a $1.9 million grant from the Bill and Melinda Gates Foundation provided computers for the state's public libraries. A July 2002 grant of $991,281 from the State Telecommunications Users' Council allowed SLN to purchase servers. In addition to state and foundation grant funding, the WVLC applies annually for E-rate discounts for SLN. The average E-rate discount rate in 2009 was 76 percent. State legislators cut SLN's fiscal year 2010 budget by 28 percent or $347,000 from its $1.1 million budget in fiscal year 2009. This reduction will most likely slow the upgrading of SLN libraries' local area networks, including evaluating and replacing wiring, switches, and other critical network components. The WVLC also plans to support SLN with some LSTA funds. This funding shift will reduce amounts available for other library programmes typically supported by LSTA funds, including direct grants to local libraries.

WISCONSIN'S BADGERNET NETWORK

HISTORY

Since, as early as the 1970s, Wisconsin has been one of the nation's leaders in creating long-haul video networks to provide distance learning to schools. In 1993, to build on this success, then-Governor Thompson established a Governor's Blue Ribbon Telecommunications Task Force.

The task force was charged to:

* Develop a vision for a statewide telecommunications network for educational institutions and government agencies and
* Recommend changes in state statutes and policy to remove barriers to the realisation of this vision.

In its planning for the statewide infrastructure, the task force also was required to consider and integrate Wisconsin's existing K-12 video network—consisting of more than 8,000 miles of fibre throughout the state at the time—into the network plans.

The Wisconsin Department of Public Instruction (DPI), which houses the State Library Agency, advocated for consideration of library needs in the network's development, and libraries played an active role in the planning effort. The State Library and several members of regional library systems participated in the task force and made their concerns and interests known to the task force participants and to legislators. The task force recommended the creation of BadgerNet in 1993, and the legislature adopted most of the task force's recommendations in 1995. Libraries were specifically included in the statute as eligible to access the BadgerNet network. Shortly thereafter, the legislature created the TEACH (Technology for Educational Achievement) programme to help schools and libraries obtain and sustain their use of technology. BadgerNet was created at a time when the economy was stable and growing. This economic stability allowed the state sufficient time to undertake the 3-year effort and engage many stakeholders in the development of the statewide network.

Additionally, the positive economic climate and the growth of telecommunications services in the late 1990s allowed the legislature to add revenue to the state's universal service fund (which collects funds from in-state telecommunications providers) to fund the TEACH programme.

Following another two-year planning process, in March 2005, the Wisconsin Department of Administration (DOA) entered into a new $116.7 million, 5-year agreement with the consortium of telecommunications providers that deliver BadgerNet services for a new converged, higher-capacity data and video network called the BadgerNet Converged Network (BCN). The transition to the new network was completed on September 1, 2006. The State Library Agency helped coordinate this transition. At that time, BCN was the largest state network of its type that AT&T, the prime vendor, had under contract.

SERVICES

Wisconsin's seventeen regional library systems are required to assist their member libraries in matters related to technology in exchange for state funding. In this regard, they play an important role in addressing local public library broadband and Internet connectivity needs.

Among the services they provide:

* The regional library systems manage wide area networks (WANs) for their member libraries. The WANs are part of the regional network infra-structure that ultimately connects to the BadgerNet backbone at four locations in the state. WANs are used primarily for shared integrated library system traffic and Internet access. Of the services offered through the BCN contract, the libraries most frequently use the WAN service, which links remote libraries to the headquarters of the regional library system in a hub-and-spoke network design.
* All seventeen systems provide consulting for the purchase of computer software and hardware.
* Many systems also offer centralised purchasing for software and hardware, which allows member libraries to obtain a lower price than they could negotiate individually.
* Sixteen of the seventeen regional systems make information technology (IT) staff available as the first point of contact to assist with troubleshooting and the installation of new software and hardware.

BadgerNet also offers high-resolution, real-time interactive video to approximately 350 K-12 schools. Included in these video services are a network scheduling function and specialised equipment that permits three or more locations to be joined together in a videoconference. Classes offered over the network are an integral part of instruction, with as many as thirtytwo separate conferences linking more than a hundred classrooms during a single hour. Finally, BadgerNet offers network support and help desk service around the clock.

NETWORK STRUCTURE

BadgerNet serves state government, some local governments, universities, technical colleges and tribal nations, and most of the state's K-12 school districts and public libraries. All state agencies are required to use BadgerNet; 900 state agency remote locations use the data network capability of the system to connect to their agency headquarters in Madison.

In total, the network exceeds 2,400 end-points spread across each of the state's 72 counties. Although library participation is voluntary, about 97 per cent of Wisconsin's public libraries have connected to the Internet via BadgerNet since, the mid-1990s. As noted, the libraries generally use a WAN topology such that individual library circuits connect back to the headquarters of the regional library system. The regional system then aggregates the Internet traffic of its member libraries and provides a direct connection to the Internet service provider (ISP). This can be seen in figure.

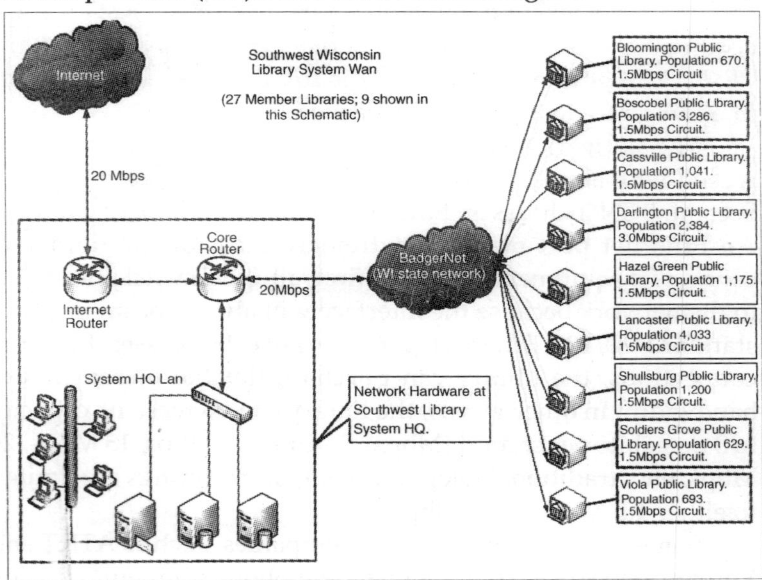

Fig. 2.3. An Example of BadgerNet's Structure.

AT&T serves as BCN's prime contractor, although additional services are provisioned by a consortium of telecommunications providers that includes other local telephone companies. Fortunately for the regional public library systems, the BCN contract allows the local provider to provision service in a variety of ways while ensuring that each library's interface is always the same 10/100 Ethernet port. Routing of traffic through the aggregation and core layers of the network is always the same as well, regardless of the access layer technology. Without exception, Wisconsin's regional library systems have adopted the hub-and-spoke WAN design. Choosing one library, often the headquarters of the regional library system, to act as the hub provides equipment consolidation advantages as well as bandwidth and port access to the Internet.

Two aspects of BCN are somewhat unusual and particularly beneficial to Wisconsin's library connectivity. First, the BCN contract covers all three network layers (a local access connection, an aggregation point, and a core). Most statewide networks provide the backbone, but the library or library system must acquire the local access connection on its own. BCN, through the TEACH programme, subsidises the cost of the local connections in addition to maintaining the backbone.

The network's comprehensive end-to-end service is one reason why almost every public library in the state uses BCN. Second, BCN includes an Ethernet port as the end-user interface. An Ethernet port makes it extremely easy for the library to connect its equipment (such as a firewall, local switch, or router) to the network because the interface will always be an industry standard 10/100 Ethernet port. Because BCN uses Ethernet connections, the library can purchase flexible increments of bandwidth. In other words, the library can increase its capacity to 3 megabits per second (Mbps), 5 Mbps, 10 Mbps, 15 Mbps, 20 Mbps, etc. (traditional telephone company offerings are limited to either 1.5 Mbps or 45 Mbps).

Some of the larger telephone companies, such as AT&T and Verizon, and some larger independent phone companies deploy fibre optic cables to libraries requesting highspeed circuits. Typically, fibre is deployed for sites needing 10 Mbps or greater, but some companies deploy fibre to sites with as little as 3 Mbps in anticipation of future growth.

The BCN portfolio of services does not, however, include asymmetrical services, such as digital subscriber line (DSL), microwave, and satellite technology alternatives, because it was too difficult to include every available technology and keep the service consistent. Even though these options are not available through BCN, some library systems purchase DSL services outside of the BCN contract; DSL is often used for patron wireless Internet access.

GOVERNANCE

BadgerNet is the state's telecommunications network; it does not provide Internet service. Most BadgerNet users (*e.g.*, state government, schools, and libraries) receive their Internet access via WiscNet. WiscNet is a not-for-profit association that operates under the auspices of the University of Wisconsin-Madison.

It is governed by a board of directors representing member institutions. A representative from the State Library and a representative from the regional library systems are on the board. WiscNet started providing Internet access in 1991 to 26 colleges and universities in the state. When the first BadgerNet network was built in the mid-1990s, WiscNet expanded its services to include K-12 schools and public libraries. BadgerNet is administered by the network office in the DOA.

The BadgerNet Advisory Council advises the DOA and the service provider on customer issues relating to the network contract, the operation of the network, and the process for developing timely solutions for services provided under the contract; it also provides a forum for planning. The council is made up of representatives from constituent groups, including one representative of a regional public library system and a representative of the State Library.

FINANCE

BadgerNet and its service vendor operate under a 5-year contract, and prices are stable for libraries within this contract period. Under the TEACH programme, schools, libraries, and other eligible institutions pay a reduced rate for their broadband connections; the remainder is paid by the TEACH programme. Schools and libraries pay $100 per month for a broadband connection up to 3 Mbps and $250 per month for a connection between 4 and 100 Mbps.

The BCN contract ends in 2011, and the BadgerNet Advisory Council is actively planning for the network's future contract service requirements. The BadgerNet contract charges the same rate to each library regardless of the distance between the library and the aggregation node. These postalised rates ensure that rural libraries pay the same monthly price for access to the BadgerNet network as urban and suburban libraries.

For public libraries in the state, the average membership fee in WiscNet is about $450 per year. More than 90 percent of the libraries have this fee paid by their regional library system. From its inception, BadgerNet required its vendors to build in rural as well as urban areas and to offer postalised rates.

While this helped reduce the price for rural libraries to connect to the network, it has caused problems in urban areas. Some urban libraries, especially in the Milwaukee area, are finding that they can save money by purchasing service from other providers instead of from BCN.

The TEACH programme uses state universal service funds to subsidise local access connections to BadgerNet for K-12 schools, public libraries, and regional library systems. TEACH pays for equipment, the installation costs for the local data lines and video links to BadgerNet, and a portion of the monthly service costs.

TEACH receives its funding from the state's universal service fund and from the federal E-rate programme. On an annual basis, TEACH spends approximately $13.8 million to subsidise network costs for schools and libraries. The subsidy for public libraries and regional public library systems is approximately $3 million annually.

TEACH received additional spending authority in the fiscal year 2007-2009 budget, which enabled more than 60 percent of the state's public libraries to increase their bandwidth at no direct cost to the library.

Separate from the funding for the TEACH programme, the state's universal service fund also provides an increasing amount of state aid to regional library systems. In prior years, the state universal service fund has generated $5 million for state aid to library systems. The state's fiscal year 2009-2011 budget funds the regional library systems totally out of the state's universal service fund, increasing the contribution by $11 million annually.

THE MAINE SCHOOL AND LIBRARY NETWORK

HISTORY

The Maine School and Library Network (MSLN) was created after a coordinated 2-year planning effort led by Maine's library and education communities. In fall 1994, three organisations in the library community—the Maine Library Association, the Maine Educational Media Association (representing school librarians), and the Maine Library Commission—joined forces to represent the interests of public libraries before the Maine Public Utilities Commission (MPUC). The result of these efforts was the creation of MSLN, one of the earliest and most comprehensive state programmes to improve libraries' Internet connections.

This advocacy effort focused on an investigation by the MPUC into allegations that NYNEX had overcharged its customers. After the libraries formally intervened and participated actively in the case, MPUC Chair Thomas Welch announced on May 1, 1995, that he wanted to permit NYNEX "to use up to $4 million of the rate reduction we require to provide rate reductions or other services to the libraries and schools of Maine."

It was left to NYNEX to work with others, including schools and libraries, to develop a plan for implementing this rate reduction. A group led by librarians and including schools, the MPUC, telecommunications carriers, the cable companies, and the University of Maine negotiated intensely over the summer of 1995. Ultimately, the group settled on a plan to provide 56 kilobits per second (Kbps) frame relay connections for all public schools and libraries in the state, with free Internet access, including equipment and free network support services.The Internet service provider (ISP) would be the University of Maine

System Network (UNET). The MPUC adopted the plan proposed by the librarians and others on January 5, 1996. The initial MSLN plan called for an allocation of $20 million to connect more than a thousand public schools and libraries in Maine for 5 years. Maine's Supreme Court upheld the commission's decision on March 15, 1996, when it issued a decision refusing to consider an appeal of the ratepayer case.

A parallel effort was undertaken in the state legislature to establish the legitimacy of the MPUC action. To guide this effort, the library organisations formed a Joint Legislative Committee to advocate for the expansion of the MPUC's authority to grant discounted rates and services for libraries.

A few weeks after the Supreme Court decision, the Maine Legislature approved a bill that amended the MPUC's authority. In 1999, the Maine Legislature codified the programme and provided funding to continue MSLN beyond its initial 5-year period.

The legislation allowed the MPUC to collect a surcharge on intrastate telephone services and deposit the revenues into the Maine Telecommunications Education Access Fund (MTEAF). Once the legislature had authorised this new source of funding, MSLN became known as MSLN2. Maine is now considering how to upgrade MSLN to accommodate the growth in Internet usage. The bandwidth available through MSLN "is now at its practical limits and is no longer meeting current needs of schools and libraries; in its current structure, it cannot scale to meet future needs."

The Department of Education and the Maine State Library are considering how to provide 100 Mbps capacity to all schools and libraries, but acknowledge that doing so will require a new strategy for procuring service and recognition that no single technology will best serve all regions of the state. Schools and libraries are consolidating traffic in central locations to reduce costs, but these central locations require more bandwidth than is currently available. As a result, some schools have opted out of MSLN and negotiated alternative connections from ISPs that can provide them greater bandwidth. This strategy may meet the individual school's needs, but it does not allow for economies of scale and cost efficiencies that come from a homogeneous network. The Department of Education believes that it should develop an upgrade strategy based on fibre optic technology. It believes this is a "future-proof" technology that can scale to very high data rates through upgrading of only the end equipment. The department also acknowledges that fibre may be too expensive in some areas.

It notes that wireless service can be a practical solution for service to islands off the coast of Maine, as well as some very rural communities. To move forward on this approach, the department recommends engaging in a collaborative effort with the research and education communities — something several other states, particularly Connecticut, Rhode Island, Missouri, and Iowa, are doing.

SERVICES

MSLN is one of the first statewide networks to provide Internet connections for all schools and libraries. Participation in MSLN is voluntary, and 49 of Maine's 271 public libraries do not receive MSLN Internet services. These 49 libraries have other connections, often through their community's cable company contract; a few have no Internet connection.

MSLN also offers technical support through a circuit rider service that provides advice and assistance by phone, e-mail, and in person to solve MSLN members' technical problems. Currently, MSLN funds a single circuit rider position. The circuit rider visits schools and libraries to assist them, assess their future broadband needs, and hear concerns.

The circuit rider focuses on the sites with the most serious problems and with the fewest local resources to solve those problems. Because the circuit rider cannot address the needs of every library, the programme tries to train local libraries to develop their own sustainable uses of MSLN without ongoing technical dependence on a circuit rider, and to integrate circuit rider efforts with those of other training programmes through the State Library and the Department of Education. Since, 2007, the State Library has been a community partner in WebJunction, the webbased training service for the library community.

In addition, Maine's three regional library systems offer workshops and other continuing education activities to member libraries. The State Library also offers limited training through its coordinator of learning and technology, who coordinates training efforts with the regional library systems. In addition, the Maine Association of School Libraries provides some training opportunities for school library media specialists.

NETWORK STRUCTURE

The network supporting Maine's libraries is an interesting case study since, it defies the typical rules for the establishment of a network. Almost invariably, networks emerge from a need to access a resource or application. The need exists before the network is built or significantly modified because few have the vision or the resources to build it otherwise. The State of Maine took the unusual step of creating the network first, when libraries were only beginning to need access to the Internet.

Maine thus developed a very simple design to serve its needs. Two main characteristics of successful library networks are aggregation and centralisation. MSLN achieves both of those key characteristics, but in an unusual way.Rather than three distinct layers that aggregate traffic (a local access connection, an aggregation point, and a core), MSLN allows each school and library to use a local access circuit (56 Kbps or 1.544 megabits per second) to connect directly to UNET (the ISP) and the Internet.

The flat MSLN network structure makes it easier for individual sites to connect directly to each other through the Internet, so that any library can host a resource that any or all MSLN libraries can access.

(A hierarchal design does not necessarily prohibit direct connections between locations, but it often narrows the opportunities.) As noted earlier, the original plan called for each school and library to have a 56 Kbps frame relay circuit connecting the school/library to UNET. In 1998, the MPUC approved upgrading of schools and libraries to a T1 connection if they were exceeding the capacity of their 56 Kbps connection.As shown in figure, the network aggregates library traffic to two UNET nodes within the state (located in Portland and Bangor) rather than a library system's main library.

That design, coupled with standard, ubiquitous transport (T1), allows MSLN to offer consistent service across the state for any library to use. An additional benefit of aggregating all the library traffic is a lower monthly recurring expense for Internet access. The average cost of Internet access measured by the megabit always decreases as more traffic is aggregated.The downside of a flat network structure with only two aggregation points is that traffic destined for a centrally managed library resource (or for another library) must traverse the Internet to reach its destination.

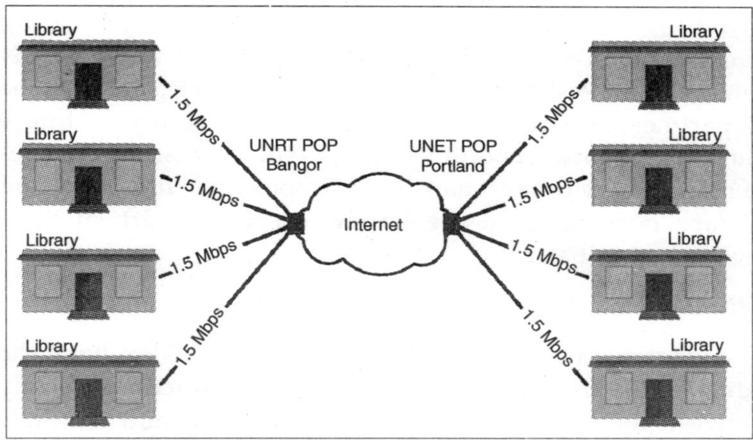

Fig. 2.4. Configuration of MSLN.

This route means that Internet traffic must travel a greater physical distance; the result is added delay, which may cause a potential drop in service. The Internet treats all traffic equally and will not recognise "high-priority" traffic even if marked as such by a library. Therefore, high-priority packets are not delivered over lowerpriority packets. While these can be genuine issues, they have not affected libraries using MSLN.

GOVERNANCE

The MPUC is the governing body of MSLN. The commission decided to retain ultimate responsibility and authority over the network since, ratepayer monies were being used to support it.

However, the commission created an advisory board with limited defined functions necessary to administer the fund and the network. In 2007, the legislature disbanded the MSLN advisory board.

The state librarian and the commissioner of the State Department of Education are now responsible for policy and for representing the interests of libraries and schools before the MPUC. Each agency has staff members responsible for assessing the needs of libraries and schools and preparing an annual report to the MPUC that outlines the network's needs and a budget request for the next year. The project manager provides day-to-day management of MSLN, including oversight of schools and libraries regarding the use of MSLN Internet bandwidth, development of recommendations to the Department of Education and Maine State Library on future bandwidth growth, coordination of circuit moves, and changes of circuits. The project manager also consults with school and library personnel on the impact on bandwidth of their technology initiatives.

FINANCE

Libraries that decide to participate in MSLN have the advantage of requesting service from a contract held jointly between the Maine Department of Education and the State Library. Compared with other library networks, Maine's is unique in many respects but not when it comes to aggregating its purchasing power.

MSLN offers a significantly lower price for T1 service than an individual library could ever hope to obtain for the same service because the MSLN contract offers the telephone company the opportunity to provide the service on a statewide basis. Offering 900 T1s is more economical for a carrier than providing one T1, and the carrier's contract pricing reflects that cost savings. In Maine, T1 services are purchased from FairPoint for any location in the state, even if the provider is an independent telephone company. MSLN can offer a fixed price for T1 service to any library in the state regardless of the local provider.

This aggregation also relieves the individual library of the burden of requesting and evaluating proposals for connectivity to meet the federal E-rate requirements. Certainly one of the factors for success for libraries in Maine is the ability to purchase or upgrade standard service from an existing contract anywhere in the state. MSLN is funded by two surcharges on telecommunications services: the federal E-rate programme surcharge on interstate services and the Maine Telecommunications Education Access Fund (MTEAF) surcharge on intrastate services.

E-rate discounts pay for approximately 60 percent of network costs, and the state programme funds the remaining 40 percent. No later than March 1 of each year, the Department of Education and the State Library file a joint proposal for support for the next fiscal year.

After a prescribed comment period, the MPUC issues an order by May 1 that establishes the amount to be collected from contributing state telecommunications carriers and a level of funding for libraries that do not apply for the federal E-rate programme. MSLN funding should remain steady for the foreseeable future as the network's revenue is generated through the federal and state universal service funds and not through state appropriations.

The MTEAF collection changes from year to year depending on MSLN needs. MSLN administrators are aware of the need to keep the assessment rate as low as possible, and they lowered the request rate for fiscal year 2008. In fiscal year 2007, the annual cost for MSLN was approximately $4.4 million. Funds from MTEAF pay for telecommunications services, Internet access, internal connections, computers, training, and content.

In addition, MTEAF funds:

* The circuit rider, who helps primarily small schools and libraries
* A consultant to assist with the federal E-rate process
* An administrator to collect the surcharges from telecommunications carriers
* A project manager to work with schools and libraries and track needs
* Free access to a variety of databases

CALIFORNIA'S PENINSULA LIBRARIES AUTOMATED NETWORK

HISTORY

The Peninsula Library System (PLS), located in California's San Mateo County, was established in 1971 to serve the county's eight public library jurisdictions and the San Mateo Community College District. In 1982, PLS decided to automate its circulation system and created the Peninsula Libraries Automated Network (PLAN).

PLAN evolved into a shared integrated library system with a union catalog that allows library users to access materials from all member libraries with one library card number. All branches of the eight public library jurisdictions in PLS have participated in PLAN since, its inception. When the network continued to slow under increased use and bandwidth limitations, PLAN libraries joined with the Community College District library in 1995 to help address the network's broadband issues.

PLAN eventually moved its telecommunications infrastructure to the Community College District. By doing so, PLAN became eligible to connect with the California Internet2 backbone and CalREN. In September 2007, PLS began to evaluate its future network capacity needs.

As part of this evaluation, planners interviewed librarians from each PLS member to assess network strengths and shortfalls. A common challenge identified by many of those interviewed was slow or failing computer applications due to insufficient bandwidth. In December 2007, PLS received two upgrade recommendations from its network consultants:

* Immediately implement hierarchical quality of service (QoS). QoS allows the most important applications to receive preferential treatment while lower-priority traffic utilises the remaining bandwidth.
* Replace the existing frame relay network with a fibre-based network, and upgrade the routers and switches that make up the PLAN infrastructure.

After issuing a request for proposals, PLS awarded a contract to AT&T of California to serve all of the PLS libraries with its fibre-based OPT-E-MAN service. Not only did AT&T offer the lowest monthly recurring service rate, but the company also waived nearly $500,000 in fibre construction fees.

AT&T's initial cost estimate to extend fibre from the curb into each of 33 remote libraries (San Mateo Community College already had an AT&T OPT-E-MAN circuit for its own networking needs at the beginning of the deployment) was $495,000 ($14,500 per library). Fortunately, management within AT&T identified San Francisco Bay Area libraries as strategically important and reduced or eliminated fibre installation costs in order to win or maintain library business.

This ability of the vendor to view libraries as strategic customers was critical to the success of the upgrade project. The only one-time costs incurred by PLS were for the purchase of equipment and professional services (device configuration and project management). The monthly recurring price offered to PLS for OPT-E-MAN service for a 5 Mbps circuit is $1,025 per month (compared with $1,100/per month for 3 Mbps under the old frame relay service).

The PLS price for a 10 Mbps circuit is $1,225 per month. At the head-end, PLS purchased a 1 gigabit link (1,000 Mbps) for $2,575 per month. By June 2009, PLS had upgraded its network to provide each of its libraries with a fibre connection. The deployment of fibre to each library and the transition to the new network took approximately 14 months. A number of issues contributed to delays in project completion.

Most of the PLS library buildings are owned by county or municipal governments, so PLS did not have the authority to give AT&T permission to pull innerduct or fibre inside the library. Any work within the building or on the library grounds had to be coordinated among various groups. Site survey meetings included AT&T's conduit subcontractor, its electrical contractor, a PLS representative, an AT&T engineer, a library representative, and the building owner. Although the need to coordinate among multiple government agencies caused project delays, PLS hired an experienced project manager who relieved the system of coordination responsibilities.

The manager had multiple years of experience with state government and telecommunications companies, and his expertise and presence contributed to PLAN's successful upgrade. In such large projects, it is essential for library systems to have their own project manager and not rely solely on the telecommunications company to provide coordination and oversight.

Once the fibre had been installed and tested, PLS converted the libraries to the new network within 2 weeks. PLS contracted for implementation services with network consultants to ensure a smooth transition from the legacy network to the fibre network. These consultants were also charged with transitioning knowledge to the local team, allowing them to maintain the network after the conversion.

SERVICES

PLAN is responsible for the day-to-day operation of the network and provides PLS libraries with a variety of telecommunications and broadband services through a centralised information technology (IT) department. In addition to the IT director, PLAN staff members include a database administrator, systems engineer, network administrator, and assistant database administrator/project manager.

These technicians supervise wide area network (WAN) services (network connectivity and network monitoring), local area network (LAN) services (switch and router hardware administration), and enterprise services (integrated library system, patron computer time management, e-mail, web hosting, and 24/7 help desk support).

In addition, PLAN staff members organise training for member library staff and negotiate reduced costs for training and equipment purchases. The community college administers firewall services for the network.

NETWORK STRUCTURE

Until the recent network upgrade to fibre-based services, PLS relied on a traditional huband- spoke frame relay design provisioned by AT&T. San Mateo Community College served as the hub of the network, and the individual libraries (spokes) were served with DS1 connections.

Today, patron and administrative workstations are placed in separate virtual local area networks (VLANs) within each library. In figure, the administrative VLAN is shown in red and the patron VLAN in blue. Creating separate VLANs for patrons and administrators reduces opportunities for security violations.

Typically, each library has at least one wireless access point, and some of the larger libraries have as many as five. PLS created a VLAN for wireless users as well, thereby isolating them from administrative traffic.

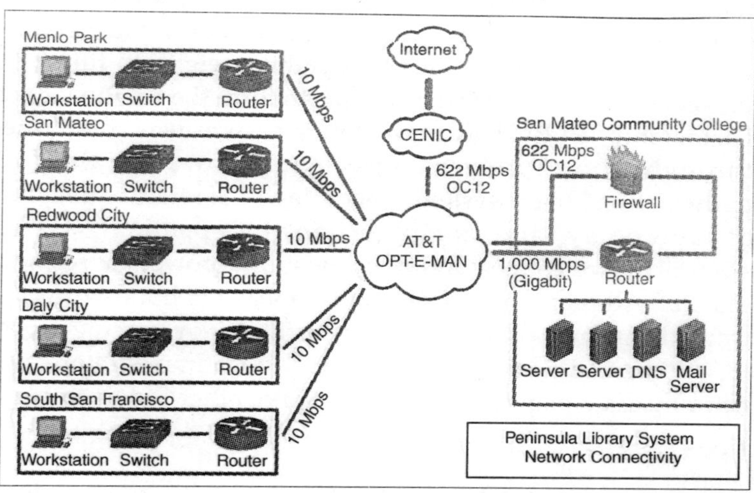

Fig. 2.5. Typical PLS Library Network Configuration.

Each library now has fibre inside the building connecting it to the network. The majority of the libraries connect at 5 Mbps, which is more than triple the 1.5 Mbps (frame relay DS1) they had previously. However, a number of larger libraries implemented 10 Mbps and have already seen usage peak at or near circuit capacity.

The process for increasing bandwidth is simple, requiring only a request that specifies the bandwidth amount desired and the date by which the increase is needed. Each PLS library pays for an increase in bandwidth. In PLAN's current hub-and-spoke design, traffic entering AT&T's fibre-based Ethernet network is routed to the core of the PLAN network at San Mateo Community College.

PLAN centralises services, such as e-mail, the integrated library system (ILS), and firewall services, at the college data center. Any traffic originating at a remote library and terminating at another remote library will travel to the network core and be redirected by the PLAN head-end router. However, most of the traffic originating from remote libraries travels to the Internet.

GOVERNANCE

PLS was one of fifteen statewide library systems authorised under the California Library Services Act. As a result of recent consolidation efforts spearheaded by the California State Library, library systems in California now number eight. In July 2009, PLS combined three library systems to form the Pacific Library Partnership (PLP). This new library system was established through a joint powers agreement; however, the four participating library systems, including PLS, retain a great deal of autonomy and maintain an independent system administrative council and their own joint powers agreement. The PLS Administrative Council, composed of library directors from PLS member libraries, is responsible for overseeing PLAN. PLAN currently serves only PLS, and PLS administrators have no immediate plans to expand it to serve other PLP members.

FINANCE

PLS supports 35 library branches. It is funded primarily by member libraries, which in turn are supported largely through local property tax revenue. PLS also receives support under the California Library Services Act, the federal Library Services and Technology Act (LSTA), and local contracts for special services. Member libraries share the up-front and ongoing maintenance costs of the central system, the connectivity costs of the transmission system, and the support staff that manage and operate the system. PLS created and maintains the network with funds from its general budget. PLS applies for federal E-rate discounts for eligible costs of operating PLAN, excluding Internet access and internal connection costs. PLS's discount rate is 50 percent.

3

Integration of Multimedia Content and E-Learning Resources in a Digital Library

INTRODUCTION

Distance education in virtual e-learning environments (such a virtual campus, for example) permits an intensive use of new technologies, especially in the field of design, creation and management of multimedia contents. The use of multimedia resources, either as learning tools in virtual environments or as basic pieces of multimedia repositories, allows us an improvement in the process of learning contents of audiovisual nature.

In this sense, teaching contents with a clear multimedia structure, such as several subjects in Information and Communication Studies, for example, requires learning tools with two desired characteristics: first, each course follows an activity oriented structure using a temporal framework and, second, content personalisation capabilities are needed to create adaptive courses but also to minimize course obsolescence. Therefore, content reusability within a course is an important issue related to course quality and management. This chapter addresses the integration between documents according to standards for multimedia content distribution such as MPEG-7, and other learning resources designed using e-learning standards such as LOM, within the context of a virtual e-learning environment that includes a digital library, which uses the Dublin Core standard for metadata. The need for metadata integration across multimedia, e-learning and library standards becomes a key factor for ensuring a proper content management and retrieval by teachers, researchers and students, the users of the digital library. All the resources in the digital library can be browsed and searched as a large repository of multimedia contents which uses structured metadata for the syntactic and semantic description of all the resources.

The use of standards for content description based on XML ensures the possibility of describing thoroughly all the elements in the virtual campus. Integration of standards for content tagging and indexation from different approaches (from the pedagogic field such as LOM, or the multimedia field such as MPEG-7) is a first step to ensure coherence and the reuse of such contents in the future.

In this chapter, we describe a proposal for promoting the integration of such standards in order to improve the indexation, classification and searching and browsing capabilities of multimedia and e-learning contents, therefore enhancing the retrieval of both such contents. This is accomplished by means of metadata standardisation, which allows us to create a hierarchy of multimedia learning objects ranging from single text, audio or video clips to complex multimedia courses.

E-LEARNING ENVIRONMENTS

The intensive use of Information and Communication Technologies such as Internet, for example, increases the possibilities for both content searching and delivery but also for interface design and implementation has completely changed the visions in the open distance education field. E-learning is one of the most promising and growing issues in the information society nowadays. The growth of the Internet is bringing online education to people in corporations, institutes of higher education, the government and other sectors. The growing need of continuous education and the inclusion of new multimedia technologies become crucial factors for this expansion.

UOC VIRTUAL CAMPUS

The Universitat Oberta de Catalunya (UOC, in English known as Open University of Catalonia) is a completely virtual campus which offers 19 official degrees, several graduate programmes and post-graduate studies, and a doctoral degree, with more than 35000 students and more than 1500 people including instructional designers, teachers, tutors, academic and technical staff.

The UOC virtual campus is an integrated e-learning environment which allows users to communicate with other users using a mail system, and includes an agenda, a news service, virtual classrooms, a digital library and other e-learning related tools.

Although the use of classical text printed books is still massive, there is also a growing use of web based e-books and other online learning resources, so the introduction of new e-learning standards and application profiles such as SCORM and IMS-LD is becoming a necessity for maintaining the constant evolution of the virtual campus. The increasing amount of multimedia content and standard based learning resources is revealing the need of new functionalities and capabilities provided by the digital library.

THE VIRTUAL CLASSROOM

Each subject has a classroom with all the needed elements for the development of the learning/teaching process: e-mails, access to documentation, the activity based teaching planning model, access to evaluation results, access to the teacher board, forums, debates, etc. The classrooms at the virtual campus are the meeting points of the learning activities.

Every subject has its own group of virtual classrooms with a maximum of eighty students and one consultant professor per classroom (although depending on the subject these figures may be very different).

From the very beginning, students receive support from their tutoring counsellor, who guides them through the complete process of enrolment, learning and being part of the UOC community.

On the other hand, the teaching counsellor offers academic advice on all matters related to the fulfillment of educational challenges, the process of integration within the university community and professional orientation on completion of a student's studies.

The virtual classroom has four access zones where all the activities related to the learning process are performed, namely Planning, Communication, Information resources and Evaluation:

* *Planning*: Shows a calendar with all the activities of the learning process, and also the teaching curriculum for the subject.
* *Communication*: Provides access to the public e-mail system of the classroom, the list of the classmates from where anyone can e-mail the other students or chat with them, and access to the tutoring and teaching counsellor e-mails.
* *Resources*: Shows a list of all the educational material, information sources and resources related with the subject. Figure shows an example of a list of available learning resources for one subject, "Data Mining" (in Catalan).
* *Evaluation*: It offers a direct access to the mailbox for submitting the evaluation activities and access to the marks and final results of all the parts of the course.

The resources area provides access to four basic kinds of resources, two of them optional. The first, named "Subject material", contains the learning materials which are edited under the UOC format and that are directly related with the course and subject objectives.

Although most educational material is available in form of printed books, this area also includes access to the web and the PDF versions for printing, and other kinds of resources such as reading materials, study cases, etc.

This kind of resource is mandatory for all subjects. While this area is a more permanent content, which undergoes a publishing plan and an editing process, at the "Information Sources" area there is the content which is easier to change, under a dynamic management process, which allows content modification each semester under the particular needs of each subject. Under "Information sources", at the moment the sources being used are: full text articles scanned from paper publications or with direct link to the electronic version; recommended bibliography with direct access to the online circulation service; academic and professional databases that the library subscribes for the UOC community; encyclopaedias and dictionaries also exclusive to UOC users; law content and standards; and a selection of free web sites coming from the bookmarks of the teachers.

This kind of resource is also mandatory. "Tools and support elements" comprises those features that give support to the students for their homework. It provides tools such as software, exams and exercises from other semesters that can be used as samples of the evaluation process, etc., all them related with the methodology, but not directly with the basic course content.

Finally, there is also the option of providing access to a "Shared Server", a public space available to all the users of the virtual classroom which is used for updating information and adding new contents in an easy manner.

It is worth to remark that most of the information resources come from the digital library integrated in the virtual campus, which uses an ad hoc database with Dublin Core, IMS and SCORM standards and application profiles for managing the electronic resources, and a commercial OPAC with MARC 21 for the recommended bibliography. For visualising these resources at the virtual classroom, at the digital library or elsewhere at the virtual campus, both XML and a set of XSL transformations are used, in order to separate both content and presentation. When using these tools, teachers have an easy manner to maintain and update the resources, and it is also possible to work with different languages (Catalan, Spanish and English). This also increases reutilisation because the same resource can be accessible from different virtual classrooms without need to maintaining several

SUBJECT PLANNING

Figure shows a typical scheduling which includes all the activities the students need to perform in order to successfully achieve the desired learning plan goals for one subject. This scheduling, altogether with all the available learning resources form what is known as the "Teaching Plan", a document which explains all the course methodology, goals, resources, and so.

Currently, the scheduling, which is activity oriented, is not directly related to the learning resources but for a simple enumeration of the resources needed for each activity. This lack of structure makes very difficult the continuous actualisation of contents, for example, or the inclusion of any new learning resource on-the-fly.

By the moment, the digital library is used as a simple repository for all the learning resources, but without a real semantic tagging or including any formal description of the learning process. The teaching plan is the first step towards a complete formalisation of the learning process with the help of the appropriate standard extensions. The use of e-learning standards for both content description and structuring will allow the inclusion of complex learning strategies such as personalisation, for example.

THE DIGITAL LIBRARY

The UOC's digital library is the center for resources of information provided by the university so that students, teachers, researchers and staff can access all the contents and services they need to carry out their basic tasks: learning, teaching, research, continuing studies and management.

These resources include, among others:

* Exclusive electronic content, both academic and professional, from e-journals, databases and e-books, among other sources. These contents are accessed remotely using the Library on the UOC's Virtual Campus and, thus, can be accessed from any computer. These resources from the library are only available to UOC users (students, teachers and academic staff) and, therefore, cannot be accessed freely from the internet.
* Free and carefully selected resources which complement the exclusive archive and which are of particular interest to the community due to their academic value and the

information they provide. Amongst these electronic resources, are bookmarks selected by UOC teaching staff. All the resources in this section, namely "Digital Collection", are described in detail to provide users with an assessment of their contents and usefulness.

The resources in the classrooms are created upon this range of digital content and also from new additions. Both selection and new proposals for content to be placed at the classrooms are managed through and e-mail service based, posted by teaching staff to librarians, so content updating it is not immediate.

Furthermore, all content is revised and tagged before it becomes available in the virtual classroom, so the possibilities of updating content in an on-the-fly manner are dramatically reduced. The content which is also available from the digital library at the virtual campus, is usually described through MARC21 or, for the electronic resources, through the Dublin Core standard.

But, the semantic description generated by the library is not used at the virtual classroom, the place where these content is still not semantically organised but through the teaching plan. This is a clear example of metadata redundancy, as the same information (but from two different points of view, library or e-learning) must be specified twice in different formats. From the e-learning perspective, there is also the need of adding new types of content at the virtual classroom resources area, which at the moment are mostly text base material:

* Teaching materials: created ad hoc for the UOC's educational methodology, which develop the basic contents for all the subjects.
* Basic digitised articles or from the database.
* *Exclusive electronic information resources*: e-books, databases, e-journals, etc.
* Access to the latest newsletters specialising in the subject matter.
* *Recommended bibliography*: A reading list with the basic bibliography for the subject, with the option of requesting their borrowing from the classroom.
* Exams and answers to the exercises from previous semesters.

* *Frequently asked questions (FAQ)*: With the help of the appropriate tools, threads in the forum of the virtual classroom can be converted into useful FAQ documents.

All these resources are currently tagged using a minimum set of metadata for library maintenance purposes only using MARC 21 or Dublin Core. In a few subjects, these resources are also tagged using a subset of the LOM standard for educational purposes (for example, allowing students to create their own evaluation activities by selecting the appropriate exercises from a large repository), but this tagging is not integrated with the MARC 21 yet. One of the goals of the work presented in this chapter is to establish the requirements of such integration using the paradigm of interoperability among content distribution standards.

STANDARDS INTEROPERABILITY

Metadata provide controlled and structured descriptions of learning resources through searchable access points such as title, author, date, location, description and subject, but can also provide interpretative information on the potential education application of resources or include described information about the relationships with other resources.

The learning resources form a hierarchical structure when are combined to create courses using learning objects as the basic pieces. Furthermore, so there is a clear need for representing all this knowledge about each subject. In order to do so, we need to define the appropriate mappings between multimedia, e-learning and library standards in a two-stage approach: first, a set of common metadata is identified in all three standards for supporting basic browsing and searching capabilities and, second, the appropriate extensions using ontologies are created to minimize metadata overlap and inconsistencies, using the MPEG-7 standard as the basic language for content description.

THE MPEG-7 STANDARD

The MPEG-7 standard is a recent standard (the version of the final work was produced in 2003) for distribution of multimedia contents, which allows users a complete syntax of contents as well as a semantic level of code. Previous standards of the MPEG family, such as MPEG-1, MPEG-2 and MPEG-4, were focused on compression and digitalisation of video and audio signals.

MPEG-7 complements them since, it aims to standardise the description based on contents of different types of audiovisual information. Search, recovery and indexation of such multimedia contents require a tool for describing documents and let them use in an efficient manner.

The aim of MPEG-7 is to provide interoperability amongst systems and applications employed in the generation, management, distribution and consume of audiovisual contents. The main feature of MPEG-7 standard is its flexibility: the use of XML (eXtensible Markup Language) as content description language and the possibility to define a pack of descriptors adapted to requirements of tagging and indexation according to the application desired.

They provide the extension of the standard MPEG-7 to be used in diverse environments and be adapted in each case to the particular use requirements. The use of XML allows users to have a structured access towards the information contained in the MPEG-7 document in an efficient manner, and ensures a connection with other standards of description through the use of transformations XSLT. MPEG-7 uses a Description Definition Language (DDL) to allow the creation of Description Schemes (DSs) and Descriptors (Ds) when new extensions are needed. An example of the relationship between these elements is shown in figure.

These descriptions are based on catalog (*i.e.*, title, creator, rights), semantic (*i.e.*, the who, what, when, and where information about objects and events), and structural (*i.e.*, the colour histogram of an image or the timbre of a recorded instrument) features of the multimedia content. The DDL defines the syntactic rules to express and combine Description Schemes and Descriptors. A DDL file is encoded in XML and more specifically uses the constructs defined in the W3C's XML Schema Language.

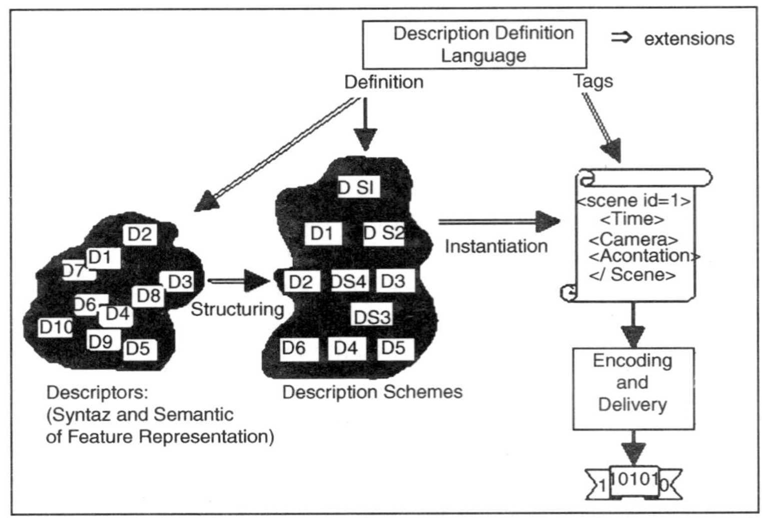

Fig. 3.1. MPEG-7 Elements.

The XML Schema Language defines a language for defining the structure, content, and semantics of XML documents. XML Schemas express shared vocabularies and allow machines to carry out rules made by people, expressed in the schema language. An XML Schema is, itself, an XML document.The importance of XML Schema language to the MPEG-7 DDL is because of the stability of the XML Schema language, its potential wide-spread adoption, availability of tools and parsers, and its ability to satisfy the majority of MPEG-7's requirements led to the decision to adopt XML Schema as the basis for the DDL.

Regarding efficiency issues, the use of BiM (Binary Format for MPEG-7) ensures a fast access because it enables the streaming and the compression of any XML documents, enabling also a parametrised transmission of any XML document and, therefore, the same contens can be accessed in many different ways, as shown in figure. This is a clear sign of the large flexibility offered by the MPEG-7 standard which can be used to build complex multimedia courses following a hierarchical structure.

E-LEARNING STANDARDS

As a very complex scenario in nature, the description of the e-learning process and the interactions between all its elements is not a simple question. Two basic levels of description can be identified: the first level, pointed towards learning objects, describes the aspects directly related to the educational content. The second level describes the interactions between such learning objects and the users within the framework defined by the learning process.For the first level, the LOM standard defines a structure for interoperable descriptions of learning objects. In this case, a learning object is defined as any entity, digital or non-digital, that may be used for learning, education or training. Notice that we do not use the definition of learning object from Wiley because it does not include non-digital resources. Nevertheless, although there are several other definitions for learning objects, all of them coincide in a single desired behaviour: reusability. Metadata for a learning object describes relevant characteristics of such learning object to which applies, pursuing reusability. Regarding the LOM standard, such characteristics may be grouped in general, life cycle, meta-metadata, educational, technical, educational, rights, relation, annotation, and classification categories.

Nevertheless, the LOM standard has been criticised because of the lack of specific metadata for educational purposes (the current educational category is very limited) and several authors have proposed extensions for covering such limitations. On the other hand, application profiles such as SCORM or the IMS-LD standard, which is based on EML, try to describe the aspects more related to the learning process in itself, such as sequencing or role playing.

It seems clear that this information cannot be stored in the learning objects, but in a higher semantic level. The use of ontologies for representing all the richness of the learning process scenario is a clear example of separating the concepts of resource, activity and role. Although the IMS-LD standard may seem too complex, its flexibility and multilevel description capabilities allow the specification of any learning process ranging from simple educational itineraries to complex learning processes including personalisation and collaborative working capabilities. Furthermore, in the simplest level, it is easy to convert any IMS-LD schema into a SCORM compatible course, which is already in development in the UOC virtual campus, ensuring compatibility.

DIGITAL LIBRARY STANDARDS

Finally, regarding the Dublin Core and MARC 21 standards, both of them have been typically used for content tagging in digital libraries. On the one hand, the Dublin Core is a metadata element set. It includes all Dublin Core Metadata Initiative terms (that is, refinements, encoding schemes, and controlled vocabulary terms) intended to facilitate discovery of resources. The Dublin Core has been in development since, 1995 through a series of focused invitational workshops that gather experts from the library world, the networking and digital library research communities, and a variety of content specialties.

The Dublin Core is a content description metadata model for the recovery of electronic resources. It is being used by formal resource description communities such as museums, libraries, government agencies, and commercial organisations. The Dublin Core is based on XML language. It is possible to use several different syntactical forms for a DC document: resource description framework (RDF), DTD and XML schemas. On the other hand, MAchine Readable Catalog (MARC) is used for coding, storing and exchanging bibliographic data since, 1968. MARC was born at the Library of Congress for interchanging bibliographic machine readable references between libraries. MARC 21 is a result of the evolution of the MARC with the main difference that is enhanced for cataloguing electronic resources. Both standards are in fact interoperable as it is possible to convert the metadata in one format to the another using the appropriate mapping.

EQUIVALENCES AND INTEROPERABILITY AMONG STANDARDS

Interoperability can be defined as "the ability of two or more systems or components to exchange information and to use the information that has been exchanged". Interoperability ensures that the data is entered only once in one application and that can be automatically propagated or queried to/from other applications.

Such a scenario requires a common semantic model, in order that metadata from one repository can also be interpreted by any other repository. As all the three standards share the same basic goal (content tagging), it is possible to establish a common set of functionalities covered by all of them, as described in.

Table. 3.1. Basic Metadata Equivalences between Dublin Core, LOM and MPEG-7 Standards.

Dublin Core	LOM	MPEG-7
Identifier	General. Catalog Entry	Media Information. Media Identification Identfier
Title	General. Title	Creation Meta Information. Creation. Title TitleText
Description	General. Description	Creation Meta Information. Creation Creation Description
Format	Technical. Format	Media Information. Media Profile. Media Format File Format
Format	Technical. Size	Media Information. Media Profile. Media Format Duration
Creator	Life Cycle. Contribute. Entity	Creation Meta Information. Creation Creator
Date	Life Cycle. Contribute. Date	Creation Meta Information. Creation Creation Date
Date	Life Cycle. Contribute. Date	Usage Meta Information. Publication Publication Date
Language	General. Language	Creation Meta Information. Classification. Language Language Code
Coverage	General. Coverage	Creation Meta Information. Creation. Creation Location Place Name
Rights	Rights	Usage MetaInformation. Rights Rights ID

Table 3.1 shows a basic subset of common descriptors for the three standards. For each field in the Dublin Core standard, the equivalent field in the LOM standard (category and element name) and the path and the equivalent field in the MPEG-7 hierarchy structure is shown.

Notice that the MPEG-7 standard is much richer than the other two standards, and that it can be even extended through the DDL.

Nevertheless, although the MPEG-7 standard could be extended to represent all the descriptors and the description schemes to include all the metadata available in both LOM and Dublin Core, only a basic subset of both standards is really necessary for basic content tagging. We are currently working in the definition of such basic subset (for the LOM standard) which will become the new set of Ds and DSs elements in the MPEG-7 proposal.

Following the ideas described in, the MPEG-7 standard needs to be represented through an ontology, in order to ensure both interoperability and scalability with other systems.

In fact, any extension of the MPEG-7 standard (or any other standard) is better defined by means of the equivalent ontology, as stated in.

Therefore, once the basic set of Ds and DSs had been defined, as suggested, extend such ontology to incorporate these new elements.

EXTERNAL RESOURCES AND INTELLECTUAL PROPERTY

Usually, digital libraries are not only structured repositories of contents, but also gateways to external databases and other external information providers. It is important to remark that the use of all the available resources is restricted by the applicable intellectual property rights policies. In the case of internal learning resources, generated within the virtual campus by teachers and students, they are always asked in advance for permission for using their work without changes in other classrooms, without making any dissemination through Internet, and only for educational reasons and providing always the author of the material. UOC policy ensures that all content generated within the learning process context becomes part of the UOC community and, therefore, it can be shared among all the users of the virtual campus. But in the external case, there is a clear need for adopting intellectual property licences that allow the modification and redistribution of such content for different purposes.

Therefore, there is a need for using a type of licence that lets the teaching staff to distribute and build new content upon the work of other teachers and external resources. UOC is promoting the adoption of content sharing licences such as Creative Commons or the General Public Licence (GPL), for example, in order to ensure a simple but effective intellectual rights policy. For those contents with more restrictive rights, the system should ensure the proper use through the appropriate standards.

In this sense, the upcoming MPEG-21 standard is intented to provide a normative open framework for multimedia delivery and consumption for use by all the players in the delivery and consumption chain. This open framework will provide content creators, producers, distributors and service providers with equal opportunities in the MPEG-21 enabled open market. As stated in, MPEG-21 can play a role in the design and development of digital library applications to ensure proper digital rights management within any organisation.

PROPOSED FRAMEWORK

Therefore, we propose to use the MPEG- 7 as the basic standard for content description in the digital library. Using the appropriate DDL based extensions, the MPEG-7 standard can represent also the required fields of Dublin Core, MARC 21 and LOM standards.In order to do so, we propose a standards integration project development in three stages:

* Basic metadata identification: once the specific requirements for both librarians and teachers have been identified, a basic subset of the needed metadata for the three standards will be described using the DDL, extending the MPEG-7 standard. This stage is currently

under development involving both librarians and teachers, but also instructional designers and usability experts, in order to ensure a tagging oriented towards the concept of activity. The resulting MPEG-7 extended standard will be represented through the appropriate ontology, hiding all metadata details from pure content, and simplifying also the access to such content from different scenarios (the virtual classroom or the digital library interface, for example).

* Ontology extension: starting from the ontology described in, as suggested, define the adequate extensions to incorporate the richness of the learning process, using the IMS-LD standard first level functionalities as the basic requirements of our system.
* Prototype development: finally, using the new available Ds and DSs, a set of learning resources is tagged accordingly to all the needed criteria: for library purposes, e-learning and multimedia content description. Then, a basic educational itinerary will be described for such learning resources using the ontology. This prototype will be probably implemented using any available IMS-LD player with the appropriate XSL transformation, using the ontology for representing all the elements in the learning process. In order to test the multimedia capabilities, a subject with audiovisual content will be chosen as the course prototype.

Therefore, all the small fragments of content which are used as learning resources in any subject or course will be tagged according to the extended MPEG-7 standard, including metadata for both pedagogical and library purposes. In fact, using the appropriate transformations (*i.e.*, a subset of the available metadata), it will be possible to generate the Dublin Core or MARC 21, or the LOM record for any learning resource in the digital library, as they are partial descriptions of the complete tagging using the extended MPEG-7 standard. All these resources will be structured and integrated in another MPEG-7 document created from the extended ontology, in order to represent all the possibilities of the learning process, including sequencing and temporal requirements, following the same approach than the IMS-LD standard.

Therefore, any subject could be seen as a single MPEG- 7 document, and the digital library will become a content producer, and students (but also teachers) will become consumers using both push and pull application paradigms. We expect that the creation of a large repository of learning resources and MPEG-7 documents for the different formative itineraries will follow the prototype course, once the proposed framework has had been validated.

CONCLUSIONS

Large e-learning environments such as the UOC virtual campus, for example, usually include the use of content repositories where very different kinds of learning resources can be found, ranging from printed books to multimedia contents. These resources are used by students as the basic educational materials for each subject they are enrolled to, following a predefined teaching plan and a scheduling.

Currently now, this information and learning resources are stored in the digital library as isolated documents, without any structuring. In this chapter a proposal for standards integration has been presented. The use of the MPEG-7 standard capabilities for describing all the metadata needed by the learning resources used in the virtual classroom seems to be the most efficient option, integrating all the knowledge managed from three different points of view: the digital library, e-learning resources and multimedia content. Three stages have been identified: first, the identification of a basic subset of metadata for content tagging, and its representation using the MPEG-7 standard by means of the DDL. Second, the extension of the MPEG-7 ontology mapping to incorporate all the aspects related to the learning process, such as activities, roles, and so, as defined by the IMS-LD standard. Finally, as a third step, as suggested, implement a course prototype for a selected subject in order to validate the MPEG-7 standard as the basic language for multimedia and e-learning content description in a digital library. The work presented in this chapter is still in the first stage of the proposal, although several aspects related to the second stage are currently under development. The main lines of present and future research in this project cover the study of the forthcoming MPEG-21 standard, still under development, which includes aspects related to contract and distribution services, or author rights management. The use of complex ontologies for the description of the relationships between producers and consumers of e-learning and multimedia content using the appropriate description standards is also an interesting research subject.

4

Building a Multimedia Digital Library

INTRODUCTION

Multimedia knowledge resources as document surrogates and as significant knowledge sources in a library needs no emphasis. In the present academic and special library setting the educational videos, instructional visual aids and audio learning resources form a significant collection. Time is fast catching up the world over that the traditional forms of collection development techniques and collection maintenance strategies need replacements with the upcoming trends in the profession. Consequently, the traditional information service options are no longer acceptable to a large majority of the users or that there is a strong demand for newer forms of services which are not so familiar to the libraries. Libraries therefore are now forced to be friendly and familiarised themselves with all relevant and current popular multimedia formats.

As technology marches past at a tremendous pace, the traditional meaning and definitions of a library's collection range also undergo a great deal of change. Interactive and multimedia learning resources are one of the most rapidly changing and exciting areas of education in the world today. The recent entrants are computer-based training (CBTs) materials/Web-based training (WBTs) materials, especially interactive multimedia programmes that run on personal

computers. These new technologies offer students, teachers and researchers access to materials as never before. Multimedia can deliver large amounts of information in ways that make it manageable, approachable, and useful. And by making it possible to access illustrations and photographs, sound and video, as well as large amounts of text, interactive multimedia programmes present learning information to teachers, students, and scholars in newly engaging and meaningful ways. The integration of multimedia programmes into libraries and classrooms promises not only to change the kinds of information that is available for learning, but the in which that learning takes place.

MULTIMEDIA COLLECTION: FEATURES, PROBLEMS AND PROSPECTS

Predominantly multimedia collection of a library comprise video resources (educative as well as entertainers), audio recordings, computer-based training materials (CBTs), Web-Based Training materials (WBTs), illustrations, photographs, etc. Depending on the nature of the parent institution's goals, academic focus, research thrust its resource allocations and financial capabilities, their collection strength may considerably vary. In most cases, the collection-building process of the multimedia resources may follow the normal traditional mode. In the case of e-Resources the purchase may be restricted to licensing and only online access to the product may be available to the library.

Publishers usually enforce stringent copyright and IPR restrictions to multimedia resources. Multimedia collection, especially the analogue knowledge resources, poses a variety of practical and operational constraints to libraries. One of the major limitations is their sole dependency on a host of gadgets such as media players, viewers, etc.

They also suffer from reach and visibility limitations as they can be viewed or listened to by a single or fewer number of viewers/listeners simultaneously. Further more, there are shortcomings with respect to resource discovery possibilities other than the basic indexing offered by their catalolgues (traditional as well as digital). Collection maintenance and long-term preservation of these special collections are always a concern for librarians. Multimedia resources in the newer breeds of media formats such as the CBTs, WBTs, digital videos/audios, etc., have the added advantage of being dynamic and mobile with respect to their flexibility, portability and efficiency of access/dissemination. The current information environment also unequivocally prompts libraries to leverage on the latest digital technologies towards building multimedia digital libraries and in setting up dynamic electronic information systems.

These newer information services offer lots of power and visibility to libraries and the user community without compromising on their quality and performance. Yet, they also pose a multitude of problems in the course of their preparations while submitting them in a digital library. Swift developments in mediarelated technologies, rapid obsolescence and their redundancy, time-to-time media and format migrations, resource intensive maintenance, etc., add up the complexity and complications of these collections. This chapter attempts to share the IIMK experience in developing, implementing and maintaining the multimedia collection as a part of its digital library development activities which comprise the entire publication types, formats and media.

OPEN SOURCE PHILOSOPHY OF IIMK

IIMK is an ardent proponent of the Open Access and the Open Source Software philosophies which is sweeping the world now. It was a chosen decision not to go in for a proprietary software for its digital library applications. Accordingly we evaluated some of the popular Open Source Software for digital libraries, which were in use internationally. 'Dienst', 'Eprints', 'Fedora', 'Greenstone', etc., were the candidates for the preferred software. Obviously Greenstone outscored the group and we formally adopted the software for creating the IIMK digital library (Greenstone). The Greenstone Digital Library Software (GSDL) is a top of the line and internationally renowned Open Source Software system for developing digital libraries, promoted by the New Zealand Digital Library project research group at the University of Waikato, headed by Dr. Ian H. Witten, and is sponsored by the UNESCO [Witten]. Greenstone software (versions starting from 2.30) along with Java Run Time Environment (JRE) were deployed for the purpose. The software suite is available at the open source directory 'Sourceforge' [Sourceforge].

DIGITAL LIBRARY AT IIMK

The primary objective of the IIMK digital library was to enhance the digital collection in a substantial way, by strategically sourcing digital materials, conforming to copyright permissions, in all possible standards/formats so that scalability and flexibility is guaranteed for the future and advanced information services and are assured to the user community right from beginning.

The digital library was planned in such a way that it would integrate and aggregate the existing collections and services with an outstanding user interface. Accordingly, necessary strategies were adopted towards working out the digital library system. This implied that the digital library system should have a strong collection interface capable of embracing almost all the popular digital standards, digital formats and software platforms, in line with the underlying digital library technologies in vogue. This was crucial in the case of multimedia integration, which was again important as it was planned to host a digital audio and video library as part of the core library collection.

The Digital Library Project at IIMK took off during September 2001. The first few months were mainly devoted to infrastructure build-up such as hardware and software, digitisation strategies, strategies regarding collection building, and finalisation of the variety of content categories. Since, the campus intranet and the Internet connectivity were robust, there were no worries on those fronts. The IIMK DL was slated to be populated with e-Books, ('born digital' as well as digitised), e-Journals, management cases, technical reports, working papers, faculty publications, teaching notes, CBTs, WBTs, educational videos/audios, value adding the existing OPAC, speeches, presentations, etc. It took around two/three months for us to install and get proper command over the software. The collection comprises multiple digital formats such as HTML, XML, PDF, PS, RTF, JPG, CIF, MPEG, etc.

The DL has now got a sizable collection of over 500 e-Books covering almost all areas of business and management, literature, classics, and Information Technology. Cross collection pointers were given to project Gutenberg (classics and literature) and to other GSDL example collections (social science, environmental science) and hence, the virtual collection strength is over 15000 e-Books. IIMK has plans to host the IIM Consortium (led by the six IIMs in India) digital archive and studies are underway on the feasibility of putting the IIM Consortium digital content under Greenstone (IIM Consortium).

A rigorous collection development drive is being worked out with most of the popular electronic publishers specialising in business and management. One of the major bottlenecks to the speedy collection development is the non-availability of proprietary and trade literature in Greenstone acceptable formats such as HTML, Word, or PDF. Most of these publishers put their materials in their own proprietary e-Book reader formats, from which the text extraction becomes almost impossible.

RESOURCE DISCOVERY

Leading edge technical skills and technology backing on campus demand sophisticated human resource requirements and high-end IT infrastructure. The quality and performance of a digital library is measured in terms of its information retrieval logistics. Multimedia digital libraries also indeed require the strong footings of Resource Description Framework (RDF) vision supplemented with descriptive metadata standards such as Dublin Core, Metadata Object Description Schema (MODS) or Metadata Encoding and Transmission (METS). They also need the strength of Extensible Markup Language (XML) encoding schemas, related Document Type Definitions (DTDs) and Extensible Stylesheet Language (XSL) transformations between the non-traditional datastreams and the Hypertext Markup Language (HTML) front-end.

MULTIMEDIA DIGITAL LIBRARY WORKFLOW METHODOLOGY

One of the salient features of this collection is that the multimedia digital library is carved exclusively out of open source software (except for the media conversion utility) and open digital library standards. The untiring support and hard work of the IIMK's Digital Library team in the Library and the Computer Center need special mention.

COLLECTION STRATEGY

The videos/audios multimedia collection was planned as a 'metadata' collection. The digital objects (video file) were stored in a separate media server so that the digital library server is not overloaded or overburdened. Hyperlinks were given to the Streaming Server where the audio/video objects were kept in JPEG format.

SOFTWARE AND STANDARDS

As discussed earlier, the Greenstone Digital Library Software (GSDL) was deployed for the digital library application. "PlayTV-USB-Pro" software was used for converting the analog videos to digital files.

Videos were first converted to AVI files and subsequently made to JPEG format. "Unreal Media Server" software was used for streaming the videos from the media server. "Streaming Media Player" software was given with all the retrieved pages for the users to download and stream/view the file. Each Video file was built as an HTML embedded page and XML was used for metadata encoding purposes. "Dublin Core" was the metadata standard used.

DUBLIN CORE METADATA AND XML TAGGING

To create indexes for section and sub-section (document hierarchy and structuring) in Greenstone the document should be in HTML format. Obviously now the Source File has to be edited as a HTML file structure.

For the section and sub-sections, the source file has to be edited appropriately, giving XML tags passed as comments in the body of the HTML file.

Unqualified version of Dublin Core Metadata standard was deployed for resource description of the multimedia digital library. The Section Tagging pattern used for the video collection is given in fig. 4.1.

```
<Section> <Description>

<Metadata name="Title"><a HREF="ums:\\TCP:streamserver:5119\video\V83.mpg">1. 20
        Steps to better management : Solving problems and thinking creatively(NEIF)
        V201 </a></Metadata>
<Metadata name="Subject" mode="accumulate"><font size=l>
        Creativity<Ifont><JMetadata>
<Metadata name="Subject" mode="accumulate"><font size=l >Strategic
        Management</font></Metadata>
<Metadata name="Subject" mode="accumulate"><font size=l>
        Strategy</font></Metadata>
<Metadata name="Subject" mode="accumulate"><font size=1> Innov
        ation</font></Metadata>
<Metadata name="Subject" mode="accumulate"><font size=l ><Ifont></Metadata> <Metadata
        name="Publisher" mode="accumulate"><font size=l> NEIF</font></Metadata>
<Metadata name="Resource Identifier" mode="accumulate"><font size=1> V 201
        </font></Metadata>
<Metadata name="Source" mode="accumulate"><font size=l>
        </font>NEIF</Metadata>

</Description> </Section>
```

Fig. 4.1. XML based Section Tagging of Dublin Core Metadata.

Unreal Media Server is an open source server software which ensures efficient multimedia deliver over the network, LAN as well as WAN. UMediaServer is a streaming server for Windows operatin systems.

Unreal scores high over its proprietary counterparts such as Microsoft and Real, with it efficiency in streaming high quality content.

SYSTEM ARCHITECTURE

Transmission Control Protocol (TCP), Hypertext Transfer Protocol (HTTP) and Real Transpo] Protocol (RTP) and Multicast transport protocols are used for streaming content from Media Server t clients. Incoming content is not stored on the client computer's hard disk and the user is not allowe to save media locally, thus author's rights are fully protected. User authentication and access restriction enable trusted access to media resources. User logging provides the means to track user activity. For the client workstations, Unreal Media Player client software was provided. The System Architectur of the multimedia digital library is given in fig. 4.2.

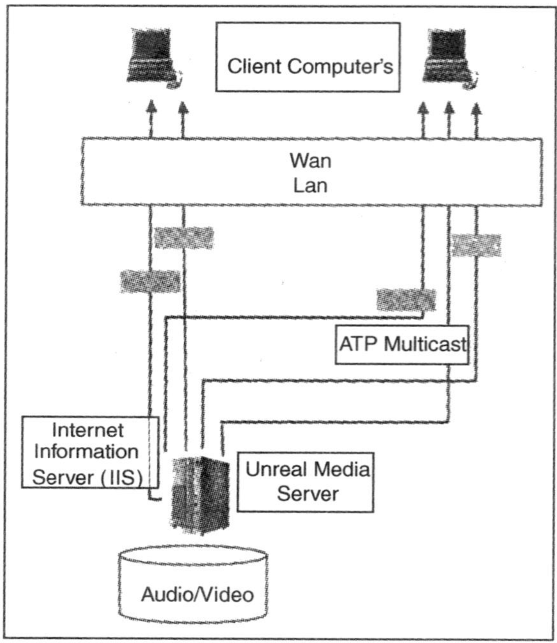

Fig. 4.2. System Architecture of the Multimedia Digital Library.

CREATING LINKS TO MEDIA RESOURCE

While setting up the Streaming Media Player it registers a custom URL protocol on the user's machine. This is a UMS protocol, allowing launching Streaming Media Player directly from the hyperlink on the web page. Though the most comfortable way for the users to access remote media is to click on a link in the Web browser, for this application we gave the hyperlink embedded in the Dublin Core metadata element 'title' as follows:

```
<Metadata name="Title"><a HREF="ums:\\TCP:
streamserver:5119\video \V83.mpg">1. 20 Steps to better
management: Solving problems and thinking creatively
(NEIF) V201</a></Metadata>
```

In the Metadata Tag, 'UMS' is the custom protocol of the UMediaServer Software. Streaming is achieved using the 'TCP' protocol. 'Streamserver' is the media server holding the multimedia digital objects. TCP's default port '5119' is the port utilised. For HTTP, default 80 is the port specified. Using Media Server Configuration tool, you can create virtual folders and map them to the different physical locations on the server machine.

Alternatively, the physical location can be anywhere in the server machine's LAN. 'Video' is the folder where the digital videos are located and 'V83.mpg' is the object being streamed to the client.

ACCESS METHODS

The multimedia collection is one of the important and appreciated services of the IIMK Library Portal. Users are able to visit the multimedia digital library and select the videos/audios of their choice by browsing alphabetically or by searching the author, title/free text, keyword, source or publisher. The Dublin Core metadata description facilitates efficient subject approach to information retrieval of the important resources with fanciful titles too, such as 'Eye of the Beholder', 'Just in Time' etc.

Retrieval of cross collection resources is another special feature which is seldom achieved through traditional methods. The digital library at IIMI< has been able to strike great impact amongst the user community on campus. The academic quality of the resources coupled with flexibility, convenience and efficiency of access across the entire campus are the major reasons for this scenario. User education and product orientation sessions held at regular intervals by the library, both online as well as live, have paid rich dividends in the increased awareness and resource utility.

The usage and usability of the digital resources have increased extensively as per server logs and monitoring statistics. The multimedia collection now streams out over hundreds of world-class educational videos, as well as audio resources.

The distinction of this work is that it has used only open source digital library softwares and open digital library standards across the entire workflow and operations. This has significant impact and implications as the proprietary softwares and standards are exorbitantly expensive and beyond the reach of most of the academic and special libraries in developing countries.

5

Digital Libraries and Reference Services

INTRODUCTION

Reference services, sometimes referred to as "reference and information services", refer to the personal assistance provided to users in the pursuit of information. Provision of such personalised information services has remained the central theme of the library and information profession. The importance of these services grew over time with the introduction of new technologies and services in libraries.

Researcher categorised reference services into three broad groups:

* Information services that involve either finding the required information on behalf of the users, or assisting users in finding information;
* Instruction in the use of library resources and services; and
* User guidance, in which users are guided in selecting the most appropriate information sources and services.

Reference questions can range from the simple fact-finding type to complex questions requiring consultation, and often analysis, of one or moreinformation sources. An important part of a reference service is the reference interview, which involves a personal discussion between a user and the reference librarian. Through the interview the reference librarian not only tries to understand the specific information need(s), but also collects information about the user, such as the user's subject knowledge, the purpose of finding the specific information, and so on. Based on the reference interview, the reference librarian is often able to filter the retrieved information in order to pick up the most appropriate source(s) for the given user at the given point of time. While reference service is largely a reactive service, *i.e.*, assistance or the service is provided when asked for by the users, libraries have also played a key role in providing information services in anticipation of user needs.

Such services include various forms of current awareness and selective dissemination of information services. These types of service that aim to keep the users abreast of the latest developments in their areas of interest, however, have not been provided only by libraries: online search services like Dialog and institutions like the Institute of Scientific Information (ISI) have provided such services, for example *Dialog Alerts, Current Contents* and so on. With the increasing availability of electronic information services, and the emergence of the Web and digital libraries, an obvious question arises: is there a need for such personalised services? To put it in the words of Arms, who is an active researcher and a strong proponent of digital libraries: "could we conceive of an automated digital library that disintermediates all the services that reference librarians now provide?".

This is a very pertinent question for the future of digital libraries as well as the library and information science profession. This is the central theme of this chapter. It is obvious that the current digital libraries, and most of the digital library research projects, have focused on access to, and retrieval of, digital information rather than on the services that have been provided to the users by traditional libraries. Perhaps the reason for this is the narrower definition of digital libraries formulated by the digital library projects themselves.

This chapter looks at some definitions of digital libraries. However, since, the definitions of digital libraries have been critically analysed by Borgman, the present chapter begins from there. It also looks at some definitions of digital libraries that emphasise services, implicitly or explicitly. The Web has altered the notion of traditional reference services, and a number of Web-based "expert services" are now offered by many non-library organisations. This chapter briefly reviews some currently available Web-based reference services. Although these reference services are not necessarily offered by libraries, and they are termed differently, for example, as "expert services", they are used quite heavily, and they do not require a visit to the library to get answers to the questions.

So, what should be the role of digital libraries? Should they stop providing reference services altogether or should they concentrate only on certain types of reference questions? This chapter looks into these issues. Current digital library research that specifically focuses on providing reference and personalised information services is also discussed. Finally, this chapter points out some research areas that may be looked at for second generation digital libraries in order to change the notion of digital libraries from information access points to information service providers.

DEFINITION OF DIGITAL LIBRARIES AND PERSONALISED SERVICES

While reviewing the definitions of digital libraries, Borgman noted that "in general, researchers (who primarily come from computer science and/or engineering backgrounds) focus on digital libraries as content collected on behalf of user communities, while librarians focus on digital libraries as institutions or services'". She further stressed that the current state of digital library research and development, especially in the USA, is influenced by the research definition of digital libraries.

The emphasis on the "enabling technologies" for access to digital resources rather than on the services traditionally provided by libraries becomes quite evident when one looks at the two special issues of the *Journal of the American Society for Information Science*, The two issues contain excellent articles reflecting the state of digital library research but none focus on digital library services *per se*. Even the editor of the two special issues did not discuss reference and information services. He mentioned that "digital libraries have the ability to provide a previously unattainable level of service". He emphasised access to information and suggested the various methods, tools and techniques that facilitate improved access to information in digital libraries. However, this is in sharp contrast to the views of the two editors of the special issue of *Information Processing and Management* on digital libraries. Marchionini and Fox in their editorial stated that "digital library work occurs in the context of a complex design space shaped by four dimensions: community, technology, services and content".

The fact that digital libraries should not be regarded only as point of access to digital information was emphasised by a definition of digital libraries given by Borgman as early as in 1992 whereby she contended that a digital library are:

* A service;
* an architecture;
* A set of information resources, databases of text, numbers, graphics, sound, video, etc. and
* A set of tools and capabilities to locate, retrieve and utilise the information resources available.

The definition of a digital library that came up in the March 1994 Digital Library Workshop emphasised that a full service digital library must accomplish all the essential services of traditional libraries and also exploit the well-known advantages of digital storage, searching and communication.

There are many other definitions of digital libraries that mention the services aspect, either explicitly or implicitly. Pointing out the lack of emphasis on reference and information services, Sloan lamented that "human interaction in the digital library is discussed far less frequently. One would almost get the impression that the service tradition of the physical library will be unnecessary and redundant in the digital library environment". He emphasised the point that "technology and information resources, on their own, cannot make up an effective digital library". Emphasising the need for personalised services in digital libraries, Lombardi mentioned that, "helping clients find resources in a digitally chaotic world is the first priority".

In a Delphi study of digital libraries it was revealed that "the primary roles librarians play in digital libraries include organisation, selection and acquisition and acting as gateways to the provision of services involving information". This study also revealed that "the best reasons for developing a digital library include: increasing access to information, serving end users' needs and bringing organisation to the unstructured universe of electronically available information".

Thus, this study shows the importance of "serving end users' needs", and the need for the librarians to act as "gateways to the provision of services involving information" in a digital library. Another study conducted by Downs and Friedman indicated that "in the absence of human intermediaries, there is a need for end-user instruction on the use of digital libraries". Covi pointed out that "digital libraries will be used only when workers can readily integrate into social legimitated and legitimatable ways of working". She further suggested that subject specialists, as digital library service providers, help users formulate disciplinary search strategies and provide assistance in developing new resources.

Arms, while trying to answer the question "whether or not we need reference librarians in a digital library", pointed out that automatic tools are steadily reducing the need for reference librarians in fields like medicine that required a significant amount of intermediation in information searching. The essence of Arms' paper is that while computers can do a lot in performing most of the traditional jobs of reference librarians, their skills may be required in case of complex information searches.

Arms, however, believes that there have been significant improvements in the end-user search facilities, provided by electronic database search services and Web search engines, and hence, the need for human intermediaries in information searching has reduced significantly. Perhaps the most comprehensive view of the need for and the nature of personalised services in a digital library has been delineated by researchers.

They maintained that:

* Services reflect the functionality afforded by systems serving the community of users. Access services that

facilitate search and browsing have been central to digital library research thus far, but there is great need for attention to reference and question-answering, on-demand help, and fostering of citisenship and literacy and mechanisms to simplify participatory involvement of user communities.

REFERENCE AND INFORMATION SERVICES ON THE WEB

A number of reference and information services are now available on the Web. Interestingly, many of these services are provided by non-library and commercial organisations. While some are free, others need payment.

Detailed discussions on such services are available in a number of publications, McKiernan maintains a site that provides categorised listing of libraries that offer real-time reference services using chat software, live interactive communication tools, call centre management software, bulletin board services and other Internet technologies. Most of these services are designed for registered users of the libraries concerned.

Researchers categorised online reference and information services into three broad groups:

* Reference and information services from publishers, database search services, and specialised institutions;
* Reference services provided by libraries and/or experts through the Internet; and
* Reference and information services where users need to conduct a search and find information through theWeb.

Researchers discussed several online information services that belong to the first category.

They have listed various current awareness and SDI services such as: the contents page service from commercial publishers, such as Elsevier's

* Contents Direct Service, IDEAL Alert from Academic Press, and so on;
* Information on new books available free from publishers and vendors, such as the *Wiley Book Notification Service* and Amazon.com;

* SDI services fromonline search service providers, such as Dialog;
* *Current Contents* and *ISI Alerting Services* from ISI, and so on.

Some of these services, particularly the contents page services from publishers of journals, are free, while for others, such as *Dialog Alerts* or *Current Contents* from ISI, users need to register and pay.

Table 5.1 provides a quick overview of some online reference and information services currently available. This is not an exhaustive list, but the table shows the different types of services and some of their characteristics.

Table. 5.1. Characteristics of Some Web-based Reference Services.

Service	Subject	Payment	Organisation	Service Providers	Question Input	Mode of Delivery
Ask me	All	Free	Askme.com	Experts (volunteers)	Select a subcategory and input query through a Web-based query form	E-mail
All Experts	All	Free	Allexperts.com	Experts (volunteers)	Select a subcategory and input query through a Web-based query form	E-mail
Inforocket	All	Fee-based (from $5 to $75)	Inforocket.com	Experts (volunteers)	Select a subcategory and input query through a Web-based query form	E-mail
Ask Auntie Nolo	Law	Free	Nolo.com	Subject experts	Input query through a Web-based query form	E-mail
Find/SVP	Business	Fee-based ($250 per question)	Findsvp.com	Business experts	Input query through a Web-based query form	E-mail, phone, fax, courier
Professional City	Law, accounting, marketing	Fee-based ($25 for the first 15 minutes and $18.75 per additional 15 minutes of cybrarian's time)	Professional City.com	Cybrarians	Input query through a Web-based query form	E-mail

It provides the following facts about theWeb-based reference services listed there:

* The listed Web-based reference services are offered by dotcom companies;
* These services use the Web only for communication between the user and the system/answer provider, while the information service is provided by a human expert;
* While most services are free, some charge as high as $250 per question;
* in many cases services are provided by (self-proclaimed?) volunteer experts;
* There are some services offered in specific subject fields.

In addition to those in table, there are also some Web-based reference services where users need to conduct a search for a reference query. Such services provide free access to various online reference sources, and allow users either to select a specific source or conduct a search on a range, or all, of the reference sources.

Examples of such services include the following:

* Internet Public Library.
* Infoplease
* Britannica
* Bartleby Reference.
* Internet Library for Librarians.
* Electric Library.
* Mediaeater Reference Desk.
* ReferenceDesk.
* Xrefer.

While most of these Web-based reference services are available free, some charge a small fee. For example, the Electric Library charges $79.95 for an entire year of unlimited access. Janes *et al.* reported a study of 20 Web-based "expert services". By asking 240 questions to 20 selected expert services, they noted that the sites gave verifiable answers to 69 per cent of factual questions. An interesting observation of this study was that the kind of reference interview that takes place in traditional reference service environments is non-existent in Web-based reference services.

In fact, the sites did not come back for any discussion or clarification after receiving the initial queries. As a justification, the authors suggested that Web-based information services have been built mainly to answer factual questions, and therefore the experts concerned do not need to go through the reference interview process. Nevertheless, the high rate of success of factual questions shows that more and more end-users will move towards these expert services rather than to libraries for answers to simple types of questions.

SEARCH ENGINE SERVICES

Although Ask Jeeves is basically a search engine, many researchers also see it as aWeb-based information service because of two reasons:

* Unlike in other search and metasearch engines, users can ask a question in Ask Jeeves, and in many cases can get an answer right away; and
* Users can ask a question on a given topic, and Ask Jeeves comes up with a list of questions on the same or similar topics; the user can select any of the those predefined questions, and then Ask Jeeves provides answers to that.

This is an interesting service and may be considered as a useful model for digital library reference and information services.

The Ask Jeeves site maintains that:

* Ask Jeeves is a unique question-answering system that allows users to ask questions in plain English, and then delivers the answer. As one of the most sophisticated navigation systems on the Internet, Ask Jeeves combines a unique natural language engine with a proprietary knowledgebase.Taken together, this mechanism processes the meaning and grammar of real questions in plain English; provides intelligent responses for user confirmation; links directly to relevant, high-quality answers; and, perhaps most exciting of all, becomesmore intelligent as its knowledgebase expands with each question asked and each answer delivered.

The site further says that Ask Jeeves processes each query syntactically and semantically, and then Ask Jeeves' answer-processing engine provides the question template response. When the user clicks on a response, the answer-processing engine retrieves the answer template that contains links to the answer locations. Thus, Ask Jeeves helps users select a query from a pre-defined set of queries on a given topic.

However, there is a debate on whether the kind of service provided by Ask Jeeves matches reference services provided by libraries. Kresh reported an interesting finding: "One consortial system in northern California conducted an informal test of Ask Jeeves by sending it 12 questions its libraries had answered. There were no trick questions, none were arcane, just questions typically received by those libraries. Jeeves was unable to answer any of the questions".

Nevertheless, the techniques and the technology used by Ask Jeeves may be very useful for introducing reference services in digital libraries. Webhelp.com is another service that claims to offer "real-time search assistance with a real live expert I any time, day or night". About.com is a service that shows a number of pre-defined categories related to a search topic given by the user. For example, a simple search on "e-commerce" not only produces a list of sites, but also provides a set of topics related to "e-commerce", such as e-commerce definition, e-commerce security, advantages of e-commerce, e-commerce disadvantages, e-commerce statistics, etc.

DIGITAL REFERENCE SERVICES AND LIBRARIES

A number of libraries have now begun to offer Web-based reference services and a number of recent studies report the current practice of reference services provided by libraries. Although this is not an exhaustive review of all the Web-based reference services provided by libraries, the following section provides a quick overview of some that are currently available.

DIGITAL REFERENCE SERVICES FOR THE GENERAL PUBLIC

Ask A Librarian is a Web-based reference service, primarily designed for UK residents, provided by a network of public libraries in the UK. The site says: "Mail us your factual question and we'll send you an answer within two working days, if not before". A user has to put the query through an enquiry page, which is automatically routed to one of the participating libraries, which receives it as an e-mail message. Within two days the library sends an e-mail message to the user with its response to the enquiry. The British Library provides special reference services for business, patent, scientific, technical, medical and environmental information. These services range from answering simple questions to finding answers to complex questions involving online database searching, etc. While some of these services are free, for others users need to pay. For example, users can ask simple business questions using a form, and can expect an answer within ten working days. Similarly, users can send e-mails with simple environmental queries.

A typical answer in such a case may include:

* A list of bibliographies from a British Library catalogue literature search; and/or;
* A list of organisations to contact for more detailed information, and/or
* Information retrieved from Internet sources.

Users are not charged for this kind of service. However, for complex queries users need to pay.

For example, the British Library provides a Science Technology Medicine (STM) search service for which users need to pay at the following rate:

* J 82.00 per hour of staff time divided into 15-minute periods;
* Plus costs of online searching;
* Plus Value Added Tax (VAT).

As stated in the Web site most searches take at least 30 minutes and therefore cost J 41.00 for staff time + costs for online searching + VAT. The site also mentions that the average list of references costs J 80.00 for medical subjects, and between J 100.00 and J 150.00 for other subjects.

Users are also charged a fee if the results are to be faxed. In order to obtain an STM search service, the user has to fill in a form that has three parts. In the first part users need to fill in their personal details, etc., in the second part, users need to enter the query, and in the third part they need to specify the modes of delivery, payment, etc. In the second part of the form, users can enter the detail specification of the query using Boolean operators and specifying date, language, etc., as limiting factors.

DIGITAL REFERENCE SERVICES FOR USERS OF ACADEMIC LIBRARIES

Academic libraries have also begun to offer Web-based reference services. Wasik and Wasik and Lankes discuss the value of digital reference and AskA services in the K-12 educational environment. They described how AskA services are built and maintained, and also explain how the service works in the classroom.

Archer and Cast emphasised the importance of the personal touch in reference services and discussed how Web technology and the personal element of reference services can be combined to provide Web-based reference services. Tenopir and Tenopir and Ennis reported a survey of the current practices of digital library services in 70 academic libraries in the USA.

These studies noted that the university libraries allow their patrons to pose reference questions in a variety of ways: 99 per cent offer e-mail reference, 96 per cent offer reference services by appointment, and 29 per cent of the libraries offer real-time virtual reference. Breeding briefly described the various customer relationship management (CRM) software, such as eGain, LivePerson and WebLine, that are used by libraries for providing Web-based reference services. He also suggested that while the CRM software offer a great deal of sophistication to the virtual reference environment, they are more complex and expensive compared to lower-cost chat-based utilities that allow a managed two-way text conversation between the reference provider and the remote library user, thus replacing the need for a face-to-face communication.

Smith discussed the current technologies, such as chat and video conferencing software used by libraries for providing digital reference services. Richardson *et al.* examined the information technology aspects and the key organisational issues involved in establishing an electronic reference desk service in a library. They also reviewed the usefulness of some electronic reference services. Breeding provided an overview of some methodologies and collaborations currently in use to extend assistance to patrons in learning to use virtual resources and in finding the information they need.

DIGITAL LIBRARY SERVICE BY CO-OPERATIVE LIBRARY SYSTEMS

In order to deal with the rising cost of reference sources and staff and also of the huge initial investment required for introducing new services in libraries, many have gone for a co-operative model of digital reference services. Oder and Weissman described the 24/7 Reference Project at Metropolitan Cooperative Library System, a consortia around Los Angeles, and the Bay Area Libraries Project at San Francisco that are co-operative projects for providing Web-based reference services to customers.

One of the advantages of Web-based reference services is that users can ask for such services from a remote location at any time of the day. However, Rogers presented an interesting report of a study analysing Web-based reference services in academic libraries in Illinois.

This study shows a usage pattern that is quite similar to the timing of usage of traditional reference services in libraries, for example, 80 per cent of all usage occurred between 8 a.m. and 10 p.m.; evening use was higher than morning use, and the busiest hour was between 2 p.m. and 3 p.m.

CURRENT DIGITAL LIBRARY RESEARCH ON PERSONALISED SERVICES

Researchers have recently reviewed the status of some digital libraries from around the globe. These reviews reveal that while the digital libraries have very good information access and retrieval mechanisms in place, there is almost no provision for quality reference and information services.

However, these studies show that there is a trend towards the personalisation of digital library service, as in case of HEADLINE and GEMS (presently called iGEMS, a digital library developed at Nanyang Technological University in Singapore).

Some recent research efforts have been directed at building personalised digital library environments. These studies can be grouped into three categories: user needs assessment, personalised user interface and personalised digital library, researchers reviewed literature on user interfaces, particularly in a digital library environment, and suggested the need for a task-based digital library.

Researcher discussed the personal digital library (PDL) that acts as a front-end to other electronic library systems and manages the user's information needs. Barry and Barbara discussed the creation of personal digital libraries. The North Carolina University Library developed MyLibrary @NCState as a portal application to the NCSU Library's information resources. This portal allows user profiling to build a dynamic, customised gateway to both general and discipline specific resources. MyLibrary is a Cornell University Library initiative to provide personalised library services to their students, faculty and staff on the basis of a focus group study to gauge library users.

The MyLibrary project has two components, MyLink and MyUpdate. MyLink allows patrons to save useful information resource links that they found themselves or those suggested by the librarians via a targeted notification in their personal space. Users can access this personal space from any place. MyUpdate periodically queries the online catalogue and notifies users, utilising a pre-defined user profile. Headline is one of the eLib Programme's Phase 3 projects, developing a hybrid library system called the HeadLine Personal Information Environment (PIE), This PIE uses portal-type technology to present an information environment that is personalised to the user's needs and allows user customisation. This project presents users with pages of resources relevant to their courses/department. PIE users are also provided with an "all resources" page that contains all the library resources.

Users can create their own lists of resources on their own pages. Meyyappan reported on ongoing research at Nanyang Technological University in Singapore on the design and development of task-based digital library organisation and a digital work environment (DWE). The major objective of these research projects is to allow users to personalise digital library access so that they can view their preferred resources, and hence, information is automatically filtered. These projects aim to select automatically a subset of the DL collection based on the nature and characteristics of a user.

The user then can add new resources, or delete recommended resources, to his or her page. The DWE project is somewhat different from others in the sense that the main objective of the DWE is to provide filtered access to the local digital library collections, to remote digital libraries, as well as to traditional libraries, and,most importantly, to the vast information resources on the university intranet. The system also allows users to create their own personal workspace to store selected information resources for future use.

CURRENT DIGITAL LIBRARY PROJECTS ON DIGITAL REFERENCE SERVICES

Some research projects aimed at providing reference and information services as part of the digital library services have recently begun. The most prominent is the Collaborative Digital Reference Service (CDRS) project launched by the Library of Congress.

CDRS

Researcher commented that "by applying the best of what libraries and librarians have to offer to the labyrinthine universe of unstructured and unverified information on the Internet, we can begin to bridge the gulf that exists between providers and users of information". With this end in view, the Library of Congress has launched the Collaborative Digital Reference Service, the mission of which is to provide "professional reference service to users, anywhere any time, through an international, digital network of libraries".

The CDRS is a library to library network for asking and answering reference questions. It has three main components:

* *Member profiles*: That contain information on member strengths and features.
* *Request Manager*: A software for entering, routing and answering reference questions.

* *Knowledge base*: A searchable database of question and answer sets.

The system is designed to work in a very simple manner. A participating library sends a question to the system on behalf of a user. The system looks into the knowledgebase for a match. If the answer is found, a response is sent to the querying library by e-mail. If the question is not found in the knowledgebase, then it is passed on to the Request Manager, which forwards the query to an appropriate library selected from the profiles of the participating libraries and their collections, expertise, etc. This library receives the query, finds an answer and sends it back to the results store, which then sends the response back to the asking library, and stores the query and the answer in the knowledgebase. Hence, the strength of the system lies in the knowledgebase and the Request Manager. Since, June 2000 CDRS has been a "working" pilot with a current total of 220 active members who are routing real questions and answers. The next generation on CDRS is being co-developed by Library of Congress and OCLC. It will integrate local and global e-reference networks, and will be released as a full production service in June of 2002.

AUTOMATIC REFERENCE LIBRARIANS FOR THE WORLD WIDE WEB

The Automatic Reference Librarians for the World Wide Web, a DLI-2 funded project at the University of Washington. The central objective of this project, according to them, "is to create software agents that posses reference intelligence I a limited understanding of complex technical topics, but a very sophisticated understanding of how and where to find high-quality information on theWorld Wide Web". Etioni and Weld reported the basic working principles of the proposed system, which works on a wrapper technology.

The basic steps involved are:

* The user asks a question;
* The Query Router assigns a topic to the query;
* The topic maps to a number of relevant wrappers;
* The parallel Web search module sends requests via wrappers to the sites;

* Responses from the sites are obtained and sent to the fusion engine for collation;
* User gets the response.

SIFTER is an interdisciplinary research collaboration among faculty and students in the Computer and Information Science Department and the School of Library and Information Science at Indiana University. The broad aim of the project is to develop information agents that would perform a number of functions such as culling information from complex resources residing in diverse locations, and conducting analysis, synthesis and customisation according to the requirements of the user.

The specific objectives are:

* Dealing with heterogeneous information sources that may change over time;
* Handling shifting requirements and interest of users with minimal human involvement;
* Creating a robust agent architecture for reactive, proactive and collaborative filtering;
* Supporting agent collaboration based on natural or artificial economic frameworks for multi-agent tasks.

VIRTUAL REFERENCE DESK

The Virtual Reference Desk (VRD) is a project sponsored by the US Department of Education, and its objective is "the advancement of digital reference and the successful creation and operation of human-mediated, Internet-based information services". VRD defines a digital reference service as Internet-based question-and-answer services that connect users with experts. The basic idea of VRD is that when a given user asks a question that cannot be answered by a participating centre, it is forwarded to the VRD network for assistance.

VRD services include the following:

* *Collaborative AskA Service*: A network of AskA services and volunteer information professionals.
* *The Learning Center*: A Web site for the K-12 community with curriculum-related Web sites, frequently asked questions, and other previously asked questions.

* *AskA+ Locator*: A searchable database of high-quality K-12 AskA services.

VRD also supports research on interoperability standards, metadata and other aspects of digital reference services.

LEVERAGING THE DOCUMENT SELECTIONS OF EXPERT PROBLEM SOLVERS

This is a DLI-2 project at the Oregon Health Sciences University and Oregon Graduate Institute. The goals of this project are "to understand how experts select information in a large and complex information space and to develop tools that assist them in this process", The project aims to capture the trace of information used by experts in the health field, for example medical doctors. The basic idea is that as medical experts traverse the large and diverse collection of documents, they make explicit choices about which information resources to examine more carefully and which ones to ignore.

These choices create a subset of documents relevant to a given problem and this subset of documents may be of interest to other users concerned with the same or similar problem. Thus, by capturing this information that is inherent in the selection of appropriate information resources for problem solving, this project aims to come up with models that may be useful for other users.

The project proposed to develop:

* A trace that describes the path taken by an expert in solving his/her problem by using the available information resources;
* A precis of information about each document, its content, and the history of its use by experts; and
* Navigation tools that would assist subsequent problem solvers using the collection by exploiting the knowledge inherent in the existing traces.

Though the project specifically deals with medical experts and looks into their problem-solving processes, the project team expects that the resulting technology will be scalable, because the value of a set of precis and bundles within a collection should increase as the document collection grows and as more experts use the collection.

QUESTION ANSWERING SYSTEMS

A number of question answering systems (QA) are now being developed that aim to provide answers to natural language questions. Research in this area will have tremendous impact on the future of digital reference services. QA systems often use a variety of natural language processing (NLP) tools and techniques to get the correct answer from the source texts. Breck *et al.* reported a QA system that uses techniques from knowledge representation, information retrieval, and NLP. Research reported in the QA track of Text Retrieval Conferences show quite encouraging results. The goal of research in the QA track is to "retrieve small snippets of text that contain the actual answer to a question rather than the document lists traditionally returned by text retrieval systems".

The basic technology involves analysing user queries in several stages. First, cue words/phrases like "who", "when" are identified to guess what is needed; and then a small portion of the document collection is retrieved using standard text retrieval technology. This is followed by a shallow parsing of the returned documents for identifying the entities required for an answer. If no appropriate answer type is found then the best matching passage is retrieved. This approach works well as long as the query types recognised by the system have broad coverage, and the system can classify questions reasonably accurately. In TREC-8, the first QA track of TREC, the most accurate QA systems could answer more than two-thirds of the fact finding type of questions correctly.

In the second QA track, the best performing QA system, the Falcon system from Southern Methodist University, was able to answer 65 per cent of the questions. These results are quite impressive in a domainindependent question-answering environment. However, the questions were still simple in the first two QA tracks. In the future, more complex questions requiring answers from more than one document will be handled by QA track researchers. Such robust QA systems can be used to provide reference services in digital libraries.

EVALUATION OF DIGITAL LIBRARIES AND THEIR SERVICES

Evaluation data of digital libraries and their services are not yet widely available. In fact, very few evaluation studies of digital libraries have taken place so far. The most prominent publications reporting some digital library evaluation experiments appear in *Library Trends*. Saracevic discusses a number of issues related to the methodology and criteria for evaluation of digital libraries. Arguing that digital libraries were still at the stage of research and evolution, he commented that the best practice standards have yet to develop against which the performance levels are to be measured. Carter and Janes reported a study that analysed the log of over 3,000 reference questions asked of the Internet Public Library (IPL), which is one of the most widely used reference services on the Web.

This study has identified different categories of reference questions, such as common questions, quick questions, regular questions and unanswered questions, which were handled by IPL. The study revealed that users seem to have difficulties in assigning subject categories to their questions, and also in determining whether they are factual or require detailed information searching.

Since, the greatest part of reference and information services in the past has revolved around assisting users in their information search, and because of the fact that in a digital library environment end users need to search information resources all of which are online, it may be wise to take a quick look at some recent studies involving end-users' search behaviour in the online and Web search environment.

Pending any data from large-scale digital library evaluation experiments involving users, findings of these studies may help us assess the users' online information search behaviour.

Gordon and Pathak compared the retrieval effectiveness of eight search engines: Yahoo!, Excite, Magellan, HotBot, AltaVista, Lycos, Infoseek and Open Text, and noted, among other things, that there were no statistical differences in the retrieval effectiveness among users for recall, though there were for precision.

Although this study talks about the performance of the selected search engines, this observation is very important as far as the need for personalised help in digital library searching is concerned. It shows that the Web search tools differ in terms of search precision, and who can argue that in an online search environment of today, precision is a very important issue since, no one will ever have time to sift through the hundreds of thousands of documents retrieved by an online search tool at any given instant.

One million Web queries to discern how the public searches the Web and had some astonishing findings, as follows:

* A great majority of Web queries are short, not much modified, and very simple in structure;
* Very few queries incorporate advanced search features, and when they do so, half of them are mistakes;
* Despite gathering a large number of Web sites as answers to their queries, users do not view beyond the first or the second page of results;
* Web users are notmuch interested in relevance feedback.

Yet another study reveals similar findings. The usage of the MelvylWeb catalogue at the University of California at Berkeley. During the 479-day study period users conducted about 2.5 million search sessions, during which about 7.4 million search statements were executed.

The findings of this study reveal that:

* The length of time research searchers spent at a session grew from six to ten minutes during the 16 month study period;
* During the study period, about 7.4 million database selections were made, out of which the catalogue database accounted for 32 per cent (about 2.4 million uses), Medlars for 22 per cent, magazine database for 10 per cent, periodicals database for 8 per cent, Inspec for 4 per cent and *Current Contents* for 4 per cent;
* The time users spent on each database also varied: about 3 minutes per search in the Medlars database, while 2.2 minutes for the catalogue database;

* Users displayed about four to five citations for each search they performed;
* The length of time users spent displaying results was 30-40 seconds.

The observations of these studies are very useful for designing digital library services. One of the major problems of a digital search environment is the absence of human intermediaries who play a major role in traditional online search services. Appropriate online support for query formulation and modification may improve digital library search results. Again, since, most users do not look at more than a handful of records, appropriate mechanisms have to be developed for filtering retrieved output.

CONCLUSION

The reference librarian in the new millennium will need the ability to read the situation a user is in and find the right information for that situation. Considering this view and also to keep in pace with the rapid appearances and developments of Web-based reference and information services provided by non-library organisations, many library and information science professionals have now turned their attention to the provision of e-reference services. Oder and Weissman suggested that "the year 2000 brought the advent of live reference.

Several libraries, especially academic ones, have used or adapted chat or commercial call centre software to communicate with surfers in real time and send Web resources to their browser. Indeed, this is a time when digital library researchers should think of the best ways and means to make the optimum use of the technology and experience and expertise of human intermediaries in improving digital libraries from mere access centres to information service providers.

Many recent projects have taken the approach to building software agents to do much of the work of reference librarians. While this is a useful approach, and such programmes will reduce the workload of human experts, it is doubtful whether digital libraries can totally replace human experts and personalised services.

So far as the information filtering aspect of the personalised services is concerned, the personal digital library approach of automatic filtering based on user nature, and the DWE approach of information filtering based on user categories and tasks, seem to be quite promising.

Recent research on online search behaviour of users re-emphasises the need for user training and assistance in online searching. This is in contrast to the views of Arms, who proposed that information retrieval tasks can now be successfully performed by end users without the assistance of reference librarians. User training, or information literacy programmes, may be conducted regularly and sophisticated online tutorial programmes using digital video technology may be developed to assist users. For assistance in conducting complex subject searches, the current practice of e-mail communications, online chat, videoconferencing, etc., are useful and may be deployed depending on the nature, number, location, available IT resources, etc., of the end users.

The approach taken by Ask Jeeves in the use of templates for storing queries, and the knowledgebase for storing the queries and their answers may be adopted by digital libraries. The strength of Ask Jeeves is the knowledgebase which, according to the site, "contains links to more than 7 million answers, which contain information about the most frequently asked questions on the Internet". Library and information professionals are trained in organising information and a new research may be conducted for finding the best way to organise reference queries and answers on various topics.

A facet analysis technique may be used in formulating different templates around a given search topic and they may be stored in a knowledge base. A knowledge base, developed on such an approach, will grow fast initially, but after a certain time the growth rate will be minimum. Only when new aspects of a given topic appear in the research and literature will there be a new impetus.

Co-operation in providing ready reference and subject-specific reference services may be a useful cost-cutting measure. Indeed, the high cost of staff in libraries has been a major problem.

However, since, digital libraries can be accessed and queries easily dealt with from remote locations, co-operative mechanisms based on subject specialisation and other criteria may be considered. Specialised search and other forms of assistance need not always be free. In fact, especially where specialised and reliable searches can save end-users' valuable time. Payments for such services may not always necessarily come from the end users. They may be recovered from research projects, business projects and so on. Holmes-Wong suggested that, by combining Internet technology and electronic commerce, libraries may be able to offer customisable electronic reference services to users.

Nevertheless, new research for testing e-commerce models for digital library reference services needs to be undertaken. To sum up, this study re-emphasises the need for, and provision of, personalised information services in the next generation digital libraries.

The current research projects aiming at finding the best means of providing such services through digital libraries are trying a variety of techniques and technologies, including:

* Information filtering mechanisms based on users' personal characteristics and tasks;
* Agent technology for automatic information discovery, organisation, filtering and retrieval based on user nature, need, etc.;
* Co-operative models for sharing the resources and specialisations I both the content and staff;
* Internet technologies such as Internet chat, call centre management software, video conferencing, etc.

These research projects will definitely bring some useful models and approaches that the second generation digital libraries may adopt.

Further research may be carried out in a number of areas, including:

* Building appropriate packages for end-user training involving the best practices for digital library use suitable for specific user needs, characteristics, etc.;
* Testing the query template and knowledge-based approaches in a digital library environment

* Testing e-commerce models for handling the payment and cost management aspects of sophisticated and resource-intensive personalised services;
* Tracing the techniques of expert information problem-solving processes, and building models for other users in a given domain; and
* Testing traditional library classification tools and facet analysis techniques for creating question templates and knowledge bases for storing answers in specific subject fields.

6

Developing an Educational Multimedia Digital Library

INTRODUCTION

The Maryland Electronic Community (MELC) was designed to investigate how the professional development of teachers could be supported with information technology One focus of this project has been the creation, maintenance, and cultivation of a digital library for the teachers to use as they develop interactive lesson plans (ILPs). While the original emphasis was on the needs of social studies and science teachers, in recent months the community has grown to include mathematics and language arts teachers.

The digital library contains over 3,200 multimedia resources, and by August 2000 this number is expected to exceed 6,300. The collection is comprised of text documents, audio files, video segments, still images, and Web sites. There are public domain items from the National Archives and NASA; proprietary items that have been contributed by project partners Discovery Communications and Maryland Public Television; and personal contributions from MELC members themselves. Each resource is identified by a set of standard metadata elements and then indexed according to Topic, Subtopic, and Standard (corresponding to national standards). Efforts at collecting and cataloging these resources was initially the responsibility of the team at the University of Maryland, but this work is gradually being handed off to the teachers as the external project funding ends. By analysing the Web logs, we can determined that the following resources as shown in table. We are particularly interested in how the video clips are being used. Currently there are 50 videos in the library: 24 science, 25 social studies, and 1 language arts.

Seven of these are in the public domain (from the National Archives and accessible by anyone) and 45 are private (from Discovery Communications, Inc. or Maryland Public Television and accessible only by MELC members). Of the video clips downloaded, only 10 were public domain. The average video clip is about two to three minutes in length and approximately 15 MB.

The Web logs show evidence of teachers downloading new videos from the server even before CD-ROMs are available. Putting the clips on the server reduces the time it takes to make the videos available to the teachers since, creating and distributing the CD-ROMs is time consuming. We examine issues related to the use and development of the resource collection including:

* The flexibility of digitised video segments (as opposed to full-length film on the VCR),
* Appropriate indexing and metadata elements, and
* Collaborative indexing and the Quick Indexing Tool (QIT).

Table. 6.1.Resource Usage from September 1999 to March 2000.

Resource Types	Unique Resources Accessed	Total Resources Accessed
Video	158	457
Image	58	110
Web Sites	37	104
Lesson Plans	30	71
Student Activities	10	42
Audio	6	14
Other Libraries	3	4
Text	3	4

SEGMENTING THE VIDEOS

While the library contains images, audio, and video, we focus here particularly on the video because it is attractive to students, adds a unique dimension to lesson plans, and is invaluable to visual learners. The fulllength educational videos are divided in one- or two-minute segments for a number of reasons. First, we consider the video segments to be building blocks for the teachers as they construct their lessons. Second, our technology was inadequate for the task of managing digitised full-length videos, especially at beginning of the project. A third reason for using segments is that they encourage cross-curriculum tie-ins.

For example, "The Real Ben Franklin" is a film about the life of a great American and as a whole is clearly within the purview of the social studies department. However, it includes several fine illustrations of scientific principles and inventions that would be useful in a science class. As a result of the segmenting, science teachers can now use resources that they otherwise might not have been aware of or able to access. While there has been a great deal of research in computer science on segmenting videos based on scene changes, we felt that truly meaningful units could be obtained only by manual segmentation. Unfortunately, while this kind of segmenting yields useful material, it is very labour intensive, requiring approximately seven minutes of processing for every one minute of video. In order to standardise the process, we have developed a set of guidelines.

As we have teased out the threads of these educational videos (interviews with experts in the field, historical footage, animations, demonstrations, re-enactments, first-person narratives, etc.), we have come to realise many ways that these segments might be re-constructed or regrouped by the teachers. Perhaps they will string together the re-enactments of Singbe Pieh and his fellow Africans aboard the Amistad, or pull out the animated graphics that show how black holes warp time and space. Thus, we try to segment along the different interviews or footage or speakers. There were times when we chose not to segment the most discrete pieces of information, as when the sum of the whole was greater than the sum of the parts. This was most often when the medium itself, video, was providing something that could not have been captured and conveyed by other media. For example, near the end of the video "The Real Thomas Jefferson," the narrator stands on a balcony in Jefferson's American Room in Monticello.

The camera pans around the room and as it passes over the artifacts the narrator briefly identifies them. Important though the images and the identification of these ancient Indian artifacts are, of greater importance is the panoramic view of the room itself. Similarly, we tended to give priority to the video's visual presentation of information over the text or narration that accompanied whatever was happening on the screen. Words can be gleaned from books or audiotapes, moving images come only from video.

We have developed several search tools that allow teachers to view these relatively small and discrete pieces. The most ambitious tool, the Explorer gives teachers a visual representation of the entire collection, allowing them to select the data elements that will be displayed on the axes. With this tool, they can isolate all of the photographs from the African Americans in World War II photograph collection from the National Archives, or the resources that deal with aquatic habitats and that also satisfy the Personal and Social Perspectives objective of the National Science Education Standards.

METADATA AND INDEXING BY CONTENT

Effective indexing is essential for any digital library and, in general, metadata and indexing should reflect the likely information needs of the library's users. Because this project was started several years ago and was focused upon the needs of a single school system, we had to develop much of our own metadata. The original indexing system was created by library-science students who tailored it to the needs of a specific group of middle school teachers. They reviewed science and social studies curriculum objects and textbook headings to determine what the list of topics and subtopics would be and compiled a lengthy set of instructions for future indexers. The result was a 60-page manual that outlined a system for assigning metadata elements and specific details for assigning the descriptive elements:

* Description,
* Topic

* Subtopic,
* and Standard.

Although a 60-minute video in its entirety may clearly belong in the social studies category, many of the segments from it could be cross-indexed to other topics. Unfortunately, many times these topics are far beyond the scope of our index. While it is probably a hallmark of high-quality educational resources that they use the familiar to introduce students to the unfamiliar, for the MELC community this is at once a blessing and a curse. As indexers, it leaves us with lots of segments for which we have no appropriate Topic or Subtopic, or which we can only index partially. The Discovery video entitled "Unearthing South America" is full of curriculum-related segments about early Indian civilisations, but many of these segments also deal with the culture's traditions of mummification and the archeological digs that are revealing much about these ancient people. Archeology is not a unit of study in the middle school curriculum, and so we have no way of capturing this essential data. It most cases we have adopted a "best fit" mentality and tried to shoehorn these segments into related categories.

A second stress upon the indexing system has been our growth as a community. As our ranks have swelled in recent years, we have embraced teachers from other areas, most notably mathematics and language arts. We have a handful of alternatives to accommodate this expansion. One would be to slow down the processing of videos and take the time to construct an index that is similar in scope and detail to the indexes for science and social studies. However, not only is this a very labour-intensive task, but it would suggest that we have learned none of the lessons of our own recent history (what if the foreign language teachers join us next month?).

Our discussions centered on two other viable options:

* Distill the descriptive indexing down to the most basic and community-specific of categories and simply assign segments to the curriculum unit(s) where they are most likely to be used; or
* Broaden the descriptive indexing structure to encompass all possible subject areas by using a scheme such as

Dewey, which in theory covers the entire body of knowledge. In retrospect, we might have limited our index to the broadest of categories for the subject areas, including many beyond the curriculum, and emphasised techniques for keyword searching in the Description field. Concurrently, we would have enriched the descriptions. Rather than simply giving a brief one- or twosentence summary, we would have made a greater effort to get the transcripts for the videos and simply copied the relevant passages directly into the Description fields, thus providing the teachers with richer text to mine. Regardless, we have come to discover that having the transcripts for any sort of video indexing is highly desirable. Short of taking the time to implement a controlled vocabulary or develop an authority file, it is important to refer to the same entity in a consistent fashion. For example, a recent addition to the library has been a video on HIV and AIDS. In a system based on simple character string recognition, it is imperative that the teachers know if the film presents information on "CD4 T cells," "cd4 t cells," "C D 4 T-Cells." or "see, de four tea sells"? Our custom-built indexing effort may not be sustainable. We feel our efforts would be better spent indexing to some national metadata standard such as the Dublin Core or GEM. While we do index to the National Science Education Standards and the Curriculum Standards for Social Studies, we do not have sufficient data to suggest that this field is being used by the community. Similarly, we have considered searching for an indexing system that would apply beyond our middle school teachers to a high school or elementary school community.

COLLABORATIVE INDEXING

Our goal has been for MELC to become a self-sustaining community when the project funding ends. At the heart of this community of educators would be the digital library that supports their work in the classroom. In order for this project to be self-sustaining within the current framework of the Baltimore City Public School System, we believe that the indexing of new resources would have to be done collaboratively by members of the community. While our effort is on a much smaller scale than the CORC project we certainly share their vision. Perhaps there are even some parallels between the indexing of the multimedia content and the manner in which Varian has suggested that quality control in scholarly publishing can become selfregulating.

QUICK INDEXING TOOL AND COLLABORATION

Our first effort at fostering a system of collaborative indexing, the Quick Indexing Tool (QIT) is designed to let the teachers capture descriptive and bibliographic information (metadata) about resources as they add them to the digital library. Having come to know both the capabilities and needs of our users, we have designed a simple interface that lets them capture the greatest amount of information with the least amount of effort.

Along with several simple fields for each QIT submission, we have included a description field that encourages teachers to jot down a brief statement or vocabulary from the page itself (keywords) as a way of representing the content. In the second half of the form, we ask the grade, subject area (social studies, math), and unit of study (Baltimore uses the Berri Curriculum) for which they envision this resource will be useful. We anticipate that these particular required fields will not dampen enthusiasm for the tool by implying that all teachers should be expected to know about the specifics of all units of study across all grade levels and all subjects.

We anticipate that sixth-grade math teachers will be entering Web sites applicable to the sixth-grade math curriculum and seventh-grade science teachers will be entering Web sites applicable to the seventh-grade science curriculum units, and so forth. Having the resources selected by these subject experts should greatly increase the usefulness and quality of the library. The QIT was introduced to the MELC teachers in August 1999. As of March 2000, 94 resources have been added using this tool including 25 of the 27 math resources. It has helped us expand the library to include the new content areas of math and language arts by having the new teachers themselves make contributions. Each of the 27 math resources in the library have been added by math teachers who used the QIT.

PROS AND CONS OF COLLABORATIVE INDEXING

In a system of collaborative indexing, all community members would be responsible for resource acquisition and cataloguing. Resources can be found items, such as Web sites; proprietary items, such as the Discovery video segments; or self-generated items, such as the photographs of Baltimore and Europe taken by various teachers who scanned them and then entered them as digital images.

The benefits of such a system are obvious and important:

* In theory, it guarantees that each item will be have high relevance to some subset of users. Only resources that other members of the group have identified as being specifically related to the curriculum will be part of the collection.
* Not only will the items all have high levels of relevance, but they will also be of high quality. Each item will have been judged useful by a subject expert.
* Moreover, the activity of creating a QIT entry may lead to reflection by the teacher about the value of the item. The time involved in entering the bibliographic data, which includes their name and e-mail, will serve as further impetus for maintaining quality control.

However, there are a few difficulties in expecting teachers to use the QIT on a regular basis:

* Becoming a contributing member of a digital library community means more work for a group that is habitually overworked. Society, school administrations, and parents already expect them to perform a myriad of functions within their classrooms. We are asking them to perform yet one more.
* The community of users probably will not find as many resources as a library media specialist would. Although the community users will be able to index the resources they do find, they may be overlooking

many others. For example, the media specialist knows that many valuable sites are only available to users who know to execute a search on the main page or by searching the site index, and that these pages cannot be found through the major search engines. Unlike today's librarians, teachers have not necessarily been trained to manipulate the search engine algorithms as a way to refine the search process.

* The community users probably will not find resources of the same quality as a media specialist. The reason for this is similar to the argument made in the previous point.
* The community of users and the QIT will not exist in an equilibrium. As we have discovered, changes in the environment can have messy implications for the system as it was originally conceived. If they are not provided with the technical skills or training to respond to these changes, then the slightest shift in the equilibrium may well overwhelm them.

CONCLUSION

Based on our experience, we envision an extended collaborative indexing system that is overseen by a professional librarian with whom they have ready access and easy communication. This professional librarian would serve as a resource to be used by the community members on an "as needed" basis, although this professional will also be an equal contributor to the endeavor and a person who will no doubt have many useful things to share when it comes to the selection, acquisition, organisation, and use of resources.

We envision an iterative process:

* An individual or subset of members approaches the media specialist with a request for information,
* The media specialist will interview them to further understand the nature of their information need,
* The media specialist will provide the user with a list of resources,
* The teacher will examine the resources,
* The teacher will select and index (with QIT) the ones

that meet his/her need, including those that he/she may have found on their own.

This scenario strikes a balance between two extremes. It leaves ultimate responsibility for resource selection to the community members, thus ensuring high relevance and importance to the curriculum, but it lets them have the option of having input from a professional whose intervention represents a great deal of "value added" to the final product. Finally, it also suggests a way that we can provide a useful framework for the local learning community, yet provide an infrastructure for a broader community.

Once a media specialist has compiled a listing of resources that would be useful for an eighth-grade lesson plan on meteorology, it is a relatively simple task to share that list with other teachers in other local learning communities. Perhaps the solution lies in a federated system of collaborative indexing communities. In this arrangement, many small groups of collaborative indexing communities join forces to benefit from the sharing of resources, expertise, and support that are inherent in a larger federation. Suppose an individual member of Community A has annotated and cataloged a resource in a way that has made it useful to the specific needs, parochial though they be, of the members of her immediate community.

An individual in Community B, upon perusing the digital library holdings of Community A, accesses this same resource but represents the descriptive data differently in his catalog. For his users, he includes information about how the resource correlates to statewide standards outlined by the governor's task force. On a macro level, the members of Community B benefit from having access to the resources in the digital library of Community A; on a micro level, they benefit from the refining process that defines collaborative indexing systems. We have plans for adding tools similar to QIT that will allow teachers to index video segments, materials from online archives, and other multimedia items. This will be accomplished by redefining the metadata fields in the top half of the form so as to prompt users to give more resource-specific information (*e.g.*, audio tapes often have narrators, computer images come in varying file formats). We continue to believe that educational video can be highly absorbing and can be an important resource for middle school teachers. However, many of the costs for the digital library (indexing, segmenting) would be better borne by a very large constituency. The issue becomes maintaining a sense of involvement from the local learning communities. The QIT is one example of a community-oriented tool. Other such tools might include social collaboration tools.

7

Management of Digital Resources

INTRODUCTION

The global information infrastructure is transforming with the growth in full text digital resources and fast communication facilities. This is so because institutions, agencies and departments in every country are busy capturing, processing, storing and disseminating information in the digital form. One of the primary methods of digital collection building is digitisation.

The digitisation means the conversion of any fixed or analogue media-such as books, journal articles, photos, paintings, microforms- into electronic form through scanning, sampling, or in fact even re-keying. Digital library is a library where the information is made available in electronic form and access to it is provided through computers and other media like Local area network or Internet.

Digitising information has become a boon to many including library and information professionals. It reduces storage space, increases efficiency of retrieval of information. The digital library offers users the prospects of access to electronic resources at there convenience temporarily and spatially. Users don't have to be concern with the physical library hours of operation and users don't have to go physically to the library to access resources. Some of the Digital library initiatives undertaken so far world-over are highlighted: Medoc in Germany, Digital library projects at the National diet library in Japan, Tsinghua University Central Library in China, Biblio theca Universalis – G7 Project, Library of Congress USA, NSW Parliament News paper clippings and press releases imaging project in Austraila, Internet Archives USA, California digital libraries.

In India, the major initiatives undertaken in this direction: Million Book Universal Digital Library project, Vidyanidhi project, National Mission of Manuscripts, Traditional Knowledge Digital Library (TKDL), Gyan Nidhi and Indian National Digital Library in Engineering Science and Technology (INDEST). The initiatives undertaken so far clearly indicate that there is a boom in funding for digital library projects.

IGM LIBRARY, UNIVERSITY OF HYDERABAD AND DIGITAL INITIATIVES

The University of Hyderabad came into existence in 1974 to promote teaching and research. The University at present has eight schools of study–Chemistry, Life science, Physics, Mathematics and computer/information science, Humanities, Social science, fine arts and communication and management studies. It offer postgraduate and research programme across a wide spectrum of discipline in area of Science, Art and Technology.

The IGM library was established in 1975 as a central facility supports teaching and research activities of the university. The library has been over years successfully catering to the information needs of the Schools/departments and students of all subjects.

It is the first University library in India to computerise all its operations and services. With modernisation and networking of the library and information system the university campus has been networked with fibre optic cable and 2MB bandwidth Internet connectivity for creating local resources, cataloguing and repackaging web resources.

All school/departments are catered network. Library holdings can now be accessed through this Local Network and Internet.

DIGITAL RESOURCES

IGM library provide access to in – house digital resources as well as external digital resources. In – house resources are stored in web server and made accessible through Network. They are books, serials, theses and dissertations, current and back volumes of periodicals, university publication, faculty publication, theses and dissertations, project reports, Lectures of visiting experts, conferences/workshops, seminars/ proceedings.

The external resources are not stored in web server. Here the digital library only act as an intermediary by subscribing these e-books, databases and provide hyperlinks to the respective databases in the web server. IGM library is subscribing to over 8000 ejournals from several publishers like EBSCO, Elsevier, UGC-Infonet, SCOPUS- A&I database, Royal Society of Chemistry, Institute of Physics and Mathscinet have given campus-wide IP based access.

OBJECTIVES OF THE STUDY

The Study was intended to collect information from the Librarian and Library staff who are involved in digitisation activity. Also to know whether they are satisfied with the digital resources currently available in IGM library.

The specific objectives of the study were the following:

* To ascertain information about the digitisation initiatives in IGM Library.
* To gather details about the existing digital library facilities in terms of collection, organisation and dissemination of the information to students, Research Scholars and Staff.
* To collect information about provisions of financial assistance and grants and other facilities.
* To review the present position of digital library facility in terms of access, preservation, retrieval of digital material.
* To find out the activities, services and area of digitalisation.

* To know the problem faced by the library staff in digitisation activity and user accessing digital material.
* To ascertain details about the future plans of the libraries in digitisation material.
* To collect the opinion and suggestions of librarians and users of digital library for improving digital library services.

METHODOLOGY

For collection of data combination of data collection was used. The data analysed on the nature and type of digital collection, the policies and programmes, planning, formats, standardisation for digital preservation. The study employed questionnaire method and discussions were made with the librarian, library staff and users to collect additional information about existing facilities in libraries. Separate questionnaires were administered to the librarian, library staff and users of the IGM library to gather data.

The survey questionnaire for the library staff covers areas like:

* Digital material policy
* Digital holdings
* Storage methods and formats
* Digital knowledge/training and
* Future needs for the services

Areas covered by the questionnaire for the users include their preferences and opinion on:

* Access to digital material
* Mode of access
* Type of material
* Problems and training
* Future needs

The scope of study includes:

* Information created originally in digital form and acquired by a repository through purchase, transfer, or legal deposit;
* Digital material created through programmes or projects that convert print, photographic and manuscript materials

to digital form. The digital conversion projects mainly to improve access to material and in terms of preservation;

* The nature of accessing, type of materials accessed and problem in accessing digital material.The present study is a case study taken up to analyse the electronic and digital library management strategies adopted by I.G.M. Library of the University of Hyderabad. Due to limitations of time the researcher could not gather the results based on the surveys of other library(s) of similar nature to evaluate and compare the services of IGML.

FINDINGS

* *Library Survey*: IGM Library is the first University Library in South India that has developed a full-fledged digital library and provide global access to it. Present study makes an attempt to study various digitisation activities of the library – Planning, Creation, Preservation and Management of digital resources.
* *Planning*: IGM library adheres to the authorised written policy documents approved by the library committee for managing digital material. The policies provide guide lines for acquiring material in digital form, converting the material from print to digital form, storage, Refreshing and migrating of material. It is ongoing and continuous. The policies of the institution meets well with the current needs. The materials selected for digitisation are not under copyright and published in house.
* *Creation of Digital Collections*: IGM Library has started creating and storing of books, serials, theses and dissertations, current and back volumes of periodicals, University publication, faculty publication, Lectures of visiting experts, conferences/workshops, and Seminars/convention proceedings in digital form. The Library is well equipped with necessary Hardware High end book scanners both flat bedded and hand held scanners, printers, P IV PCs for processing, i2s Digibook scanner, Sony digital camera, SUN server for storage, UPS backups.

* *Different Softwares used by the library includes*: VTLS: Digital library application software, OCR fine reader 7, cleaning and editing software, scanner software, LINUX, ORACLE, Publishing software, Search Engines, etc. The pages are scanned and a computer readable (digital) image of pages are produced and stored in computer. The Optical character Recognition (OCR) software convert the text image in ASCII format for editing and manipulation of information and digital document is stored in server for online access.
* *Preservation of Digital material*: IGM digital library holds the responsibility of long term preservation of digital material. They are stored in hard disk, magnetic tapes, CD ROM, Optical disk(rewritable) and WORM Optical disk (write once and read many). It accepts electronic records in any format and convert into standard format and store them in hard disk, CD ROM, Optical disc Rewritable, WORM. Digital materials are archived in TIFF, JPEG or PDF formats.
* *Access Control*: IGM Library provides access to digital resources to its students, faculty and staff. User can access the digital material through ID & Password. There is no limitation for access to the materials provided if he/she is an authorised user. The institution has chosen to mount the digital reproduction (content) for Internet access in order to support searching across the collection. Digitisation work is an ongoing, there is no specific time schedule. The IGM library receives funds from University of Hyderabad, UGC, Vidyanidhi project, Universal digital library project & SUN Micro system. It also holds preservation responsibility of digital material. Currently, approximately 621 documents with 7200 MB has been stored in PDF format. The digital library supports the metadata standards.
* *Training of Staff*: The staff are trained in digitisation work. They are given training in IIIT, Hyderabad and IIIT, Bangalore from time to time. There are training programmes to increase the level of staff expertise with

digitisation of material and preservation. The Library is also a member of digital consortia–Universal digital library (UDL), Vidyanidhi and UGC – infonet.

* *User Survey*: The IGM Digital library is large depository of information collected and stored in digital form. The study has examined the use of the digital collection by potential users (such as students, Research scholars, and faculty). A structured questionnaire was prepared taking into consideration all parameters regarding digital library use.

It may be observed from the findings that majority (53%) of users suggested that the Internet connectivity speed should be increased. Users have also requested to organise training programme on down loading, saving and printing of digital materials. Some of the users requested to increase the number of computers in the campus for accessing of digital materials. Some of the users even suggested to adopt more user friendly software for down loading of digital materials in any format *i.e.*, PDF, HTML or XML.

CONCLUSIONS

The 21st century witnessing a knowledge revolution resulting from rapid growth in information and communication technology, acceleration of technical change and intensification of globalisation. Creating digital resources for providing wider and seamless global access to digital information to the users in distributed environment became a challenging task for any contemporary librarian.

The present study is an attempt to analyse the present situation in IGM library, University of Hyderabad. Regarding the frequency of use of library and digital material in the library, it is observed that a large number of faculty and research scholars are accessing and using regularly both in-house and external digital resources.

This indicates the optimum utilisation of library resources. IGM Library has framed regulations to allow access to the digital material to the registered users of the university. The library provides access to the digital material to its users regardless of their geographical location.

It is also observed that the problems faced by users using Digital Libraries are quite similar to the traditional libraries with some changes due to electronic rather than physical resources. The nature of problem can be broadly categorised as slow access, inadequate number of systems, inefficient display of information and lack of awareness in access, use and downloading information from digital resources. There are number of managerial and technical issues that are to be addressed by the digital librarians to provide satisfactory services to the users. The workflows and processes are only one aspect of digital libraries but there are number of issues that need to be considered. When creating a digital library like users, management support, staff authority and responsibility, policy related to IPR, security, finance, leadership and coordination, etc. Before starting to create a digital library it is important to evaluate the hardware and software aspect so that the digitisation process can run smoothly without further investment for it. There is another important aspect of the digital library, *i.e.*, preservation of digital contents. Therefore, the preservation technology must also be addressed while planning the creation of a digital library. There are two main methods for transferring information contained on magnetic or optical media onto new media; harvesting and migration seem to be the only logical answers to preserve the information. Migration is an active system-based approach.

Migration preserves information by continually moving it between one system and its replacement. The difference between the two methods is that migration preserves the structure of the file and its information while harvesting merely copies the information. Building a digital information is a complex process involving requirements analysis, careful planning, and well informed choices. Ultimately, every library's goal is to meet the information needs of its users. The digital library infrastructure will assist staff in creating the tools and supporting applications to manage a growing collection of library work in digital form, will help to ensure long term preservation, and will provide new and innovative library services to the users.

Acquiring and implementing application development tools for programming staff, testing implementation of digital content that use the core software defining the library's corporate requirements for electronic document management and determining the best approach for implementing an electronic document management system. All hardware and software dependencies should be avoided and all digitisation equipment must be capable to support the requirements for long-term preservation. The library professionals should pay keen interest to understand the various provisions about the copyright act, patterns, and designs, etc.

The liabilities and safeguards in regards to the librarians and libraries should be taken care of to avoid the infringement of the copyright act. The Government of India has passed the copyright law before attaining independence and amended in different periods to protect the copyright till date. In digital and new worked environment, it would be ideal if there is a single world law on copyright to safeguard the intellectual property rights, at the national, and international level. The role of Library professional is also changing in the digital library environment. Library professionals with their expertise, knowledge and techniques of where to look up and how to find out information for a given query can help the users in their search for information by extending personal help and assistance. Library professionals should acquire such skills in handling the information sources and users tactfully and render satisfactory information service in the fast changing digital library environment.

It is also necessary for their very survival and survival of the library profession. In a Country like India where resources are limited, funds are inadequate; librarians have to take careful and judicious decisions in selecting library materials for digitisation. However, taking into consideration the user's information needs other requirements, university libraries may plan for digitisation projects. Only through digitised information, university libraries can share their resources with other libraries and make their resources available to a large number of users through the web.

8

Open Access Movement and Open Access Initiatives in India

INTRODUCTION

Prior to the advent of the Internet publishers and academic societies dominated scholarly communication, and researchers channeled their research output solely through authoritative publishers and academic societies. Now when Internet has become a part of our lives, it continues to make changes in every aspect of our society and reshapes scholarly communication in many ways. Chan states that scholarly communication and publishing are increasingly taking place in the electronic environment. With a growing proposition of the scholarly record now existing only in digital format, serious and pressing issues regarding access and preservation are being raised that are central to future scholarship.

On the other hand exponential growth of scholarly literature has put a severe hindrance on their accessibility, and the libraries, particularly in the developing countries is vexed with the problem of providing access to the vast amount of literature. In addition, the increase in the prices of academic journals by their publishers has posed a major threat to libraries which support academic researcher's research activities. Today journals are being published electronically and distributed in bundled databases controlled by large commercial publishers and libraries and users are facing restrictive licensing terms on their access and usage. Therefore in words of Ramachandran 'even though the bundling includes a very large number of indifferent and low-impact journals, institutions around the world, including many in India, have entered into such agreements to gain access to a large number of journals. But the price rise in these bundling schemes seems to have outpaced inflation. These journal bundling deals, while being profitable from the publisher's perspective do not meet the specific needs of the libraries.

Therefore to overcome what is often termed as 'commercialisation of scholarly publication' or 'serials crisis' and to communicate the fruits of scholarly literature to a world wide community of researchers and scientists the *open access* (OA) initiative emerged as a revolutionary movement that promotes free access to scholarly publications over the Internet, removes the price and permission barriers and ensures the widest possible dissemination of research. OA literature and journals and are expected to be read more often than those with subscriptions thereby having a higher impact rate. Additionally OA significantly accelerates the publication and use of new research by reducing the time lag between the actual completion of a piece of research and its publication.

OPEN ACCESS

Open Access (OA) was initiated in the developed countries and was marked by three notable declarations known as Budapest Open Access Initiative (BOAI) in 2002, Bethesda statement in June 2003, and the Berlin declaration in October 2003 and since, then the issue is spreading through the world and many developing countries including India have joined the effort.

OA has made significant progress in the area of public policy and support, copyright, publisher alliance and technology standards. Most OA definitions have key features in common, *i.e.,* open access exists where there is free, immediate and unrestricted availability of digital content. According to Suber 'Open access to scientific article means online access without charge to readers or libraries. Committing to open access means dispensing with the financial technical and legal barriers that are designed to limit access to scientific research articles to paying customers'. Bjork defines OA as that a reader of a scientific publication can read it over the Internet, print it out and even further distribute it for non-commercial purposes without any payments or restrictions.

At the most the reader is in some cases required to register with the service in question, which for instance can be useful for the service providers in view of the production of readership statistics. The use of the content by third parties for commercial purposes is, however, as a rule prohibited. Thus OA is simply the free online availability of digital contents, scholarly journal articles, research results, which authors publish without expectation of payment and is based on 'an ethical argument that research funded by the public should be available to the public'. OA operates within the legal framework and own the original copyright for their work.

Authors can transfer the rights to publishers to post the work on the web or else can retain the rights to post their work on the archives. Open access requires several enabling technologies and metadata interoperability protocols like open source software for establishing and managing digital archives, open source software for online journal publishing, metadata schemas and OAI Protocol for Metadata Harvesting which collects the metadata and enables it to be searched.

OPEN ACCESS MECHANISMS

There are various mechanisms by which the open access is achieved. Harnard and et. al identified two main roads to OA 'gold' and 'green'. The gold road refers to OA journals which are openly accessible immediately on publication. The green road refers to OA self archiving. The green road is faster and cheaper, whereas the gold road is more costly, but better maintained and managed.

The OA mechanisms can be classified as:

* Open access periodicals providing complete and unrestricted access to web based OA journals, *e.g.*, journals such as D-lib, PLoS Biology.
* Domain-specific, subject-specific institutional and digital

repositories where the authors or authors institutions or institutions administered by an organisation or scholarly society make publications available free online *e.g.*, Arxiv.

* Limited access, *i.e.*, conventional journals that allow open access to certain sections of their issues, e.g. Nature.
* Delayed OA version is another mechanism, *i.e.*, periodicals going OA after a specified period of time from the date of publication, e.g. Highwire press journals.
* Dual mode is subscription based print on paper edition along with OA online edition, e.g. British Medical Journal.
* State of economy based access is a mechanism where conventional periodicals are made available as OA periodicals to countries based on economic criteria, e.g. HINARI, AGORA.

OPEN ACCESS MODELS

OA is free for users of scholarly, but it is not free for publishers. It facilitates a few OA operational models such as the author pays model in which publication fee is paid by the author, author's institution or research programme. But this model is disliked by the authors and there is a possibility of low quality literature being provided.

Another model is external funding, *i.e.*, seeking financial support from external sources like private foundations, corporate funds, governmental and institutional grants. For, *e.g.*, 10 per cent of DOAJ journals are supported totally or partially through external funding. Institutional repositories are often supported by academic or research institutions, *e.g.*, the repository ArXiv is funded by Cornell University and National Science foundation, USA. The third model is fee-based support model, whereby the publishers fund OA project through additional services or products for sale online including advertising, e-commerce, off-line media and software, etc. BioMed Central offers advertising services on its web site. This model makes use of the media and technological resources to generate revenues to support OA. The voluntary work is another model where the volunteers with relevant knowledge and expertise contribute to the OA projects without expectation of any monetary rewards. It is supposed to lack rigorous accountability. Finally, personal web sites of author publications, which is the most common OA channel today. However it is widely scattered on the web and it is very difficult to search and locate information from them, metadata is seldom assigned and it may not be updated regularly thus lacking quality.

OPEN ACCESS INITIATIVES IN INDIA

In India poor access to international journals and the low visibility of research papers are the major problems facing Indian researchers. OA is viewed as a solution to remedy this. Rajshekar explained that India's challenge is to reciprocate the information flow and improve access and thereby the impact of Indian research. To meet this challenge and to generate a national R&D resource base, an open access approach in line with the Budapest Open Access Initiative is being promoted.

Various Indian R&D organisations, leading scientific research institutions are now taking part in the open access movement by establishing institutional and digital repositories to provide worldwide access to their research literature. Several Indian publishers have already adopted the open-access philosophy for the electronic versions of their journals. Unlike some open-access journals in other countries, in which authors pay to publish their papers, Indian open-access journals use government grants and subscriptions to their print version to cover publishing costs.

INSTITUTIONAL REPOSITORIES

The first Institutional Repository endeavor to be successfully implemented in India is the e-prints repository of research outputs from the Indian Institute of Science, IISc, Bangalore. The archive is maintained by National Center for Science Information (NCSI) and it supports self-archiving by IISc's scientists of research publications and supports metadata for browsing and searching through subject, year, author, keywords and by the latest addition. E-prints@IISC is well populated with almost 3645 publications which are growing.

Not all publications are available for open access, some are for registered users only, and others are linked to publisher's web sites. NCSI allows deposits by e-mail with attachments. Another endeavor of IISc, is the e-theses repository ETD@IISc which covers 153 records of theses and dissertations at present, mainly in the area of science and technology. It offers theses templates in both MSWord and Latex. It also has a browse function by guide and by subject which has been customised for local use by NCSI. Librarian's Digital Library (LDL) at DRTC offers search Digital Libraries (SDL), a selective harvester for archives and e-journals in library and Information sciences. Archives including E-LIS and DLIST can be browsed individually or searched together.

It includes about 236 items basically research papers, articles, reports and provides access to papers published in DRTC conference and seminar proceedings. INFLIBNET, an Inter-University Centre of UGC that serves towards modernisation of libraries through a National Network of Libraries in around 264 Universities, Colleges and R &D Institutions across the country created OAI repository Dspace@INFLIBNET for its post prints, preprints, new clippings, CALIBRE and PLANNER full text proceedings, training material and other scholarly publications. Repository of INFLIBNET annual reports and IRTPLA (Inflibnet Regional Training Programme on Library Automation) course material is also maintained. Another subject specific repository of Indian Medlars centre (IMC) caters to the information need of the Indian Medical community is the e-print archive OpenMed@NIC which stores and provides access to biomedical literature.

It has value added features such as MESH classification and offers RSS feeds to its users. Another Significant document type repository Vidyanidhi Project of the University of Mysore, is designated to act as a national repository for e-theses providing support to universities which may not have resources to manage their own repositories. Apart from the wider dissemination of research particularly among Indian researchers, the project hopes to improve the quality of theses and to protect duplication of research. There are other repositories from national level institutes and various Management Institutes and IIT's have joined the tally.

OPEN ACCESS JOURNALS

As far as the Journals are concerned there are a few open access journals providers in India. The prominent open access journal initiatives have come various institutes like Indian National Science Academy, Indian Academy of Sciences, Indian Medlars Center, Medknow Publications and other smaller ventures.

Indian National Science Academy (INSA)

INSA's project, "Building Digital Resources: Creating Facilities at INSA for hosting S&T Journals Online" has strengthed the open archive movement at the national level. The National Information System for Science and Technology funds the project. It facilitated digitising S&T journals published by INSA and hosting them on a web server. At present INSA publishes 4 journals including the proceedings of INSA. It launched the OA versions of their journals in December 2003 in PDF format. User registration is required to access the journals. INSA also encourages other professional societies having their own web sites to get a link on INSA's site to facilitate a single point of access.

Indian Academy of Sciences (IAS)

Indian Academy of Sciences (IAS) publishes 11 journals in all front-line scientific disciplines which are open access and the full text is available as PDF. Indian Academy of Sciences does not charge authors for publishing their papers. The cost of publishing is met by government funding and subscriptions to their print journals. Current Science, published by the current science association in collaboration with the IAS, has entire back volumes from 1932 and has been online since, 1999. Many other journals including the Journal of Chemical science, Sadhana, Pramana, Journal of Biosciences, etc. have back volumes online.

Indian Medlars Center of NIC

National Informatics Center (NIC) and Indian Council of Medical Research (ICMR) has initiated INDMED @NIC that indexes 77 biomedical peer reviewed journals since, 1985. Another recent project MEDIN@NIC provides full text contents of 38 biomedical journals which are indexed in IndMED.

Medknow Publications

Medknow Publications a company based in Mumbai, has helped 29 peer-reviewed scholarly biomedical journals, including the Journal of Post Graduate Medicine and Neurology India, make the transition from print to electronic open access. These journals provide immediate free access and do not charge the author or author institutions for publication of the articles. These journals also permit authors self archiving by the online submission of manuscripts through their respective web sites. Medknow e-journals offer a professional interface with many value-added advanced linking features. Full text is available in both HTML and PDF.

They have adopted the Open URL standard making it easy for libraries to link users from the citation to full text of the article, and DC metadata for easy retrieval linking of eponyms in the text to sources that provide origin of the terminology, linking of scientific names to species databases, citation information and PubMed links from references cited are other enhancements provided. Searching for medical images, multiple journal search and table of contents alerts are offered as options. 15 Medknow journals are archived in the OAI compliant Bioline International e-prints archive hosted at the University of Toronto.

There are other isolated efforts from learned societies such as the Indian Statistical Association which provides full text access of its journal Sankhya. The Journal of the Indian Institute of Science is also available online. Indianjournals.com provides access to multidis-ciplinary journals published by different Indian Societies and Institutions. Another Delhi based publisher Kamla-Raj enterprises provide access to 8 social science journals which are OAI compliant. The publication wing of CSIR (Council of Scientific and Industrial Research); NISCAIR brings out 11 research journals in different S&T disciplines. Though full text is not currently available online, bibliographic information and abstracts can be accessed and searched. In addition, some Indian open-access journals are using international agencies such as JournalServer.org, an online library of academic journals, to gain greater visibility.

INDIAN OPEN ACCESS SCENARIO: PROGRESS AND FUTURE

Various institutions in India have established open access institutional repositories to disseminate research outputs of their institutions as the technical infrastructure for setting them is now in place with minor costs. This is because there are a number of free open source software applications for setting up the archives. The most widely used software in India is e-prints made available by the unit of Southampton and Dspace by MIT. At present OA to full texts is uneven in Indian repositories and in some cases access is only available on the intranet or by registration. Copyright ownership is a subject that is under intense discussion. Recent growth in India research repositories are covered by ROAR-Registry of Open Access Repositories and Directory of Open Access Repositories. The number of Indian repositories registered in ROAR is 20 at present and India is placed at 8th position in the list of countries with OA repositories registered on ROAR. USA tops the list with 184 repositories, followed by 69 in UK, 63 in Germany, 42 in Brazil, 31 in France, 25 in Australia, 25 in Sweden, 20 in India, 5 in China, 4 in South Africa. Both ROAR and OpenDOAR do not completely represent open access initiatives in India as they depend on voluntary registration. ROAR also includes archives in testing or developmental phase which may not be openly accessible. Though India is placed at the 12th position for overall number of journals among the top 25 publishing countries, its position falls down to 18th for its scientific journals with online content. Surprisingly, its position in the list of open access journals is 5th, well ahead of countries such as the Netherlands, China, Germany, Australia, and so on. No matter the number or quality of OA journals and repositories in India, it has shown a great commitment amongst the developing world.

India has set up some OA operational examples and methodologies for the developing countries. OA movement has made the Indian journals reach the target audience of the world's communities and now more than hundred Indian journals provide free access to full-text contents. For example the Journal of Post Graduate Medicine which has been made open access from Medknow publication, has not only increased the visibility of papers published but there has also been a steady rise in number of submission of articles. The journal is indexed by Abstracting and Indexing services including PubMed, and is OAI compliant through the Bioline International e-prints archive. Statistics showing the number of visitors and downloads can rival some of the better known international medical journals. Moreover the number of citations to articles published in JPGMonline has been increasing every year and so has its projected impact factor.

Now even outside submissions from outside India are publishing in JPGM. Some journals have insisted free user's registration whereas some have browsing facilities without user registration. Another significant development in open access scenario has been the Open Course Ware (OCW) which has gain momentum with the announcement of availability of learning resources on the Internet by two important national level organisations, namely IGNOU and NCERT. There have been efforts to popularise OA archives through various conferences and seminars and workshops in India over the past two years. A special session on OA was held at 93rd Indian Science Congress in January 2006, which came up with the following recommendations for 'Optimal National Open Access Policy' Government of India including DST, DSIR, CSIR, DBT, DoD, DAE, DRDO, ICAR, ICMR, UGC, IITs, IISc and NITs) expects authors of research papers resulting from publicly-funded research to deposit electronic copies of any research paper into an institutional open access repository immediately upon acceptance for publication. Grant holders are encouraged to publish in OA journals and the grant will cover the publication costs. Journal indexing services, index metadata, search engine harvest are being experimented.

A metadata harvesting service harvests metadata from OAI compliant archives through harvesting software that supports

OAI-PMH. Ghosh and Das mentions a few metadata harvesters installed in various archives in India such as Search Digital Libraries (SDL) of DRTC which harvests library science subject specific open access archives and repositories. The SDL currently has 6816 papers from 13 archives indexed. Knowledge Harvester@INSA harvests metadata from 3 archives and currently has 2011 papers indexed. SJPI Cross Journal search service is a recent initiative from NCSI at the IISc that harvests metadata from 13 Indian OA journals and has currently 1047 papers indexed. IIT, Delhi has initiated a metadata harvesting service called SEED. It currently has 5019 papers from 4 archives indexed.

The entire 4 metadata harvester in India use a harvesting system that is PKP Harvester, developed by public Knowledge Project (PKP) from Canada. Informatics has recently launched Open J-Gate OA journal indexing service which covers 3, 000 OA academic, research and industry journals. Out of the 1500 are peer reviewed scholarly journals. These OA initiatives need to be vastly expanded. The future of the OA movement is to fill up repositories, providing open access to full-text and diversification of content where it does not exist. There is a long term commitment to maintaining repositories with the robust systems having backup facilities.

The expansion of content through an extension of the INDEST consortium is being pursued. IISC is committed to put its entire publication online for its centenary year 2009. Ejournal publishing is also expected to increase. INFLIBNET mandates to improve computer and networking facilities in Indian libraries. Further the DRTC plans to include open access journals in library science. CSIR plan to set up a national digital repository of research literature which include theses and dissertations and various other initiatives are likely to arise in future which is supposed to establish a strong OA scenario in India.

OVERCOMING THE BARRIERS

In spite of various institutions having initiated and set up institutional repositories, the response from the community of authors has been far from encouraging. Although OA has gained popularity in the library profession, it is relatively a new concept among the scholarly communities.

Probably there are reasons for this, which need to be addressed if the movement has to grow and succeed.

* Authors have limited familiarity with the concept of OA publishing and surrounding issues and OA policies have little impact on author's decision for submitting papers. There is a misconception that it will be difficult to assess the impact of research if it isn't published in conventional journals. Some unawareness also lies in the fact that the attitude of the journals is changing and renowned journals also permit the authors to archive both preprints and post prints.
* Intellectual property issues continue to dominate the OA landscape. As a result many archives are either in the development stage or on the intranets pending clarification of IPR issues.
* There are copyright violations concerns. Fears to be stolen of the preliminary research ideas might prevent author submissions and there exists the perception that research in smaller institutions may plagiarise the work of the premier institutions
* Barriers to the widespread implementation of IR at universities include a lack of leadership and poor infrastructure. Many universities and research institutions in India lack both computers and high bandwidth Internet connectivity.
* At present there is not much support for adopting a national approach to e-prints archives in India and distributed repositories are being favored.
* Lack of expertise and training issues in organisations for the promotion, installation and maintenance of repositories

To a significant extent these problems could be overcome if universities and research organisations are encouraged to develop Institutional repositories with the software and technical support. Well known authors should be targeted to archive their papers which will set good examples in supporting OA. Showing value to authors, convincing them on OA's value and wide applicability and the increased visibility it provides and creating public opinion and mandating deposits by funding agencies such as UGC, CSR, DBT, ICSSR, DAE etc, self-archiving support from top levels of administration and increasing training opportunities among staff by holding workshop and providing education to open access will surely boost the OA landscape in India.

Research visibility can be provided by registering repositories with open access registries such as ROAR, Open DOAR and federated services such as OAIster. OAIster is a cross-archive search tool, which facilitates to search e-print collections in almost 300 institutions worldwide. Further academic and research libraries should be encouraged to join such coalitions as SPARC that promote OA.

CONCLUSION

A large number of open access developmental projects are underway with the active support of government funding agencies, learned societies and publishers to make the fruits of scientific progress equally available to all. These efforts are to be consolidated and other important Indian organisations and funding agencies which have a strong research base with a large output of science and technology papers can set up institutional archives and provide subscription free journals.

Arunachalam states that as research originating in India often go unnoticed, even by other researchers in India, therefore creating institutional archives and providing open access journals would help to reduce the isolation of our scientists. Raja Simhan says that OA archiving should be given much higher attention in policy circle so that they would raise the profile of Indian research. Open access to scientific journals is beneficial to scholars and has wide support as a concept, but it needs viable revenue models and great commitment among its promoters. Therefore the emphasis should be primarily on setting up open archives rather than on persuading journal publishers to make their journals open access.

While we realise the importance and value of expanding OA to scholarly research, it is equally important to address the many questions that are being raised about the prospects of OA. Its principal strength will continue to derive from technology that enables accessing and sharing distributed resources by the community of scientists. Though the OA concept is still debated and there is no consensus within the scientific community or a proven model, indeed, the benefits of open access to results of research cannot be denied.

9

A Techno-Savvy Approach of Traditional Cataloguing

INTRODUCTION

The Dublin core metadata initiative began in 1995 with a little fanfare, but today it is widely recognised as International Standard. The continuous explosion of electronic media, internet and the www has brought a revolutionary change in the method of cataloguing and managing the information electronic resources. The term metadata simply means data about data that aids in the identification description and location of networked electronic resources including long term preservation. Some of the most popular metadata schemas include: Dublin Core, AACR2 (Anglo-American Cataloging Rules) – a standard set of rules for cataloging library materials, GILS (Government Information Locator Service), EAD (Encoded Archives Description)–a metadata scheme for collection finding aids, IMS (IMS Global Learning Consortium), AGLS (Australian Government Locator Service).

Out of these DC metadata schema is very easy to create due to its simplicity, usability and flexibility. The elements of Dublin Core are easily identifiable and are clear enough to be understood by even non-catalogers, if proper awareness programmes and training are provided. The metadata also improves resource discovery. Metadata sets are also being developed for administrative control, security, personal information, management information, content rating, rights management, preservation. Due to its simplicity the Dublin core Metadata is becoming very popular outside the library community amongst researchers, museum curators, and music collectors because it does not require knowledge of highly specialised descriptive systems like AACR2. DC Metadata is synonymous of cataloguing. The only difference is that cataloguing is for physical objects and metadata is exclusively for electronic resources. Metadata is structured information that describes, explains, locates or otherwise makes it easier to retrieve, use or manage an information resource.

METHODOLOGY

This is a conceptual study based on participant observation. The research for this paper is based on interpersonal and intrapersonal communication with the Library Professionals, Metadata Analyst, and Metadata Librarian, at various academic libraries. Important journals, periodicals, publications and research volumes, online journals internet and project reports are explored thoroughly to build up the first hand information for further analysis. The objective of this study is to define the new way of cataloguing, the Dublin core metadata. A new insight is given to library professionals to adopt better polices to create DC metadata on web. Several pointers to further literature and web sites complete the overview.

METADATA DEFINITION

After exploring many definitions, Jane Greenberg's definition is found to be the most appropriate. He defines metadata as "Structured data about an object that supports functions associated with the designated object". Structured data implies a systematic ordering of data according to a metadata schema specification. The object is any entity, form, or mode for which contextual data can be recorded. The universe of objects to which metadata can be applied is radically diverse and seemingly endless, ranging from corporeal and digital information resources, such as a monograph, newspaper, or photographs, to activities, events, persons, places, structures, transactions, relationships, execution directions, and programmatic applications. Functions associated with the designated object emphasis here is on the ability of metadata to support the activities and behaviours of an object. For example, "author", "title", and "subject" metadata facilitate the discovery of an information resource. In this example, metadata promotes specified functions surrounding the life of the designated object – the information resource. Michael Day in the British electronic journal Ariadne, points out the connection between today's metadata and the traditional library bibliographic record.

When the library and information community discuss metadata, the most common analogy given is the library catalogue record. Priscilla Caplan has defined metadata as a neutral term for cataloguing without the 'excess baggage' of the Anglo-American Cataloguing Rules or the MARC formats. The most well-known metadata initiative, the Dublin Core Metadata Element Set, has the specific aim of supporting resource discovery in a network environment.

DUBLIN CORE METADATA

The Dublin Core metadata element set is a standard for cross-domain information resource description. It provides a simple and standardised set of conventions for describing things online in ways that make them easier to find. Today Dublin Core is widely used to describe digital materials such as video, sound, image, text, and composite media like web pages. Implementations of Dublin Core typically make use of XML and are Resource Description Framework based.

The main objective of Dublin Core is to define a simple set of data elements so that authors and publishers of Internet documents could create their own metadata records with out extensive training.

The Dublin Core approach is to have the level of bibliographic control midway between the detailed approaches of MARC and 'structured' TEI (Text Encoding Initiative), and the automatic indexing of locator services such as Lycos. Library catalogue follows Anglo-American Cataloging Rules, second edition revised AACR2R to describe resources in a standard way, these descriptions are encoded in the Machine Readable Cataloging (MARC) format. Bibliographic utilities like OCLC and RLIN are first checked before the library cataloger creates a bibliographic record for the resource.

If the bibliographic description already exists, the record is modified or adapted and exported into the Online Public Access Catalogue (OPAC) of the library.

Some libraries, rather than using OCLC and an integrated library automation system to hold their OPAC, may use proprietary database using SQL or other technologies. DC emerged as a simpler alternate to MARC to describe electronic resources and is now used widely to describe all types of resources, including books.

DC stands for Dublin Core, a standard from the National Information Standards Organisation (NISO) and the International Organisation for Standardisation (ISO). Initially, there were 15 DC elements such as Title, Creator, Subject, Description, Publisher, Contributor, Date, Type, Format, Identifier, Source, Language, Relation, Coverage and Rights; but afterwards it extended to one more element, Audience.

DC standard has two levels in creating metadata. When 15 DC elements are used in metadata creation, the level is called Simple, this can be considered equivalent to minimal level cataloging. When the 16 DC element Audience, refinements to the original 15, such as qualifiers and encoding schemes (for example, the vocabulary term and name of the vocabulary from which it is derived), are used, the level of DC use is called Qualified, think of this as full level cataloguing. This chapter provides directions for use of a level of DC that is Qualified and yet very simple and straightforward to practice. Simple DC does not help in the goal of information discovery and not all born-digital resources, *i.e.*, electronic resources, have a print equivalent or share the characteristics of books, serials, videos, computer files, and other information resources traditionally organised in the library, and thus require more complex descriptions than simple.

WHY DUBLIN CORE METADATA

The Dublin Core metadata schema is easy to create due to following advantages

* Due to its usability, flexibility and simplicity, non-cataloguers used them freely. It is expected that authors or Web-site maintainers unschooled in the cataloguing arts will be able to use the Dublin Core for resource description making their collection more visible to search engines and retrieval systems. DC includes sufficient flexibility to encode the additional structure and more elaborate semantics appropriate to such applications.
* All elements are repeatable means if there is more than one person who created the resource and the Creator element can be used as many times as is needed to record the names of multiple creators. Similarly, all other elements (title, subjects, etc) may be repeated as many times as needed.
* All elements are optional, but allow each site to define which elements are mandatory and which are optional.
* It is not intended to supplant other resource descriptions, but rather to complement them. It is intended to describe the essential features of electronic documents that support resource discovery. Other important metadata such as accounting and archival data, were deliberately excluded to keep the schema as simple and useable as possible.
* Due to syntax independence its use in the widest ranges of applications.
* The elements of Dublin Core are easily identifiable by having the work in hand, such as intellectual content and physical format.
* Due to its clear designing of semantics of these elements a wide range of untrained users can understand easily.
* The elements may be modified in limited and well-defined ways through the use of specific qualifiers, such as the name of the thesaurus used in the subject element. Refinement qualifiers may be vocabulary terms from registered lists such as standard library tools like the Library of Congress Subject Headings and Dewey

Decimal Classification, these two may be used to the subject element. There are other vocabularies that may be used. The name of vocabulary used is the encoding scheme qualifier.

* It can be extended to meet the demands of more specialised communities. From the very beginning, the Dublin Core creators recognised that some resources could not be adequately described by a small set of elements. The Dublin Core creators came up with two solutions, number one, by allowing the addition of elements for site-specific purposes or specialised fields. Number two, by designing the Dublin Core schema so that it could be mapped into more complex and tightly controlled systems, such as MARC.

HOW TO CREATE DC METADATA

It is very pathetic to observe the paradoxical attitude of some of the library professionals and information specialists who continue to believe that cataloging web resources is a waste of time, it is better to make web pages (essentially webliographies or lists) because many of the web resources are too ephemeral to be included in the library catalog. To make the maintenance of metadata for web resources much simpler, new tools such as URL link checkers are used. The users are suggested to start with the library catalogue as a single gateway to the universe of knowledge. The usage of DC refinements and principles advocated in this chapter is both integrative and time saving. It will save the time of the library cataloger and the user because it recognised the lessons learned by the library, archival and museum cataloging communities and tries to incorporate them into DC metadata creation. Cataloging is synonymous for the activity of metadata description. Resource descriptions are synonymous for DC records. Instead of 999 tags in library MARK, 16 elements of Dublin core have been used. The best of cataloguing practice, however, be captured in the following simple guidelines. Required information should be filled normally, failing which an element becomes meaningless.

GUIDELINES TO CREATE DC METADATA

There are three main guidelines to create DC metadata as discussed below:

* *Guidelines 1*: A comprehensive Resource description is required. The data should be absolutely complete to avoid confusing meaning of the element. For example, if there is no title, make up a title. Leave the element blank only as a last resort.
* *Guideline 2*: Consistent resource description should be provided taking into consideration the inconsistent nature of humans beings, the principles of consistency is used in cataloging and classification to avoid cognitive overload. There are many techniques for ensuring consistency and the simplest is to use words from a predetermined and authoritative list whenever possible for controlled values.
* *Guideline 3*: All of the DC elements is optional, repeatable, and modified by qualifiers. All 16 elements are described in detail and each element includes the following categories of instruction and information. Main categories of Instruction for creating DC Metadata are shown in fig. 9.1.

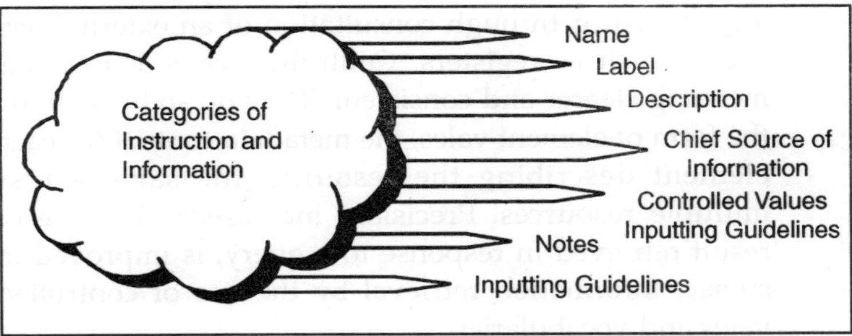

Fig. 9.1.Categories of Instruction for Creating DC Metadata.

MAIN CATEGORIES FOR CREATING DC METADATA

The Main Categories for creating DC Metadata are Name, Label, Description, Chief Source of Information, Controlled

Values Inputting Guidelines, Notes, and Inputting Guidelines.

* *Name*: Name is the name given to the element in DC standard.
* *Label*: Label as seen in an integrated library system or a bibliographic utility such as OCLC for entering this information. Somewhere elements name is same as the Label and sometimes it may be different
* *Description*: Description is the definition given in the DC standard Comments also come for the DC as appropriate.
* *Chief Source of Information*: Instruction modeled after the technical reading of the item for cataloguing practices, AACR2 is the chief source of information. The process of technical reading provides specific guidance to the sources of information the exact places in the resources from which the metadata for each element may be selected.
* *Controlled Values Inputting Guidelines*: Controlled values is also modeled after AACR2R and MARC to some extent and allows the metadata creator to know if the element uses a list of controlled values, a classification, or controlled vocabulary. These values may be made enforceable by the software or humanly selected from a given list or through consultation of an external list/ source such as registers. Controlled vales help make meaning clearer and consistent. They do so by keeping the form of element vales, the metadata content for each element describing the resource, the same across multiple resources. Precision, increased relevance of result retrieved in response to a query, is improved in subject information retrieval by the use of controlled vales and vocabularies.
* *Notes*: Metadata Creator Notes or creation guidelines discuss how much of the cataloguer's (metadata creator) judgement is involved in creating the metadata for each element. Metadata creation is often subjective rather than objective. Without clear rules and standards, two different catalogers may describe the same resource

quite differently. The term subjective is used to indicate that a particular element can be described based on the personal judgement of the resource cataloger and objective is used on the personal judgement of the resource cataloger and objective is used to denote objectivity, when the data or content is found on the resource or may be identified in a similar manner by all resource metadata creators and catalogers.

* *Inputting Guidelines*: Inputting guidelines provide special directions that must be followed to enter the resource description. These illustrate the general principles of DC metadata creation.

ELEMENTS-BY-ELEMENTS DESCRIPTION OF DC METADATA

Description and how to create DC metadata (Notes) and inputting guidelines with examples for electronic (web) information resources for all DC elements are discussed below.

Element: Title

* *Description*: A name given to the resource.
* *Inputting Guidelines*: Enter the title information as found in the resource. Use capitalisation and punctuation as found in resource.
* *DC Creator Notes*: Generally, there should be no individual judgement involved as the metadata creator is merely transcribing the title, when the resource has a clearly presented title. Many electronic resources, however, may not have a title clearly visible or the title may be generic for the whole and not the specific part being catalogued. In these cases, creating the metadata for the title, where the cataloger must create or supply title, can become subjective. Follow the guidance prescribed in the Chief source of information and generally take title from the actual information resource whenever possible. Example: Title= "The Art of Music"

Element: Creator

* *Description*: An entity primarily responsible for making the content of the resource.
* *Inputting Guidelines*: Enter the Creator as found in the resource. Use capitalisation and punctuation as found in resource. If Creator is an organisation, enter the name of the organisation.
* *Metadata Creator Notes*: Objective. Cataloging the creator becomes a subjective activity should the creator not be listed in the resource, while it is possible through extra research to find out this information, generally this would take too much time and hence, most cataloguing is only done based on actual examination of the resource. If creator can not be readily determined from this, leave this element blank. Many electronic resources do not have the creator easily identifiable. Example Creator= "Mishra, Rajeshver"

Element: Subject

* *Description*: The topic of the content of the resource.
* Inputting Guidelines: Input subject from LCSH or from resource as Keywords.
* *Metadata Creator Notes*: Objective when the terms are found on the resource. Subjective, if cataloger supplied. Most often will be cataloger supplied. Example: Subject="Library Automation"

Element: Description

* *Description*: An account of the content of the resource.
* *Inputting Guidelines*: Provide abstract, table of contents, or description of the resource.
* *Metadata Creator Notes*: Objective if taken from resource. The information in this element may be subjective if it is a summary provided by the cataloger. Example Description" The chapter defines metadata, examines the relationship between creating metadata and cataloguing, provides definitions for key metadata

vocabulary terms and explores the topic of metadata generation. Cataloguing is for physical objects and metadata is exclusively for electronic resources"

Element: Publisher

* *Description*: An entity responsible for making the resource available in its present form such as Publishing House, a University Department, or Corporate entity.
* *Inputting Guidelines*: Enter the Publisher as found in the resource. Use capitalisation and punctuation as found in resource. If Publisher is an organisation,enter the name of organisation.
* *Metadata Creator Notes*: Objective, may become subjective. It is often difficult to find the name of the publisher for electronic resources. For example, consider the homepage. Who is the publisher? We generally consider the organisation or individual who is hosting the web page to be the publisher. Thus the publisher of this author's home page is the University of Kanpur. Example Publisher="Kanpur University"

Element: Contributor

* *Description*: An entity responsible for making contributions to the content of the resource.
* *Inputting Guidelines*: Enter the Contributor as found in the resource. Use capitalisation and punctuation as found in resource. Contributors play different roles and can be indicated by using parenthesis, following the name. Thus, some roles are Editor, Translator, and Illustrator. Example Contributor= "Anand, Anoop (Editor)"
* *Metadata Creator Notes*: Objective. There are a great many more roles that Contributors can fall into. But, to keep the activity of metadata creation simple and save time, the three are sufficient.

Element: Date

* *Description*: A date associated with an event in the life cycle of the resource.

* *Inputting Guidelines*: Follow the YYYY-MM-DD format and choose from list what type of date is being recorded, whether the date is the date the resource was created or modified. If no date is available, leave blank, if multiple dates are found, enter the most recent only and indicate type. Enter 00-00 for month and date when it is not found on the resource easily.
* *Metadata Creator Notes*: Objective. Keep cataloguing simple and only specify one or two dates, when found, based on your local user needs. Example Date= "2007-07-27"

Element: Type

* *Description*: The nature or genre of the content of the resource.
* *Inputting Guidelines*: DCMI Metadata terms TYPE Vocabulary has a list, from which select as many as types. They are Collection, Dataset, Event, Image, InteractiveResource, MovingImage, PhysicalObject, Service, Software, Sound, StillImage and Text that can be found in the resource.
* *Metadata Creator Notes*: Objective. Example Type= "Image"

Element: Format

* *Description*: The physical or digital manifestation of the resource. Typically, format may include the media-type or dimensions of the resource.
* *Inputting Guidelines*: Select one or more of the formats.
* *Metadata Creator Notes*: Objective. Example: Format="Image/gif" or Format="2KB"

Element: Identifier

* Description: An unambiguous reference to the resource within a given context.
* Inputting Guidelines: Give full URL starting http://.....
* Metadata Creator Notes: Objective.

Element: Source

* *Description*: A reference to a resource from which the present resource is derived.Recommended best practice is to reference the resource by means of a formal identification or call number system.
* *Inputting Guidelines*: Enter the title followed by a comma and the URL. If no title or URL found or the original source is a print or other format, describe in own words. Many electronic resource are born-digital and have no print or other digital counterpart. Hence, source may often be left blank.
* *Metadata Creator Notes*: Objective. Example: Source="Image from page 34 of the 1922 edition of Romeo and Juliet"

Element: Language

* *Description*: A language of intellectual contents of the resource.
* *Inputting Guidelines*: Select the language of the resource.
* *Metadata Creator Notes*: Objective. Note that many learning resources are available in versions other than English, therefore record the language to match the object being catalogued. Do not use the language element to record version information. Example: Language= " en" for English and "fr" for French.

Element: Relation

* Description: A reference to a related resource.
* Inputting Guidelines: Select the appropriate relationship between two or more resources. A resource may have multiple relationships. Add Title and URL.
* Metadata Creator Notes: Objective. Example: Title="Electronic AACR2" Relation="Anglo-American Cataloguing Rules, 2nd edition"

Element: Coverage

* *Description*: The extent or scope of the content of resource.
* *Inputting Guidelines*: Select the appropriate spatial, temporal, jurisdiction coverage of the resource and use the words in the resources.

* *Metadata Creator Notes*: Objective. For some types of literary materials, this might be subjective.

Element: Rights

* *Description*: Information about rights held in and over the resource. Typically a Rights element will contain a rights management statement for the resource, or reference a service providing such information. Right information often encompasses Intellectual Property Rights IPR, Copyright, and various Property Rights.
* *Inputting Guidelines*: May be either a text statement or URL pointing to a right statement, or a combination, when a brief statement and a lengthier one are available.
* *Metadata Creator Notes*: Objective. Example Rights="Access limited to teachers"

Element: Audience

* *Description*: Intended user for resource.
* *Inputting Guidelines*: Look for this information on the main resource page, if none is found, browse the resource and select one or more of the values from the Controlled values list - Elementary, Middle, High School, Undergraduate level,Graduate Level, Professional, General Education.
* *Metadata Creator Notes*: Subjective, if not found explicitly stated in resource. Example: Audience=" General Education"

FUTURE

There has been growing awareness in the library and information community of the importance of metadata, not only for resource discovery but also as an aid in the management of networked digital resources, including long-term preservation. In future the job titles of cataloger will be replaced with Metadata architect, Metadata librarians or Metalogger. The term Metalogging will be introduced in place of cataloguing in metadata community.

But these new terms follow the cataloguing profession to a certain extent, the general consensus is that they are not the same fields of endeavour. DC is not a simplified cataloguing format. As expressed by Gradmann in his IFLA paper 'Cataloguing vs. Metadata: old wine in new bottle'. The concept of metadata is meant to provide machine understandable description It is not just to be read by humans, but interpreted by computers which will then act on it, for example, to differentiate between good and untrustworthy sites. The continuous increase in production and proliferation of electronic information results in creation of new innovative simpler standards research resource description to accomplish the goal of universal bibliographical control and information access. Metadata just like currency will continue to make the world go around, because it is the medium of exchange for connecting searchers with the information they need. Metadata will be shared, reused and redistributed in user community because it is very simple and economic and saves time and money.

CONCLUSION

Gone are the days when long hours were spent in creating catalogue cards.In the present technosavvy ambience of the academic world even the cataloguing practices are also influenced. The traditional library catalogue, over the last 100 years, has evolved to fulfil the function like Finding, Identifying, Locating, Selecting, and Collocating. Equating creating metadata and cataloging makes sense because these activities have the same end goal – to produce a set of structured descriptive data that will facilitate object discovery and other desired functions. The first objective to be fulfilled by the traditional library catalogue is to help the user in finding, identifying and locating materials when the author, title or subject is known. The second objective is to bring similar materials together in collocation and aid in selection. Dublin core also fulfills the traditional library catalogue system.

As Find covers DC elements like Title, Creator (author etc) other Contributors, Subject for primary search categories and for secondary search Language, Coverage, Format. Identify includes Date, Type, Format, Identifier. Select includes Description, Coverage. Obtain In networked environment, obtaining a resource should be fully supported by the inclusion of an accurate address in the Identifier element. Most of the effort in this area has gone towards assuring that the identifiers assigned to electronic resources are – and remain over time – accurate. Both cataloguing data and DC metadata support the four tasks, although DC is only designed to support the finding and obtaining of electronic resources. In the digital library more importance is given to the information discovering function and finding and locating.

Metadata has been and will continue to be an enabling tool for extending the usability of the Web in the areas of resource discovery and access. Resource metadata creation is an ongoing process. Metadata for electronic resources are more similar to serials catalogue records, which require constant maintenance, changes and updates as serials evolve throughout their life. In this paper more emphasis is laid to bring harmonious relationship between cataloguing and metadata creation by outlying some important ways in which DC metadata can be created. In the development of DC metadata standard by the DCMI, initial emphasis has been laid in getting minimal bibliographic control over electronic resources. So we can say Metadata is a fancy name for an inferior form of traditional cataloguing.

10

Developing Digital Libraries for Global Children

INTRODUCTION

The International Children's Digital Library (ICDL) was initially created by an interdisciplinary research team at the University of Maryland in cooperation with the Internet Archive. Members of the team include computer scientists, librarians, educational technologists, classroom teachers, graphic designers, and graduate students from the University of Maryland's (UMD) College of Information Studies (CLIS) and the UMD Human-Computer Interaction Lab (HCIL), a leader in children's interface design. The mission of the International Children's Digital Library Foundation (ICDL Foundation) is to support the world's children in becoming effective members of the global community - who exhibit tolerance and respect for diverse cultures, languages and ideas by making the best in children's literature available online free of charge.

ICDL: FOUNDATION

* *Collection*: To create a collection of more than 10,000 books in at least 100 languages that is freely available to children, teachers, librarians, parents, and scholars throughout the world via the Internet. The materials

included in the collection reflect similarities and differences in cultures, societies, interests, lifestyles, and priorities of peoples around the world. The collection's focus is on identifying materials that help children to understand the world around them and the global society in which they live.

* *Education*: To develop a greater understanding of the relationship between children's access to a digital collection of multicultural materials and children's attitudes towards books, libraries, reading, technology, and other countries and their cultures.
* *Technology*: To collaborate with children as design partners in the development of computer interface technologies that support children in searching, browsing, reading, and sharing books in electronic form.
* *Business*: To provide a platform for operational excellence that insures the Library grows in strict accordance with it strategic priorities and in a manner that leverages its outstanding human and intellectual resources to achieve the Library's mission of reaching as many children as possible with the best of children's literature.

CONTEXT OF EVALUATION

Digital libraries are complex social, institutional and technical systems. No evaluation can possibly address all of these aspects together. Thus, different approaches have been used for different evaluation goals.

Context includes selection of a goal, framework, viewpoint or level(s), basic approach or perspective of evaluation. There are different types of approaches of digital library evaluation on the basis of different aspects.

No single approach can exhaustively evaluate the all aspects of any digital library. Here we try to incorporate most of the approaches as possible.

The approaches are:

* *System-centered approach*: Most prevalent. Involves study of some aspect of performance. Includes assessing

effectiveness and/or efficiency of some feature or some specific design or some technological component. Applied in a number of studies with results that may inform specific choices in design or operations.

* *Human-centered approach*: Also widely applied. Involves study of behaviour in respect to given information needs, such as information seeking, browsing, searching including performance appraisal of given tasks, either predetermined or observed in natural settings. Used in a number of studies that illuminated human behaviour, requirements, needs, or difficulties encountered. Provides implications for design, but indirectly rather than directly.
* *Usability-centered approach*: Involves assessment of different features, particularly in respect to portals, by users. It is a bridge between systems- and human-centered approaches. Used in several studies with mixed, or self-evident results.
* *Ethnographic approach*: Involves study of life-ways, culture and customs in a digital library environment. Also involves study of impact of a digital library on a given community. Applied successfully in a few studies, with illuminating results, particularly as to impact.
* *Anthropological approach*: Involves study of different stakeholders or communities and their cultures in relation to a given digital library. Applied in one study with interesting results illuminating barriers between stakeholder communities.
* *Sociological approach*: Involves assessment of situated action or user communities in social setting of a digital library. Applied in one study with disappointing results.
* *Economic approach*: Involves study of costs, cost benefits, economic values and impacts. Strangely, it was applied at the outset of digital library history (*e.g.*, project PEAK) but now the approach is not really present at all.

CRITERIA FOR EVALUATION

Criteria reflecting performance as related to selected objectives. They include:

* What parameters of performance were concentrate on?
* What dimension or characteristic were evaluate?

Criteria refer to chosen standard(s) to judge things by. Criteria are then used to develop measures. The importance of criteria follows from this truism: there can be no evaluation without explicitly or implicitly having some criterion or criteria first.Since, 1950's evaluation of IR systems uses relevance as the basic criterion for evaluation. Libraries use a variety of (more or less) standardised criteria for evaluation of components, such as a collection, or services, such as reference. Digital library efforts have not as yet developed anything similar as to evaluation criteria. A summary of most often used criteria follows.

USABILITY

Usability has been used widely in digital library evaluation, but there is no uniform definition of what does it cover in digital library context. Usability is a very general criterion that covers a lot of ground and includes many specific criteria – it is a meta term This was pretty much the umbrella under which usability was used in digital library evaluation. Here is a list of specific usability criteria applied in various studies:

* Content (of a portal or site):
  - Accessibly, availability
  - Clarity (as presented)
  - Complexity (organisation, structure)
  - Informativeness
  - Transparency
  - Understanding, effort to understand
  - Adequacy
  - Coverage, overlap,
  - Quality, accuracy
  - Validity, reliability
  - Authority
* *Process*: Carrying out tasks such as search, navigate, browse, find, evaluate or obtain a resource, etc.
  - learnability to carry out
  - Effort/time to carry out

- Convenience, ease of use
- Lostness (confusion)
- Support for carrying out
- Completion (achievement of task)
- Interpretation difficulty
- Sureness in results
- Error rate

* Format:
  - Attractiveness
  - Sustaining efforts
  - Consistency
  - Representation of labels (how well are concepts Represented?)
  - communicativeness of messages
* Overall assessment:
  - Satisfaction
  - Success
  - Relevance, usefulness of results
  - Impact, value
  - Quality of experience
  - Barriers, irritability
  - Preferences
  - Learning

SYSTEMS FEATURES

As digital libraries are systems, many traditional systems evaluation criteria were used.

Some pertain to performance of technology others to performance of given processes or algorithms using technology.

* Technology performance:
  - Response time
  - Processing time,
  - Speed
  - Capacity
  - Load
* Process/algorithm performance:
  - Relevance (of obtained results)
  - Clustering

  - Similarity
  - Functionality
  - Flexibility
  - Comparison with human performance
  - Error rate
  - Optimisation
  - Logical decisions
  - Path length
  - Click throughs
  - Retrieval time
* Overall system:
  - Maintainability
  - Scalability
  - Interoperability
  - Sharability
  - Costs

USAGE

A number of studies concentrated on use of a digital library, considering this as evaluation.

Usage in itself is a criterion involving studies of:

* Usage patterns
* Use of materials
* Usage statistics
* Who uses what, when
* For what reasons/decisions

ETHNOGRAPHIC AND OTHER CRITERIA

Several ethnographic and anthropological studies used criteria derived from those fields. Among others, these involve determination of conceptions and misconceptions in and between different groups, their practices and environments, their culture, their language and frames of reference, priorities, learning, impacts and similar aspects that provide comparative evaluation in a broader context of a digital library..

ICDL: EVALUATION METHOD

The range of methods used in digital library evaluations is wide. It would be hard to find a scholarly evaluation method that was not used. It involves: What measures and measuring instruments were used? What samples were used? What procedures were used for data collection? What procedures were used for data analysis? In the present study involves mainly limited user study and systematic study of web site of ICDL with respect to Intel Pentium PCs with MS Windows having 14", 17" and 19" monitors.

Actually methodology includes:

* Surveys, including direct questionnaires and online surveys
* Structured interviews
* Focus groups
* Observations
* Task accomplishment
* Think aloud
* Case studies
* Transaction log analyses
* Experimentation
* Records analysis
* Usage analysis
* Documents, meeting, communication analysis (anthropology)
* Economic analysis

DATA COLLECTION

As the scope is very much little as per time span for evaluation and other constraints, only user survey and web site study were used for data collection.

ICDL: ANALYSIS AND EVALUATION

AUTHORITY

The ICDL was initially created by an interdisciplinary research team at the University of Maryland in cooperation with the Internet Archive. Members of the team include computer scientists, librarians, educational technologists, classroom teachers, graphic designers, and graduate students from the University of Maryland's (UMD) College of Information Studies

(CLIS) and the UMD Human-Computer Interaction Lab (HCIL), a leader in children's interface design.

The ICDL is now the principal activity of the independent not-for-profit ICDL Foundation, which continues to work closely with the University of Maryland by providing generous support for ICDL related research in the Human Computer Interaction Laboratory and the College of Information Studies. (The ICDL is a five year project funded primarily by the National Science Foundation (NSF) and the Institute for Museum and Library Services (IMLS) for creating a digital library of international children's books.

This five-year research project, created in collaboration with the Internet Archive and conducted by the University of Maryland, has five primary goals):

* To create a collection of more than 10,000 books in at least 100 languages that is freely available to children, teachers, librarians, parents, and scholars throughout the world via the Internet;
* To collaborate with children as design partners in the development of computer interface technologies that support children in searching, browsing, reading, and sharing books in electronic form;
* to better understand the concepts of rights management and "fair use" in a digital age;
* To evaluate the impact that access to digital materials may have on collection development and programming practices in school and public libraries;
* To develop a greater understanding of the relationship between children's access to a digital collection of multicultural materials and children's attitudes towards books, libraries, reading, technology, and other countries and cultures.

An initial prototype of the ICDL was introduced at a celebration at the Library of Congress in Washington, DC, in November 2002. At that time, the collection consisted of 181 books, which were provided by national libraries and other government agencies, public library systems, collaborating publishers, and individual authors and illustrators. Approximately half of the titles were within copyright protection and half were freely available in the public domain.

The materials selected for the prototype generally were in compliance with the selection criteria established for the collection by the National Advisory Board of Librarians; however, efforts were made to acquire and digitise as diverse a collection as possible to ensure that the functions of the ICDL interface could be effectively tested. Now International Children's Digital Library Foundation manages ICDL. From very beginning ICDL was developed and powered by well-reputed institutions. The ICDL Foundation has famous and scholar personalities in Foundation Directors and Board of Advisors.

AUTHENTI CITY

The information in the web site are very much authentic because the metadata regarding each item/book are explicitly stated with each and every book. Again authority and authenticity are correlated to each other.

COLLECTION/RESOURCES

The collection in the ICDL is comprised of different children books written in different languages. All books consisting of the scanned pages arranged serially. At the end of the initial research period, it is anticipated that the collection of the ICDL will consist of approximately 10,000 materials in at least 100 languages.

Materials within the collection are made available through the Library over the Internet to all users without charge. The project does not support downloading, copying or printing of any materials in the collection.

The materials selected for inclusion in the ICDL are those that:

* Support the understanding of similarities and differences among and within countries, peoples, and cultures;
* Promote tolerance and acceptance;
* Are considered relevant to children in today's world;
* Have a high degree of appeal for children of an age between 3 and 13;

* Meet professionally accepted quality standards in terms of content, format, and presentation; and,
* Can be presented effectively in a digital format.

Relevance

Librarians, teachers, authors, illustrators, publishers, and children from all over the world suggest books that they think should be considered for our collection. Each book must be carefully evaluated before it can be added to the Library. In accordance with the goal of the ICDL, all information are relevant. Again as per the audience is concerned, the books included in the library are of basically children books. The metadata associated with the item are reasonable and relevant.

Formats

The formats of the books in the ICDL are of scanned image. The digitised formats are obtained through:

* *Choosing books*: The ultimate selection of the books to be scanned.
* *Scanning books*: Books have to be scanned and saved TIFF image format into our database in order to get the book pages into our computers. Scanners take very detailed pictures of pages and save the images in a way that the computers of ICDL can recognise. Some of the books that are scanned for the ICDL are cut up and sucked into a scanner one page at a time to be automatically scanned. Other books are scanned one page at a time without destroying the books. Some of the really old books in the collection have to be repaired before they are scanned because the scanning process could cause them to fall apart. Sometimes the people who donate books scan them for ICDL. Other times the people who work at the ICDL scan them. Sometimes ICDL pay another company to scan books for the library. The technical specification including formats, naming convention and guidelines for scanning are enumerated below:

- Technical Specifications:
  a. *File Format:* Uncompressed TIFF
  b. *Pixel depth*: 24 bit colour
  c. *Spatial resolution*: 300 dpi
  d. *Example*: Caralic-0001.tif (11.5 MB)
- Naming Convention:
  a. Filenames should use the format <id>-####.tif where:
     i. <id>

Guidelines

* Scanning of the book cover to cover, including blank pages. Scan 0001 is assumed to be the front cover. If all pages are scanned, there should be an even number of scans.
* All scans should represent a single page, even if an image spans multiple pages.
* Cropping of the scan to the edge of the page. Clear direction is given to make all scans, including the cover page, the same size and dimensions (*i.e.*, number of pixels), or as close to the same size as possible.
* Scanning of pages with rotated images as they appear in the book.
* Provision of address for contact ICDL authority at icdl-rights@cs.umd.edu if senders have any questions.

Library Materials Selection

Selection Criteria for the ICDL

Materials selected for inclusion in the ICDL collection during the first five years of the project must support the research goals of the project and must be appropriate for one or both of the primary audiences identified as users of the Library.

The materials in the International Children's Digital Library, which are intended primarily to be used by children, parents, teachers, and school and public librarians, should:

* Support the understanding of similarities and differences among and within countries, peoples, and cultures;

* Promote tolerance and acceptance;
* Contribute to children's understanding of the diversity of the global society;
* Have a high degree of appeal for children of an age between 3 and 13;
* Meet professionally accepted quality standards in terms of content, format, and presentation;
* Be considered relevant to children in today's world;
* Be appropriate for the age levels of the intended audience for the collection;
* Be presented in their entirety and not adapted or abridged from their original published form; however, works originally published as abridgements or adaptations of other works may be included in the collection; and
* Be presented effectively in a digital format.
* Expand the scope and variety of cultures represented in the collection;
* Have achieved historical significance;
* Represent exemplary artistic, historic, and literary qualities, such as award winners; or
* Contribute to the project's research priorities.

Acquisitions Process

Materials included in the collection may be:

* Freely available in the public domain;
* Contributed by a National Library or another national agency that holds the rights to the materials;
* Acquired by the ICDL under a contractual agreement with the creator(s) or publisher(s) of the work or with another entity that has legal authority for its intellectual property rights; or
* Collaboratively acquired by the ICDL and other private or public special collections through a contractual agreement with the rights holders

Reconsideration of Materials

Objections to materials included in the collection will be considered by the ICDL National Advisory Board of Librarians and/or the International Advisory Board.

The Board(s) will use the established selection criteria in determining whether the item is appropriate for the collection. The recommendation of the Board(s) will be given to the Director of Collection Development for the Library. The final decision concerning the retention or withdrawal of a work will be made by the Director of Collection Development.

USER INTERFACE

All web sites particularly a digital library is only as good as its interface. The interface is the entry point into the library. The user interface is the aggregate of means by which people (the users) interact with a particular machine, device, computer programme or other complex tool (the system). The user interface provides means of: Input - allowing the users to control the system, Output - allowing the system to inform. The junction between a user and a computer programme.

User interface design important for several reasons.

* First of all the more intuitive the user interface the easier it is to use, and the easier it is to use and the less expensive to use it.
* The better the user interface the easier it is to train people to use it, reducing your training costs.
* The better your user interface the less help people will need to use it, reducing your support costs.
* The better your user interface the more your users will like to use it, increasing their satisfaction with the work that you have done.

The ICDL uses Graphical User Interface (GUI) that takes advantage of the computer's graphics capabilities to make the programme easier to use. In ICDL, as maximum users are of 3-13 years age group, the GUI is appropriate.

The ICDL interface uses most of the basic components of GUI such as:

* *Pointing device*: The mouse that enables users to select objects on the display screen.
* *Icons*: Small pictures that represent commands, files, or windows. By moving the pointer to the icon and pressing a mouse button, users can execute a command or convert the icon into a window.
* *Desktop*: The area on the display screen where icons are grouped is often referred to as the desktop because the icons are intended to represent real objects on a real desktop. The ICDL interface is comprising of well-grouped desktop.
* *Windows*: In ICDL interface no such frames are used by dividing the screen into different areas where in each window user can run different programmes. But there is the possibility of opening separate window for certain purpose.
* *Menus*: Most graphical user interfaces let the users to execute commands by selecting a choice from a menu. The ICDL uses different menus and drop-down sub-menus in each menu for various information. The animated presentations of menus create a attracting and elegant effect.

Presentation

Overall presentation of web site is quite satisfactory in ICDL. It includes:

* *Information flow*: Information flow throughout the web site is very much impressive.
* *Navigation*: One can search or browse the required information directly by using different attributes that are relevant for the children. Different types of book reader are there for presenting the pages of the book. Again the options like next page, zoom in, zoom out etc are present for smooth navigation.
* *Visuals and icons*: Meaningful icons and graphics are used that create a pleasant flavour to the eye.

* *About texts*: Texts are legible and nicely looking.
* *Working with colour*: Colours used for the different components are really attractive and eye appealing mainly for the children.
* *Screen design and layout*: The ICDL uses tables for accommodating various elements of the web page.

Consistencey

Consistency must be acquired in many fields like visual appearance, control, and functionality, etc., for increasing the recall of the users. It includes:

* Different functions keys always have the same effects throughout the site.
* Prompt and help messages appear in the same way and the same place throughout
* Different colours used in the web site always have the same meaning
* Consistent use of headings
* Consistent use of terminologies and abbreviations throughout
* The main menus appeared on the top portion of the home page is absent in the other subsequent pages.

Organisation

The organisation of the information and different components of the web pages are very important for the users. The proper organisation may lead easy navigation of the relevant information the user needed.

It includes:

* Relative positions of different information in the page are nicely organised.
* Right linking of relevant information
* Well positioning of functional keys
* Inclusions of all relevant information in the small space mainly in case of advance search.
* Getting of information by minimal mouse clicking
* Systematic organisation of information so that users get the information they need by minimum scrolling of pages

Interactiveness

It includes dynamic nature of pages where web page cans response to the users. It is very much effective a informative web site like digital library. The ICDL has provisions of interactivity. In the searching mode, the Boolean search is very much interactive to the user's search query.

Attractiveness

It includes overall getup of the site.

It may comprising of:

* Use of proper colours in accordance with the children's liking and choice
* Use of different graphics instead of texts.
* Use of colorful cartoon-like icons
* In location search there is the provision of graphical search by using world map which is very attractive to the children

User Friendliness

User friendliness is the ultimate aims of user interface. The design should be synchronise with the user's needs and behaviours. The ICDL web site is very user friendly. The target audience, *i.e.,* children of different geographical and linguistic regions of the world, can easily find their relevant information through easy navigational tools.

There are various provisions of browsing and searching of books. In case of Boolean search, the search phrase formulation is shown in the page explicitly (e.g. Main collection AND Ten to thirteen AND Pink covers AND hobbies and crafts = 1 Books). In every searching and browsing mode there is the provision of language of the book, which is very much user friendly as per the children of diverse linguistic regions are concerned. Again country wise books are also useful for the wide range of children.

USE, USAGE AND USABILITY

The usage and usability of digital library is gaining the focal point of study. Actually the use of any digital object is the ultimate objective of any web site or digital library. Therefore the information must be uniform, consistent and well-organised, so that one can retrieve the relevant information by using navigational tools. The ICDL can be accessed through the commercial search engine like Yahoo, Google, etc.

The following search data are shown:

* Google search engine:
  - Search by the term 'ICDL' fetched 775000 listing in 0.12 seconds.
  - Search by 'international children's digital library' lists 3520000 sites in 0.11 seconds
  - Search by exact phrase "international children's digital library" through advanced search fetched 96800 listing in 0.14 seconds
* Yahoo Search Engine:
  - Search by the term 'ICDL' fetched 775000 listing in 0.12 seconds.
  - Search by 'international children's digital library' lists 3810000 sites in 0.02 seconds
  - Search by exact phrase "international children's digital library" through advanced search fetched 63500 listing in 0.31 seconds
* Use and users' statistics:
  - The ICDL has been visited by over a million unique visitors since, the launch in November, 2002.
  - Google is the number one Web site directing Internet users to the ICDL, followed by Farsibooksonline and Yahoo.
  - The users come from 166 different countries, most frequently from:

    a. United States (50%)

    b. South Africa (15%)

    c. China (7%)

    d. United Kingdom (6%)

    e. Canada (5%)

    f. Iran, Islamic Republic of (4%)

    g. Taiwan (4%)

h. Philippines (4%)
i. Australia (3%)
j. Egypt (2%)

- *Top books visited*: Our book preview pages have been visited over 650,000 times.
- *Book reader*: Our standard book reader is chosen most of the time to read books in the ICDL. The book readers receive the following use:a.Standard reader (52%) b.Adobe reader (23%) c.Comic reader (15%) d.Spiral reader (9%) e.Plus reader (1%)
- *Registered users*: On May 25, 2005, we launched a new interface that allows library users to log in with a user name and password. Currently, registered users can choose their preferred search interface and what language the library appears in. Kids can also choose a monster to guard their password. In the future, users will be able to personalise their search results, save favorite books on a bookshelf, and return to the last page they were reading. Here are some facts about our registered users:
  a. 1082 adults, 508 children -1031 females, 560 males,Preferred languages (of the nine languages the library is currently available in):
     i. English (72%)
     ii. Spanish (11%)
     iii. Chinese (5%)
     iv. Persian (4%)
     v. Arabic (4%)
     vi. Filipino (1%)
     vii. French (1%)
     viii. German (1%)
     ix. Hebrew (1%)
  b. Adults can choose their preferred search interface, and they choose Simple Search 73% of the time, followed by Advanced (24%), and Location (3%).
- Connectivity: The connection speed of our users breaks down to 17% dial-up, 40% high-speed, and 43% unknown.

From the data we can conclude that the library is used by varieties of users in all respect. We can say that the usability of ICDL is good as the aims of the Foundation is concerned. But still there are some scope of attaining the degree of usage and usability of the library.

Different usage and usability criteria used in ICDL and gaps if any are enumerated below.

* Graphics,
* Text,
* Content/Information
* Updates
* Layout/Space
* Presentation of information: It concerns the implications of using colours, fonts and display styles to present information. The colours used in the ICDL pages are very much eye soothing and also attractive. The display styles for pages in the book are very lucrative in the spiral reader.
* Categorisation of Information
* Navigation,
* Colour,
* Visual Appearance,
* Advertisements/Pop-ups/Animation,
* *Downloading Time*: It includes factors in designing that impacts speed of downloading. As all pages of books in the library are of scanned images, it takes some amount of time to be downloaded.

SECURITY/PRIVACY

Security/privacy is the vital issue for any digital library. The ICDL states "Feel secure using the ICDL knowing that we protect the privacy of our members, especially children". The International Children's Digital Library (ICDL) is committed to protecting the safety and privacy of the users, especially children. The ICDL does not require anyone to provide any personal information to use the site and no one is excluded from the site for not providing personal information. The ICDL does allow users to create an optional profile that provides access to extra features such as selecting a preferred reading language. If a user chooses to create a profile, ICDL ask them to provide the following personal but not personally-identifiable information (only a user name and password, etc., are required):

* User name
* Password
* Age
* Gender
* Preferred reading language

users who register may choose to use their e-mail address as their user name. This information will only be used for two purposes. First, it allows the ICDL to send users a new password if they forget their old one. Second, adult users who register with their e-mail address may also opt to be on our mailing list to receive announcements about the ICDL

COST EFFECTIVENESS

As information are only accessed through network, the cost effectiveness is the vital issue when evaluating a digital library. The books can be accessed in ICDL without paying any money; it is absolutely free of cost.

SERVICES: REAL LIFE SITUATION

Services are comprised of searching and browsing of relevant information using the various tools provided in the web site. This is the ultimate objective of any digital library. The search statistics may help to develop better interface.

Between May 25, 2005 and August 31, 2005, ICDL looked at what the library users were searching for. This data helped to improve the search interfaces and understood what library users are looking for in a digital library and accordingly new interface was designed on March 22, 2006. Users overwhelming prefer the Simple search interface. The usage of the various search interfaces breaks down to the following:

* Simple search (71%)
* Advanced search (15%)
* Text or keyword search (10%)
* Location search (3%)
* Author search (1%).

Availability

Most of the books included in the ICDL are always available through the searching and browsing tools. Actually I tried for 100 books and no such false link is there. As the total collection is not verified I prefer to use the term 'most of the books'.

Searchability

Searchability basically includes effectiveness in searching and browsing so as to get required pages of the books. At first it is better to enumerate the provisions of searching and browsing in the ICDL site.

Searching

Simple Search

Various search facilities are there in the simple search. The menus/icons are arranged in four sides of the page. The provisions are: Location search

In location search there are two versions

* Graphical version using globe having world map and provision for turning the globe by clicking the arrow provided for the purpose. This is effective for little children who just learning the locations in the world map.
* Text version by using names of continents and countries.

Advanced Search

Advance search is composed of using various criteria for single search. Actually it is Boolean search using only AND operator.

The criteria are:

* Keywords
* Language
* Audience: Age, collection, etc.
* Appearance: Cover colour, format, length, shape, etc.
* Content: Continents, character, countries, time period

* Type: Feeling, rating, etc.
* Subject: Culture, history, science and nature, animals, etc.

The beauty of advance search is "unified search using more than one criteria used in the simple search at a time". The stating of search formulation statement is another effective feature in the advance search. The statement (e.g. Main collection AND Ten to thirteen AND Pink covers AND Hobbies and crafts= 1 Books) may increase the confidence of the users.

Keyword Search

As the pages of the books are of scanned image in TIFF format and no provision of using OCR technology, full text search is not possible. It only includes the meta-information about the books.

Directions:

* Typing the keywords into the search box
* Selecting the language user is searching in from the pull down menu
* Clicking the Search button to search for books with matching information

Browsing

Browsing of books will be done through four ways mentioned below:

* Recently added books
* Award-winning books
* Full book list
* Author and illustrator list

The browsing through Author and Illustrator list are effective but there are the oddness:

* No such indication element for author and illustrator; names are alphabetically arranged according to the surnames but no rendering of names are there which create confusion to some extent.

Referral

The ICDL provides referral service by mentioning link through which one can get the books. When we select any book, the metadata are listed in the right side to the cover/title image of the book. At the end of metadata, there are the provisions of links stating the addresses of the organisations from which one can purchase the same.

Links

The links in the web site are very much systematic and relevant. Not so false link is there in the page so far as my verification is concerned.. The links in the 'announcement' in the home page is not retrieved. After selecting a book to be retrieved there is the provision of link to the similar books available in the ICDL. No such external links are there for similar books the ICDL has. The links among the different pages are explicitly shown in the Sitemap menu.

POLICY

The policy of any digital library like ICDL, includes the written guidelines for attaining consistency and effectiveness in the web pages. The policy in the present study is comprised of collection development, copyright, privacy and link.

Collection Development Policy

Examination of the criteria used to select books that are appropriate for the ICDL collection. All works will be presented in their entirety and will not be adapted or abridged from their original published form; however, works originally published as abridgements or adaptations of other works may be included in the collection.

Materials included in the collection may be:

* Currently available in print and within copyright;
* Out of print but within the copyright protection of the country in which they were
* Published; or
* Freely available in the public domain.

Copyright Policy

Find out how ICDL protect the interests of rights holders while sharing their books with audiences throughout the world. The International Children's Digital Library respects the intellectual property rights and other proprietary rights of others. The ICDL has negotiated rights to include the books in the collection. These rights do not allow downloading, printing, or further distribution of the books in ICDL by the users. To obtain permission to download, print or distribute the books in ICDL, the user must be contacted to the rights holders directly.

The ICDL software does not support printing, emailing or saving of material accessible through the ICDL If any user believes that his copyright has been violated by material available through the ICDL, there is clear statement on behave of the ICDL Copyright Agent with the following information:

* Identification of the copyrighted work that user claim has been infringed;
* An exact description of where the material about which user complain is located within the ICDL collection;
* Users address, telephone number, and e-mail address;
* A statement by user that he has a good-faith belief that the disputed use is not authorised by the copyright owner, its agent, or the law;
* A statement by user, made under penalty of perjury, that the information in users notice is accurate and that the users are the owner of the copyright interest involved or are authorised to act on behalf of that owner;

Privacy Policy

ICDL is always trying to protect the privacy of the users/ members, especially children. The privacy is maintained particularly for the personal information of the users. More provisions are already analysed in the Security/privacy section.

Links Policy

Links appearing on the ICDL web site must conform to the selection criteria for the books included in the collection. The sites linked should expand, enhance, and support books included in the collection. Sites linked to the ICDL must:1.Have a high degree of appeal for children from ages 3-13; 2.Support the understanding and use of books in the collection; 3.Be appropriate for the age levels of the intended audience for the collection; 4.Include content that is relevant and of interest to children ages 3-13; 5.Support the understanding of similarities and difference among and within countries, peoples, and cultures; 6.Contribute to children's understanding of the diversity of the global society; and, 7..Meet professionally accepted quality standards in terms of content, format, and presentation.

LEGAL ASPECTS

Some books are very old and others are just like those that user might find in school or public library. Most of the old books are out of copyright. This means that nobody owns these books so ICDL Foundation can put them on the ICDL without getting permission from anybody.

For the newer books, the authority must get permission from the people or the company that owns the words and the pictures in the books. All of the books in the ICDL must meet the collection development standards. These standards are the rules that use to choose which books can go into the ICDL. The Advisory Board of Librarians and International Advisory Board created the rules for the purpose. Some of the legal aspects are included in the section 'Copyright policy'.

CONSTRAINS

* No main menus in the same fashion in the pages other than home page.
* No links in few places
* The ICDL software does not support printing, emailing or saving of material accessible through the ICDL
* No born digital objects are included in the ICDL
* External hyperlinks are few
* Some contradictory data exit
* The scanned pages need to remove noise
* No provisions of audio that are interesting to the intended audience
* No provision of machine translation

RECOMMENDATIONS

The ICDL has its strong objectives and planned policy. According to the aims and objectives of ICDL Foundation, the web site of International Children's Digital Library is very impressive in all respect.

Still some recommendations are given for the overall development of the ICDL.

* Some good animations may be inserted to the menus/ icons to add the extra flavour
* Besides books, some non-book material like audio, video, animation, etc., may be included to instigate appetite of the children
* The scope will be given for inclusion of born digital books
* Digital noise in the scanned images have to be removed for better viewing the pages
* Some external links for similar information may be sited to the web page

CONCLUSION

In conclusions, as per the aims and objectives are taking into consideration, the ICDL is unparallel. They strictly follow the pre-defined policy. The ICDL always promote cross-cultural development among children, and therefore it intentionally not use the machine translation.

But it mentions some volunteer translator for the same. Within a short period of time ICDL has flourished rapidly in wellorganised way. It maintains the list having date wise addition of books in the collection. The ICDL is very transparent in its each policy and function.

11

New Option for Libraries in the Digital Era

INTRODUCTION

In the electronic information environment one of the responses to the problem of bringing large amounts of information together has been for libraries to introduce portals. A portal is a gateway, or a point where users can start their search for information on the web. There are a number of different types of portals, for example universities have been introducing "institutional portals", which can be described as "a layer which aggregates, integrates, personalises and presents information, transactions and applications to the user according to their role and preferences".

A second type of portal is a "subject portals". A third type of portal is a "federated search tool" which brings together the resources to a library subscribes and allows cross-searching of these resources. They work using the Z39.50 protocol used by database suppliers to enable communication between computers. This protocol is not always effective because database suppliers have not always adopted it consistently so other protocols are also used such as HTML, XML and SQL. Since, these tools access resources that the library pays for, some type of authentication is required to ensure. Well before the launch of the World Wide Web, librarians recognised the need for establishing a common interface to search multiple sources. The ANSI/NISO gives the international search-andretrieval protocol, Z39.50, which was originally proposed in 1984 as a standard means of interrogating bibliographic databases. Since, then it has gone through three versions, the latest of which was issued in 1995. Federated search compliments the Z39.50 facility, it offers the ability to extend search beyond the online catalog virtually to any electronic resources that can be authenticated at the point of access. This means that users no longer need to jump from one search interface to another.

Information integration over distributed sources is an urgent problem to be solved for providing access to a variety of Digital Libraries through a common search interface and portal. Federated or cross-database search tools now available on the market are the correct solution for unifying access to a variety of information resources.

These tools can search not only library catalogs but also commercial abstracting and indexing databases, web search engines, and a variety of other databases, while often merging and de-duplicating results. Federated searching started in 1998 when Webfeat Team took the initiative to connect any or all of their databases at the same time through a simple, common user interface and turned this idea into a product called Webfeat.

WebFeat, the original federated search engine, used by over 15,000 leading public, academic, government and Global 1000 libraries and information centers — including over a third of the largest 100 U.S., public libraries, 18 statewide library systems, and 2 out of every 10 Association of Research Libraries (ARL) institutions, brings you the next frontier in federated search technology.

Originally founded in 1992 as an information technology consultancy. The WebFeat concept is simple: search any or all of your library's databases simultaneously with a single intuitive interface. WebFeat can search any database, including licensed databases, free databases, catalogs, Z39.50, Telnet, proprietary databases, anything! And with SMART, WebFeat's next generation usage tracker, you can report detailed database usage within your library with just a few mouse clicks.

FEDERATED SEARCH

Federated search is the simultaneous search of multiple online databases and is an emerging feature of automated, Web-based library and information retrieval systems. It is also often referred to as a portal, as opposed to simply a Web-based search engine. It is sometime termed as broadcast search, parallel search, cross reference search, etc. Various terms are used to refer to these tools in the literature including: metasearchers, crosssearchers, cross-database searchers, portals, broadcast searchers or parallel searchers.

The term metasearcher is particularly prominent and is the term adopted by the United States National Information Standards Organisation (NISO), which has developed a Metasearch Initiative. However as Fryer explains, the term metasearcher can cause confusion due to its association with web Metasearch engines such as Metacrawler which function in a different way to federated search tools. The term federated searching is the function of search tools, which search a number of databases, particularly subscription databases, simultaneously with one interface. The content searched by federated search tools is content that could not normally be searched via a web search engine.

DEFINITIONS

Researcher defines federated search as, "Transforming a query and broadcasting it to a group of disparate databases with the appropriate syntax, merging the results collected from the databases, presenting them in a succinct and unified format with minimal duplication, and allowing the library patron to sort the merged result set by various criteria". In simple words, Federated searching will be defined as a search system using a common interface that enables the simultaneous searching of databases from a variety of vendors. Federated search technology enables users to search multiple information resources simultaneously through one search query. Users can then view search results in a single integrated list. In other words, users do no longer need to consult each information resource individually.

Instead, they can search multiple library catalogs (OPACs), Web sites (e.g. Amazon.com, Google, etc.), subscription and citation databases all at once. Federated search technology is an integral component of an Information Portal, which provides the interface to diverse information resources. Once the user enters his or her search query in the search box of the Information Portal, the system uses federated search technology to send the search string to each resource that is incorporated into the Portal.

The individual information resources then send the Information Portal a list of results from the search query. Users can view the number of documents retrieved in each resource and link directly to each search result. Metasearch, this word is synonymous to federated searching, people find no difference between federated searching but there is slight difference between federated and meta searching.

DIFFERENCE BETWEEN FEDERATED SEARCH ENGINE AND META SEARCH ENGINE

Federated search engine and Meta search engine seems to be synonymous but we found slight difference between them. Some of them are as follows:

Table 11.1. Federated Search Meta search.

Federated Search	Meta Search
* Federated search engine have cost. More, depending upon the seats, design, functionality and targets or databases and subjectc ategories and thesauri	* Meta searc h engines are a vailable "free" of cost on internet.
* Federated searches concentrate mostly on textual inforrmation and offer subscription-based premium content database searching ignored by Web oriented meta search engines that miss these invisible Web Sources.	* Meta search engine commonly found on internet. The Public at large uses meta Search engines because they run Searches via multiple web search engines that spider the open Web, including multimedia sources.
* Federated searching refers to the ability to issue a single query that concurrently searches multiple disparate and heterogeneous collections of information. This is especially important to library patrons and staff that are interested in locating resources that exist within, or are licensed by libraries or library consortia.	* This technical part is lacking in meta searching.

Table Contd...

Federated Search	Meta S arch
* Typically, these collections include the library catalog(s), commercial databases *(Ebsco, Gale, ProQuest, etc.)*, digital collections, specialised collections, and even third party systems and content (Library of Congress, Web search engines, etc.). Single-search access to multiple resources enables libraries to offer value added services that Web savvy patrons have come to expect. These include a single login, personalisation features, and the ability to remotely interact with your library Value added services not only enhance end user experience, but help ensure that the library continues to be the epicenter for information discovery in the ever-increasing digital world.	* Web meta-search tools such as and MetCrawler run across multiple web search engines at once, returning sets of results grouped individually in each search source. Names such as VIVISMO and IXQUICK also spring to mind in this context. In this context. meta-search vendors are Muse Global's Muse Search, Web Feat's Prism that is used by Dynix, and Sirsi uses Muse Search, just to name a few common vendors

NEED AND PURPOSE OF FEDERATED SEARCH TOOLS

The need and purpose of the federated searching are as follows:

* The growth of different types of databases, produced by different suppliers, with numerous interfaces and logins means that library users can find it confusing when attempting to access information;
* Library OPACs and web-pages have been alienating users with their use of library terminology and by including long lists of databases that users find it difficult to select from and search;
* The needs and expectations of library users, particularly students using academic libraries. The growth of different types of databases, produced by different suppliers, with numerous interfaces and logins means that library users can find it confusing when attempting to access information.

There are certain purposes which can be served by the federated search are as follows:-

* Transforming a query and broadcasting it to a group of disparate databases with the appropriate syntax.
* Merging the results collected from the databases,
* Presenting them in a succinct and unified format with minimal duplication,
* Providing a means, performed either automatically or by the portal user, to sort the merged result set.

In traditional search engines such as Google, only sources that have been indexed by the search engine's crawler technology can be searched, retrieved and accessed. The large volume of documents housed in databases is not open to traditional Internet search engines because of limitations in crawler technology.

Federated searching resolves this issue by the technique described above and makes these deep Web documents searchable without having to visit each database individually.

ADVANTAGES OF FEDERATED SEARCH

There are certain advantages of using Federated Searches. Some of them are as follows:

* The reduced time it takes to do a basic search is benefit enough.
* Unified access to diverse content sources.
* Simultaneous searching across all sources.
* Ability to Simple search as well as advanced search.
* Integrated results which are easy to view and use.
* Direct links to the native source for further searching.
* Ability to filter, sort, save, print, export and e-mail search results

SEARCH MODELS

Search on data bases starts with simple search formulation using single keyterm and combinations of terms. The search results thus obtained can be listed in simple predefined format or using user customised format to get desired information. Various search models indicate the interactions of users search formulations and its interface with databases in a Library or online web access to aggregated databases.

OLD SEARCH MODEL

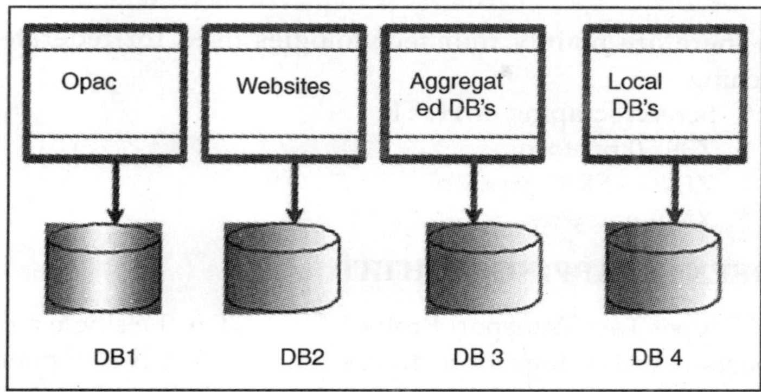

Fig. 11.1. Old Srearch Model.

Without a federated search tool, each database requires its own unique search tool - significantly complicating and slowing the search process for patrons. In this kind of search model user submit their search query to individual database or search engines etc and individually they get their required information. This kind of search tools are very time consuming and most of the time user didn't get their desired information.

FEDERATED SEARCH MODEL

Using federated search, a single tool searches and accesses all databases with one, easy to use interface.

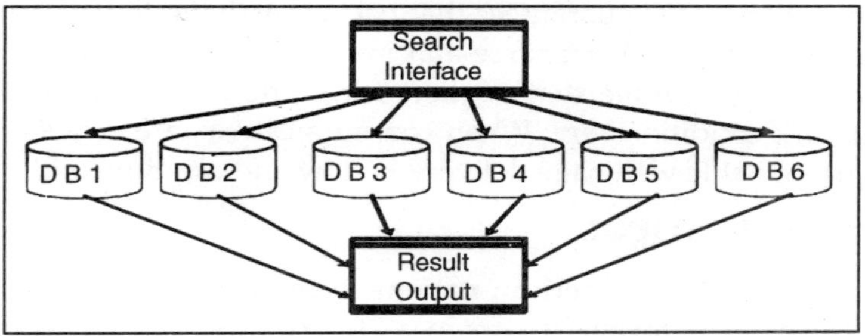

Fig. 11.2. Federated Search Model.

It provides opportunity to the users that they get their desired information from various databases, search engines, etc.

FEDERATED SEARCH TECHNOLOGIES

There are mainly four technologies used for federated searching.

* Screen scraping or HTTP
* Z39.50 protocol
* ZING - SRW protocol
* XML gateway

SCREEN SCRAPPING OR HTTP

"Hyper Text Transport Protocol" - HTTP is the single most important technology that drives the web and yet remains virtually transparent. Without this protocol HTML and XML via the web would not be able to perform the myriad of tasks that we put them to daily.

The Hypertext Transfer Protocol (HTTP) is an application-level protocol for distributed, collaborative, hypermedia information systems. HTTP has been in use by the World-Wide Web global information initiative since, 1990. The HTTP protocol is a request/response protocol.

A client sends a request to the server in the form of a request method, URI, and protocol version, followed by a MIME-like message containing request modifiers, client information, and possible body content over a connection with a server.

HTTP communication usually takes place over TCP/IP connections. TCP guarantees that packets arriving to and from the web server are error free and in the right order. It doesn't however guarantee that packets arrive no matter what the network conditions are. When communications are congested or unavailable web page delivery is slow and can time-out.

Z39.50 PROTOCOL

Z39.50 is an American national standard for information retrieval. It is formally known as ANSI/NISO Z39.50-1995 - Information Retrieval (Z39.50): Application Service Definition and Protocol Specification.

This document specifies a set of rules and procedures for the behaviour of two systems communicating for the purposes of database searching and information retrieval. As a network application standard, Z39.50 is an open standard that enables communication between systems that run on different hardware and use different software The Z39.50 standard was developed to overcome the problems associated with multiple databases searching such as having to know the unique menus, command language, and search procedures of each system accessed.

Z39.50 simplifies the search process by making it possible for a searcher to use the familiar user interface of the local system to search both the local library catalogue as well as any remote database system that support the standard. In libraries, the Z39.50 protocol is most often used for searching OPAC sources.

The important facilities offered by Z39.50 are as follows:

* *Browse*: Allows the client to scan the contents of wordlists or indexes on the server. This can be particularly useful in the case of controlled keyword lists or facets.
* *Access and resource control*: Allows authentication of users, and cost control and online charging for commercial services.
* *Sort*: Allows the client to request different orderings of query results, eg. relevance ranking, sorting by date or version number, etc.
* *Explain*: Allows the client to interrogate the server about a number of details about its contents and its level of support for the application profile.
* *Item Order*: Allows offline ordering of materials in cases where they cannot be delivered electronically, or where per-unit charging (eg. online charging) is required. Such services are being supplied in an ad-hoc fashion by online Web-based component repositories such as ASSET. The item order service provides a ready-made and semantically standardised version of this service.
* *Item Update*: Permits an authorised client to update the contents of the remote database.

SRW (SEARCH/RETRIEVE WEB SERVICE)

Search/Retrieve Web Service is a new HTTP-based information retrieval protocol providing broadly the same facilities as Z39.50, but by means of very different technology. SRW is designed to be a low barrier to entry solution to performing searches and other information retrieval operations across the internet. It uses existing, well tested and easily available technologies such as SOAP and XPath in order to perform what has been done in the past using proprietary solutions. The protocol has two ways that it can be carried, either via SOAP or as parameters in aURL.

This second form is called SRU – Search Retrieve by URL. Other transports would also be possible, for example simple XML over HTTP, but these are not defined by the current standard. The primary function of SRW is to allow a user to search a remote database of records. This is done via the search Retrieve operation, in which the client sends a search Retreive Request and the server responds with a search Retrieve Response. The request has several parameters, most of which are optional. The response is primarily a list of XML records which matched the search, along with the full count of how many records were matched.

XML (EXTENSIBLE MARKUP LANGUAGE)

XML stands for EXtensible Markup Language. XML is a markup language much like HTML and was designed to carry data, not to display data. XML tags are not predefined. You must define your own tags. XML is designed to be self-descriptive and it is is recommended by the World Wide Web Consortium. It is a fee-free open standard. XML is not a replacement for HTML. HTML is about displaying information, while XML is about carrying information. In simple words, XML is a software and hardware independent tool for carrying information. It is used both to encode documents and serialise data.

It supports Unicode, allowing almost any information in any written human language to be communicated. XML is now as important for the Web as HTML was to the foundation of the Web.

XML is everywhere. It is the most common tool for data transmissions between all sorts of applications, and becomes more and more popular in the area of storing and describing information. XML simplifies data sharing as in the real world; computer systems and databases contain data in incompatible formats. XML data is stored in plain text format. This provides a software- and hardware-independent way of storing data. This makes it much easier to create data that different applications can share.

SELECTION OF FEDERATED SEARCH ENGINE

In selecting a Federated search engine, one needs to bear in mind the following:

* The maximum number of resources the software can include
* The ease of setting up resource targets
* Availability of simple search options
* Speed of search results
* Limiting and refining searches
* Ranking results by relevance
* Export options, *i.e.,* print, e-mail, download
* Adequate statistics and reporting features

STANDARDS AND DEVELOPMENT

NISO – (US) National Information Standards Organisation launched and continue to develop initiatives in order to develop and adopt standard search and retrieval protocols for federated searching. XML – Web protocol and SOAP (Single Object Access Protocol)

ACCESS ISSUES WITH FEDERATED SEARCH

Verification, authentication and certification can be difficult for the federated search vendor. Since, federated search engines don't hold the data locally, *i.e.,* the engines perform the search, and send the results back to the portal.

The federated search engine must be able to access multiple passwordprotected databases behind the scenes, or IP validate all at the one time, and show users their results in one easy navigable interface.The challenge for federated search vendors is to provide only licensed users access to databases, as specified for each license agreement that is in place for the organisation.

AUTHENTICATION

Authentication sets federated search engines apart form other expensive and highly sophisticated search software such as Verity and Autonomy. The latter usually restricts searches to internally generated information, ignoring subscription databases that enterprises have bought in-house. All the user needs with federated searching is ID, password or IP validation along with files to be searched, and the federated search engine do the rest..

THE SET–UP PROCESS

The set up process is lengthy and time consuming for both the Library and the vendor. This is not the end of the process either! It continually evolves as databases change, or new resources are acquired and links are added to the federated search portal.

INTERFACE ISSUES

We need to decide how much time is to be devoted to design, who is the audience and should this audience be able to perform multiple searches, without having to do more than input their ID and password or IP authenticate, and type in the search query.

REMOVING DUPLICATES (DE-DUPING)

Most federated search engines will de-dupe some only when requested. However this opens up a Pandora's Box about how the results are returned. User habits indicate that the end user views only the first ten hits or results. How do the vendor and the interface designer ensure that the highest hits are returned? This area is continually evolving, and it is up to the federated search engine provider, to provide what they can, to the best of their technological ability in this regard.

HOW FEDERATED SEARCH WORKS

Federated search computer programmes allow users to search multiple data sources with a single query from a single user interface. The user enters a search query in the portal interface's search box and the query is sent to every individual database in the portal or federated search list. Access details for the individual databases must be preset in the portal by its owner.

Federated search systems either rely upon vendors to create commercial portal systems, or they rely upon government or other organisations to provide open access portals. How federated search is implemented depends upon which of the two types of organisations is providing the portal. Federated search portals, either commercial or open access, generally search public access bibliographic databases; public access Web-based library catalogues (OPACs), Web-based search engines like Google and/ or open-access, government-operated or corporate data collections.

These individual data sources send back to the portal's interface a list of results from the search query. The user can review this hit list. Some portals will merely screen scrape the actual database results and not directly allow a user to enter the data source's application. More sophisticated ones will de-dupe the results list by merging and removing duplicates. There are additional features available in many portals, but the basic idea is the same: to improve the accuracy and relevance of individual searches as well as reduce the amount of time required to search for resources.

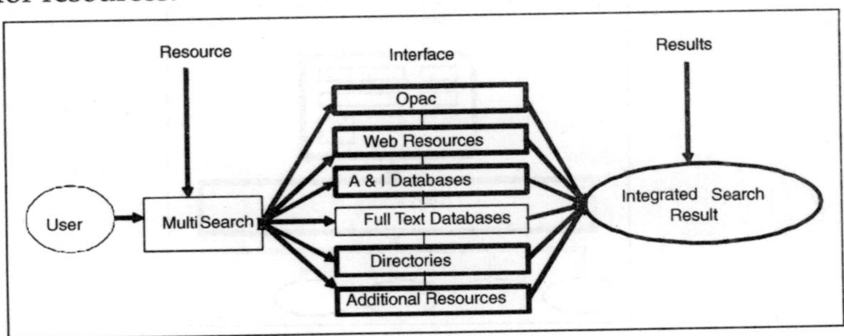

Fig. 11.3. Diagrammatic Representation of Federated Searching.

In federated searching, a wealth of information is incorporated into a single repository that can be searched. In this model, the information is processed prior to the user's search. From the enduser's point of view, federated searching and metasearching may seem similar, because both provide a single interface to multiple resources, but they actually differ in many respects.

The pre-processing taking place in a federated searching environment, which we can describe as just-in-case processing, offers new opportunities regarding search methodologies and the presentation of results. For example, a ranking algorithm can be applied to each data element stored in the repository, unrelated to any future user query. Such an algorithm can take into account the number of times that an article has been cited, the number of articles that the author has published, the number of times that a book has been borrowed, a journal's impact factor, and other parameters. A federated searching system can use the calculated rank to better evaluate the relevance of the specific item once it has been retrieved as the result of a query.The system searches a local repository that was created earlier through the accumulation of data from numerous resources. Looking back a few years, we can see that the need for a single search interface to multiple resources arose some time ago, and, in fact, metasearching and federated searching have been available for quite some time.Such systems originated in a variety of environments; for example, Elsevier, a publisher offering numerous journals, created a federated search mechanism enabling its users to search all its e-journals through its ScienceDirect service.

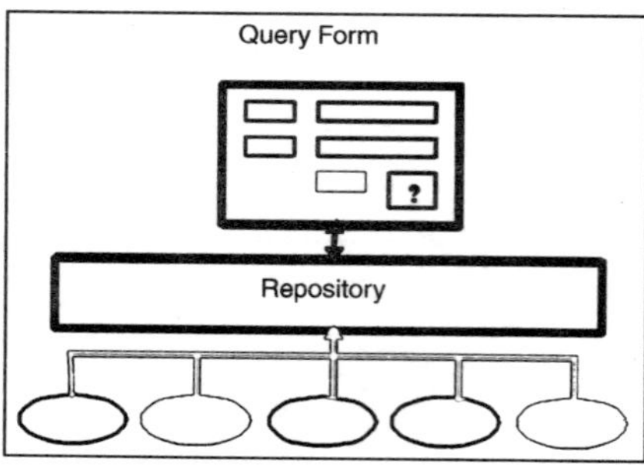

Fig. 11.4. Diverse in Form Mation Resources.

As Elsevier acquired other publishers, it was able to add their journals to the same platform. Database vendors developed similar mechanisms. For example, Ovid provides a single interface to a few hundred databases that it publishes, and still retains them as separate databases.

Commercial organisations were not the only ones that addressed the need for a single search interface; several large research institutions created a local environment based on federation.

For example, the Los Alamos National Laboratory and the Ohio Link consortium in the United States, the University of Toronto in Canada, the Technical Knowledge Center of Denmark (DTV), and the Max Planck Society in Germany all offer large, diverse collections of e-journals that they store locally. These institutions have implemented federated searching to provide a single search interface across their electronic collections. However, not all organisations have the resources to adopt this just-in-case approach.

Furthermore, with the rapid increase in the number of heterogeneous resources that institutions offer their users, a single federated searching system can serve only as a partial solution.

IMPLEMENTATION

When a federated search engine is implemented at a particular library, it then becomes a unique service. Federated-searching software allows customisation, so no two implementations are exactly the same. For example, a library may choose to include all of its online resources as targets for a federated search engine or it may choose to create subject groupings first, each of which leads to a federated search service for a narrow topic.

Gerrity, Lyman, and Tallent discuss implementing a federated search system at Boston College, where they promoted the new service as "MetaQuest".

One application of federated searching is the metasearch engine; however, this is not a complete solution as many documents are not currently indexed.

This is known as the deep Web or invisible Web. Many more information sources are not yet stored in electronic form.

'Google Scholar' is an example of a project trying to address this.When the search vocabulary or data model of the search system is different from the data model of one or more of the foreign target systems the query must be translated into the each of the foreign target systems.

This can be done using simple dataelement translation or may require semantic translation.

FEDERATED SEARCH PROVIDERS

Individual institutions have their in-house Federated option and other institutions uses global federated search options, following are the popular federated search providers:

* Google Scholar
* Scopus
* Liberty

GOOGLE SCHOLAR

Google Scholar is seen as the competition for both campus institutional repository systems (at least in terms of search and discovery) and academic library federated searching. Google Scholar provides a simple way to broadly search for scholarly literature.

From one place, you can search across many disciplines and sources: peer-reviewed papers, theses, books, abstracts and articles, from academic publishers, professional societies, preprint repositories, universities and other scholarly organisations.

Google Scholar helps you identify the most relevant research across the world of scholarly research.

FEATURES OF GOOGLE SCHOLAR

* Search diverse sources from one convenient place
* Find papers, abstracts and citations
* Locate the complete paper through your library or on the web
* Learn about key papers in any area of research

Google Scholar gives various option to the user so that they can search according to their equirements, such as time period, author wise search, subject wise, publication, institution wise etc and after giving the key term by the user, it searches that key term to various databases, search engines, journals etc and display the result on interface with name of author along with its full bibliographical description and it also provide citation information.

SCOPUS

Scopus is the largest abstract and citation database of research literature and quality web sources. It's designed to find the information scientists need. Quick, easy and comprehensive, Scopus provides superior support of the literature research process.Scopus is updated daily and it offers 15,000 peer-reviewed journals from more than 4,000 international publishers, over 1000 Open access journals, 500 Conference proceedings, over 600 trade publications and over 125 Book series. It also covers 33 million records, out of which, 16 million records include references going back to 1996 and 17 million pre-1996 records go back as far as 1869.

LIBERTY: QUEST

Liberty is a total web based library automation software which allows federated searching. In Liberty federated searching refers as "Quest" it capitalises our investment in online databases by providing library users with a single search point from with in Liberty.

Benefits of Quest:

* *Single Search Point for Multiple Databases*: Include databases that your organisation subscribes to in your Liberty3 search. Quest simplifies searching and access for your users.
* *Easy to Use*: Quest offers basic or advanced searching options, interleaves search results, and represents search results graphically. Quest allows a number of refine and sort options including sort by relevancy.

* *De-duplicate Searches*: Easily remove duplicates from search results by title or URL.
* *Customisable*: Quest offers you the option to include the library catalogue in the federated search. You can also select the databases you wish to search in your federated search.
* *Local Soft link Support and Service*: Quest is supported locally and hosted on Soft link servers. There is no need for you to worry about installation or maintenance.
* *The biggest players* in the federated searching industry are MuseGlobal (Muse Search), Fretwell- Downing (Zportal), and Webfeat (Knowledge Prism). These product offerings allow a user, regardless of vendor, to access multiple databases through one search interface. Endeavor (ENCompass) and ExLibris (MetaLib) are also in the federated search engine.
* Scirus, Wikipiedia, Pub med central, these are public domain site which provide federated searching.
* Publishers offering numerous journals created a federated search mechanism so that users are able to search their all journals. A good example is Elsivers Science Direct. As Elsivers acquired other publishers, it was able to add their journals at the same platform.
* Database vendor develop the same mechanism such as Sliver Platter provide a single interface for more than 300 databases that they published SCOPUS, etc.
* Proquest, Ebsco, Gale Cengage and Elsevier etc are such databases who offer federated search. In Gale Cengage "federated search" refers as "Power Search".
* The NISO Metasearch Initiative seeks to develop industry standards for one-search access to multiple resources that will allow libraries to offer portal environments for library users offering the same easy searching found in Webbased services like Google.
* Many public and academic libraries also utilise Auto-Graphics' federated search solution AGent Search.

DRAWBACKS OF FEDERATED SEARCH

Limitations of the current generation of federated search engines.

These include:

* The lack of a uniform authentication standard means that some databases are inaccessible to federated search engines.
* True, full, deduplication is impossible because databases download results in small sets and metadata standards vary by resource.
* Relevancy ranking is limited by the quality of the metadata, which usually does not include abstracts or full-text information.
* Although federated search systems are fundamentally software, they must be implemented and managed as a service, which takes a great deal of resources.
* Federated search engines cannot improve on the native interface in terms of search accuracy and precision.
* Federated searching is not for power searching needs. Just as with searching metasearch engines, only basic Boolean commands can be used.

The federated search has some other issues as well. First, it cannot cover all online library resources. The goal of one-stop shopping cannot be achieved completely by any federated search.

There are various reasons for this:

* Some databases do not work with any federated search at all, such as SciFinder Scholar. SciFinder Scholar does not use a web browser but rather requires its own internet client. Neither MetaLib nor WebFeat can cover SciFinder Scholar.
* If databases require a login, they will not work with the federated search.
* Some databases work with one federated search product but do not work with the other. MetaLib cannot search LexisNexis databases because LexisNexis does not allow Z39.50 or XML gateway access. WebFeat cannot search databases that do not have a search box on their front

page because WebFeat counts on the search box on the native interface to search.

* Many libraries have databases on a pay-per-search basis, and libraries normally do not want them to be searched by a federated search for budgetary reasons.
* Some databases have a limited number of concurrent users, and if these databases are included in a federated search, the limited seat(s) is/are taken immediately whenever someone logs into the federated search, and no other users can use these databases. Libraries normally do not want to include databases with a very limited number of concurrent users in the federated search.

It may not make sense to add to a federated search menu the very specialised databases that most general users would not be interested in, or the databases that require special software. One example is Inter-university Consortium for Political and Social Research (ICPSR) that requires statistics software such as SPSS to view data.

CONCLUSION

By allowing users to search multiple databases simultaneously, federated search engines may save some steps in getting results from various library resources, and may also attain search results from databases users otherwise would not try without the federated search.

Even librarians at reference desks sometimes notice a good number of search results from databases they might not expect would have many good hits. But in no way can the federated search compete with Google in Google's strengths: speed, simplicity, ease of use, and convenience. Nor can the federated search truly serve as one-stop shopping for all library databases as people hoped, because some databases cannot be searched by the federated search for various reasons. The federated search probably cannot replace information literacy education or the learning process either, partly because it cannot make searching as easy as a Google search, as serious research may require selecting various information sources beyond Google results. In a certain sense, the federated search shifts the process of selecting a database from "before" performing searches to "after" performing searches.

Users still need to learn the functions of the library OPAC and periodicals indexes with names like ABI, CINAHL, ERIC, MLA, and CHICAGO, etc. It is also very helpful for users to learn other information literacy basics, such as the ability to interpret bibliography or to tell the difference between books, book chapters, and periodical articles, in order to make better use of the federated search engine offered by their libraries.

12

Selection Criteria for Library Automation Software

INTRODUCTION

Software is a computer programme for using computers and other such hardware to their optimum capabilities. As computers do only what they are told to do and therefore, the instructions given to computer should be unambiguous. Writing step by step instructions without any ambiguity to solve a particular problem is called programming. A software package can have one or more computer programmes to solve a specific problem. A programming language provides a special type of grammar and syntax to the programmer to enable him to give instructions in a simple and understandable way. Writing programmes and developing software packages involves special training, hardwork, time and money. For developing in-house software to solve complex problems, these requirements become severe and unmanageable.

Due to these limitations, the practicing librarians or information scientists should be exposed to some commercially available software packages. Software packages are generally available as commercial products which typically provide solutions to particular application problems. Since, they are developed on a commercial scale in a competitive market for use by a variety of customers, a great amount of skill and effort is put in their development. Therefore, they are reliable, easy to use and in many instances, well-documented. Ready-made software packages are now available for a wide range of applications such as management information systems (MIS), industrial support systems, office automation systems, library automation and information retrieval operations.

CATEGORIES OF SOFTWARE

Computerisation of Library and information services, involves non-numeric data processing, text retrieval, manipulation of strings of characters and information retrieval, etc. Some general purpose software packages can be used for these purposes and for specific needs, special purpose software are also available in the market.

The various categories of such software and their features are:

* Basic software for data entry, validation, sorting and merging of files, and editing of data
* Word processing software to manipulate text-storage, recall, use and modify; alignment of margins, addition and deletion of string of characters, manipulate paragraphs, etc.
* Database management systems (DBMS) for creation and management of databases, file management systems, relational database management systems (RDBMS), network and hierarchical DBMS
* Text-Retrieval Packages for storage and retrieval 'of non-numeric records (tabular or even graphics). These are self-contained software, require minimum involvement of computer specialists, records are independent of variable length for natural language text, have access to data by context, inverted file access, user interfaces which makes them simple and easy to use. Search and indexing facilities are other important features
* Software Associated with Searching Online Retrieval System and CD-ROM Databases. Major online systems have their own software usually written in command language, provide access to external databases, private

or personal file facility, and permit editing of search files on micros

* *Library House Keeping Software*: These have provision for acquisition, cataloguing, circulation control, serials control and statistical report generation.

Library automation software or computer based information storage and retrieval systems cover two major functional areas, namely:

* Control and management of library resources, and
* Access to documents and information.

These two areas deal with library house-keeping systems and text retrieval systems respectively. Gradually, the distinction between them is vanishing. In latest software packages there is provision for both library house-keeping operations as well as public access for information retrieval. In addition, there are software packages for re-organising and presenting information in desired format, producing publications, arid to control and manipulate statistical and financial data.

Library automation software packages can also be grouped in four categories:

* Word processing,
* Library house-keeping operations,
* Management communications and support, and
* Text retrieval.

The type of software can be categorised based on the hardware or computer systems used. For example,

* Microcomputer-based software
* Mini computer-based software
* Large mainframe-based software

Each of these categories of software may be either In-house software that is owned and operated by the library, or shared with other libraries through a consortium arrangement-through a bibliographic information network.

OPTIONS FOR SELECTION

In recent times, libraries are not encouraged to develop the software for its use. In other words, libraries are advised not to waste efforts, time and money in developing in-house programmes for library house-keeping operations and public access information storage and retrieval. Software development is a costly, time consuming and risky job whose results may be uncertain. However, the options available for selection of library automation software are summarised below:

* Acquire a prewritten, off-the-shelf software package (e.g. LIBSYS),
* Acquire a turnkey package incorporating both hardware and software (e.g. MINISIS, TULIS),
* Write in-house programmes,
* Commission writing of programmes, and
* Participate in the formation of, or join a cooperative that offers access to software and/or hardware and/or databases.

Rowley discusses the advantages and disadvantages of commercially available software packages. She concludes, "It is sensible to choose a commercially available package, -since, it is too costly to write a local software package or to commission someone to do this, even though a tailor-made package designed specifically for a given application is most likely to fit all the requirements of that application."

GUIDES TO COMMERCIALLY AVAILABLE SOFTWARE

There are a large number of commercially available library automation software packages. Studies that enumerate, compare and highlight the salient features of these software packages are also in abundance. An effort is made here to review some such selected studies to enable one to fathom the length, breadth and depth of the problem of selecting a suitable software for one's use. Clossbrenner in his book How to buy software: The master guide to picking the right programme describes much general and specific application software but does not mention the library housekeeping or information storage and retrieval software packages. A number of software packages are mentioned which could be used for general applications and other areas related to library automation. These include packages for word processing, database management, statistical manipulation, online searching of databases, etc. The book is a comprehensive, user friendly master guide for selecting suitable software for specific purposes. Hansen in Microcomputer user's guide to information online lists more than 100 sources of information, and their access software. Rowley lists some text retrieval software for microcomputer and for mainframe/ microcomputer systems. Further, She adds a list of library house-keeping software, their features and suppliers. Mahajan surveys some 40 software packages.

SOFTWARE WITH CD-ROM DATABASES

The CD-ROM databases are usually provided with information retrieval and public access software. Valas gives a comparison of some well known CD-ROM information retrieval software packages. There are not many publications dealing with the comparison of different CD-ROM information retrieval software packages. Richards and Robinson suggest a model for evaluating CD-ROM software whereas, Harry and Oppenheim discuss the various criteiia for evaluating electronic databases. jacso describes the evaluation, selection and installation of CD-ROM software, data ware and hardware. Jasco searches for skeletons in the database cupboard to find errors of omission and commission.

McFaul comes out with a final report on consistent interface guidelines. Tian-Zhu limits his' formal analysis to searching capabilities and ease of use of CD-ROM user interfaces. Sieverts and others give additional programmes for testing, evaluating and comparing software for information storage and retrieval. Most of these studies are confined to user interfaces as the principle of comparison of software packages. They usually give rules on how to rank the CD-ROM publications, how to give marks for the CD-ROM databases in addition to the software. In many cases the performance factors that are most important for professional searchers are usually missing from these collection of rules. Valas emphasises the performance factors that are considered to be the most important viewpoints for a professional searcher. "A retrieval system may be as user friendly as you wish; but you will not like it if one single e search step in an intricate query may take two hours and displaying the hits may take another two; or if complicated search strategies are not possible at all."

INDIAN SCENARIO

Chowdhury and Chowdhury discuss the automated text retrieval and library management software in India. A number of software packages have been released recently by government and private agencies. The authors provides a list of 20 and a brief overview of 10 selected Indian packages released upto 1994, namely, CATMAN, CDS/ISIS, LIBRARIAN, LIBSYS, MAITRAYEE, MECSYS, NIRMALS, SANJAY, TULIPS and WILISYS. Considering the cost aspect, it is concluded that CDS/ISIS along with SANJAY (with a few modifications) might prove to be the most suitable package for most Indian libraries. The authors compare the common features such as cataloguing, OPAC, online help, acquisition, circulation and serials control of the selected packages. However, the criteria to evaluate such packages are not discussed.

Major problem areas of library automation in India are as follows:

* Funds, manpower and retrospective conversion
* Facilities for entering data in desired format
* Downloading facilities for data
* Facilities for data exchange
* Problems in creating files in packages based on DBMS due to long fields for longer data fields (*e.g.*, in Oracle), and use of repeatable fields which are common in bibliographic and text database (e.g. SANJAY, LIBSYS, CDS/ISIS)

WHY IS SELECTION DIFFICULT

Selection of suitable software for library automation is always what Grosch calls, a case of "fud" where 'f' stands for fear, 'u' for uncertainty and 'd' for doubt. This is because of the technical parameters associated with the selection of the software, such as the shape of network, computing platform, type of operating systems and various standards. Since, today's software investments are likely to be for longer term than those made some three decades ago, the overall system architecture may now play a stronger role in such selection.

The problems are:

* *A large number of software packages*: A conservative estimate shows more than 80,000 separate software packages for a variety of purposes-not all are for library house-keeping operations but a large number may include information storage and retrieval. The number of such packages is multiplying like 'coat hangers in a darkened closet'.
* *Over choice*: A large number of software packages give not only choice but over choice to select one that is suitable for the purpose.
* *Tall claims*: Advertisements for each software package tries to claim that it is one up and better than others. There is plenty of material to confuse the selector-journal articles, product brochures, direct mail solicitations and catalogues. The software producers generously distribute lot of advertising material.
* *Documentation*: Often the product manual supplied with the software does not provide adequate information for the installation and for using the software by the user on his own.
* *Cost*: At times, the software is costlier than the hardware on which it is to be used. Further, the software package is normally purchased as a one time investment.

Other common problems that make the selection of software difficult, relate to:

* Understanding the exact purpose for which it is to be acquired
* Knowing the physical and social environment in which it is to be used
* Understanding the educational and professional level, and aptitude of the persons who are going to use the software
* Knowing the compatibility, simplicity and ease of use of the software.

CRITERIA TO SELECT LIBRARY AUTOMATION SOFTWARE

To evaluate a particular software package, a simple procedure is to read the literature supplied by the manufacturer, look at the reviews and advertisements published in various computer magazines and to ask the salesperson for a demonstration of the programme. What is often found to be missing in this procedure is the basic conceptual understanding of what a computer does on a physical level and how the software works. It is not necessary to know the details of computer components, such as accumulators, registers, clock signals, instruction set of 380 microprocessors or computer programming, etc. But, when deciding on the best suitable software, more computer knowledge is required than just how to insert a disc into the slot and press a key.

However, the following general guidelines may be useful in selecting a programme.

* Locate and evaluate a knowledgeable dealer or sales person
* Thoroughly examine the documentation for the software you are considering
* Arrange for a demonstration of the software
* Prepare yourself before the demonstration
* Put the programme through its paces
* Evaluate the quality of support you can expect from the dealer or vendor.

CRITERIA FOR SELECTION: STUDY NO. 1

Glossbrener has given the following twelve sure-fire rules for selecting software.

* *Rule* 1: Do not take anything for granted: There is more hidden in the advertisements than it is revealed.
* *Rule 2:* You are not the stupid one: Don't ever let yourself feel foolish when looking at, reading about, using, or otherwise dealing with a computer programme. If its creators haven't lived up to their responsibility, it is their fault, not yours.
* *Rule* 3: How many and how long?: How many author names can you put in that file? How long can each name

be? Nothing brings a program's limitations to the surface faster than these questions.

* *Rule* 4: Forget about the sizzle and focus on the steak: Ask, what the programme can to do and how well it can do it? The advertisement may say, "This programme contains all the standard word processing features". Note, there are no widely agreed 'standard' features of any programme. In short, concentrate on performance and forget the decoration
* *Rule 5:* Whenever possible, make an effort to visualise yourself using the programme: Visualise, how much work will be involved putting all of your books, records, or magazines into database management files? Will you be able to enter each new book record? The more accurately you visualise the steps involved in accomplishing a task.the more you know about how a given programme will deal with those steps.
* *Rule* 6: Read at least two reviews of any programme before you buy.
* *Rule* 7: Get a demonstration on the identical computer, configured exactly as the one you will be using.
* *Rule* 8: Life will be easier if you stick with proven products offered by major hardware and software firms.
* *Rule* 9: Buy only the four 'building block': programmes to start with. It is easy to master a programme faster and comprehensively, if you concentrate on just one at a time. The four building block programmes are communications, word processing, electronic spreadsheet and personal filing or database management.
* *Rule 10:* Don't drive yourself crazy trying to get something to work. Ask.
* *Rule 11*: Nothing is impossible. But the game may not be worth the candle. Computers and software are so versatile that you can accomplish just about anything you want. But these will not save the time, effort and money.
* *Rule 12:* Whenever you can-WAIT! Make sure the rapidly changing software market place works for you.

CRITERIA FOR SELECTION: STUDY NP.2

There is another monumental work discussing various criteria to evaluate and select library automation software, particularly for the housekeeping operations. The eight volume series publication entitled Library Systems Evaluation Guide, is brought out by Jera.

Since, it was published in 1983, the Guide may be a little outdated. However, the principle evaluation criteria discussed are still valid. The coverage in eight volumes of the Guide is indicated in the table.

Table. 12.1. Indication of Coverage in Library Systems Evaluation Guide.

Vol. No.	Title	No. of Pages	No. of Reference
1.	Serial Control	194	60
2.	Circulation Control	261	97
3.	Public Service	267	117
4.	Acquisitions	252	96
5.	Management Services	234	88
6.	Interlibrary loan	248	98
7.	Cataloguing	261	168
8.	System integration	278	198
	Total	**1995**	**922***

Note: * No effort is made to identify the unique references. The total number of references includes a number of multiple citations.

The Guide presents basic information on the requirements and techniques of evaluation of automated library applications in a concise and easily usable format. The Guide considers 'evaluation' as 'relative in nature'. Therefore, to determine the ability of various systems to meet a library's requirements, the systems must be compared with each other or to some reference model. The latter approach to evaluation is both easier and more objective, provided a reference model is available. The Guide provides such a reference model, which could suitably be adjusted to represent the requirements of a given library and then this model may be used to evaluate one or more number of library automation software packages.

The Guide suggests an eight-phase evaluation methodology.

* *Phase 1:* Setting objectives.
* *Phase 2:* Fine tuning of components of the methodology to agree with objectives.
* *Phase* 3: Selection of candidate systems for evaluation.
* *Phase* 4: Examination of accompanying system literature and documentation.
* *Phase* 5: Comparison of candidate systems with the functions and features table, and with the checklist of data elements.
* *Phase* 6: On-site evaluation of candidate systems.
* *Phase* 7: System selection and acquisition.
* *Phase* 8: Post installation evaluation.

CRITERIA FOR SELECTION: STUDY NO.3

Rowley emphasises the need to identify systems requirements before the selection of either software or hardware. The functional requirements are important. Therefore in the evaluation of any package for a given application, priority must be given to establish whether the software is capable of performing the tasks for which it is to be acquired.

General Criteria

* *Other's experiences*: Useful in indicating the potential and problems of a software package; some users may offer help and advice in implementing the package.
* *Cost*: Comparisons of prices of packages be made. What is included in the price of the package and what is excluded should be understood. Cost of hardware and database creation are additional costs.
* *Originator*: The originator's reputation, and experience in developing software is helpful. An established software house is more likely to be able to offer continuing support.
* *Supplier*: Sometimes the supplier is the same as the originator, if the supplier is a separate agency acting as an intermediary between the user and the originator, it may hinder direct communication between the user and the originator.

Technical Criteria

In addition to the general criteria of the selection, the following technical criteria should be considered, both when selecting between packages and also in assessing whether any specific package is suitable for a given purpose.

* *Language*: The programming language in which the software is written. Whether a compiler or interpreter is available on the given system to run it efficiently in terms of machine time and storage requirements.
* *Operating System*: The package must be suitable for running under the operating system on the hardware being used. Whether it is a single user or multi-user operating system that will function on a network.
* *Hardware*: Compatibility with software, its various versions and also ability to run other necessary or useful software on the computer system.
* *Ease-in-use*: The quality of the operator - machine interface, menus, commands, screen displays, documentation, etc. will enhance ease in use of the software.
* *Supplied format*: Software must be supplied on disks, tapes, etc., that can be run on the system and when required transferred to another medium such as hard disk.

Support Criteria

It is an important criteria for using the software and to fully exploit the various features of the software.

* *Documentation*: It includes both printed documentation and online help facility. The documentation should cover introductory exploration of the basic features, a full account of all features, a list of commands, an online help system, additional tutorial support, choice to interface at different levels depending on user's experience, etc.
* *Advice to setting up*: Assistance in installing and implementing the package must be provided. This may cover creation of databases, input formats, report formats, initialisation, etc.

* Training in the use of software package.
* *Maintenance*: This may include removing any bugs or errors that might become evident in the software as it is used for a greater variety of applications and improving the software so that it incorporates new facilities and concepts (*e.g.*, mouse, windows, popup menus).
* *User groups*: Many of the larger and well-established software packages (*e.g.*, CDS/ISIS, LIBSYS) have user groups or user clubs. These groups share expertise and experience in application of the software, discuss problems and limitations in using the software and present a concerted front to the software supplier for solving problems and asking for improvements.

CRITERIA FOR SELECTION: STUDY NO.4

Grosch discusses some procurement and evaluation factors together market trends that may affect the future of library systems. The major system evaluation and selection according to Grosch is the availability of the capabilities and product enhancements of the application software at the time of its installation. The other criteria include examining hardware platform options, operating system requirements, directions of the system developers towards open systems, conversion support, training, ongoing software support, record of old and new versions of the software, ease-of-use, etc. The advice is: 'Setting realistic goals that are attainable in your selection of a system, biting off only what can now afford but providing a goal enhancement base for future years, will result in an easier systems transition'.

CONCLUSION

Electronic spread-sheets crunch numbers. Word processing programmes crunch words. Library automation and information storage and retrieval programmes crunch information. They help to deal effectively with information explosion. The purpose is important. If the selected software cannot retrieve right information at right time in right format for the right user, the sophistication and decor of the package is worthless. The categories of software explained before help in fixing the appropriate category of the software for the purpose of library automation.

Based on what one has in terms of physical environment (computer) and social environment (users, staff) and what one can afford, suitable software has to be selected. There are many options and a large variety of software packages. It is suggested to acquire a commercially available software package. These are developed for use by a variety of customers. A great amount of skill and effort is put in their development. They are expected to be reliable, easy to use, well documented and they are available for a wide range of applications. Even then the selection of suitable software is difficult because of their availability in large number, over choice, tall claims, varied cost, technicalities involved, etc. It is necessary to know the various criteria that could be applied in selecting the suitable software. The four selected studies, by Glossbrenner, Library Systems Evaluation Guide, Rowley and Grosch provide a variety of selection criteria. This wider perspective of such criteria with be helpful and provide better pitch and outfield to play the serious game of selecting the suitable player-that is, the required software package.

13

E-Resources, E-Services and the Human Factors

INTRODUCTION

The growth in online learning or e-learning, in which education is delivered and supported through computer networks such as the Internet, has posed new challenges for library services. E-learners and traditional learners now have access to a universe of digital information through the information superhighway. New information and communications technologies, as well as new educational models, require librarians to re-evaluate the way they develop, manage and deliver resources and services.

Historically, librarians have sought to provide services to distance learners that are equivalent to those available to on-campus learners, and this aspiration is grounded in the philosophical frameworks of the Canadian Library Association's *Guidelines for Library Support of Distance and Distributed Learning in Canada* and the Association of College and Research Libraries' *Guidelines for Distance Learning Library Services*. Both the Canadian and the American Guidelines recognise that distance learners frequently do not have direct access to the full range of library services and materials, and that in this situation, the goal of equity makes it necessary that librarians services that are more "personalised" than might be expected on campus. The library literature provides a rich record of service models and best practices, and there has been an explosion in publication as librarians consider ways to support learners in a networked environment. What do e-learners need from librarians? Suggestions advocating change in librarians' roles in support of distance learning in the information age appear throughout the literature: librarians "must assert themselves as key players in the learning process thereby changing their roles from information providers to educators"; they have become providers of technical support; and they have been transformed from "information gatekeepers" to "information gateways".

Researchers advocates librarian involvement in learning communities: "The librarian can shift the focus from explaining library resources to meeting the ongoing information needs of the students in the broad information environment". In responding to the need to provide ongoing online library support, librarians have worked at translating what they do in a traditional library into virtual or digital environments, while customising their services and resources for e-learners. Traditionally, libraries offer circulation services, interlibrary loans, course reserves, an information desk, a reference desk, and library instruction.

To serve learners connected to their institutional library primarily through a computer network, librarians are providing remote access to, and electronic delivery of, library resources, and are using communication technologies to deliver electronic reference services and instructional support. When we speak of providing support to e-learners, we are referring to a wider community of learners than the term "student" suggests. An academic library's learners may include students, faculty, staff, researchers, and so on.

The library is seen as a source of training and guidance to a community of learners who are concerned with navigating the complexities of locating and using digital resources and services. Moreover, the move towards an online environment has resulted in a shift from the systematic oneto- one information flow of the past to a new model in which the users and the providers of information are able to relate in a many-to-many, dynamic relationship. For example, in the traditional model, a librarian provides a bridge between learners and information providers by selecting and cataloguing resources and by providing assistance with these resources.

In the new model, the library serves as a facilitator by offering ongoing support enabling learners to interact and exchange knowledge with others, to communicate directly with the publishers and vendors of information resources, and to participate in a collaborative endeavor to make available rich collections of online scholarly information resources.

This chapter examines how libraries are responding to the challenges of delivering core services to e-learners. We look at library practices and technologies being applied in the construction of virtual libraries. We also consider challenges and opportunities virtual libraries bring to the support of e-learners, as well as the importance of providing support within a collaborative environment, which stresses human factors, such as communication and interaction.

DEFINING THE VIRTUAL LIBRARY

Gapen defines the virtual library as:

* The concept of remote access to the contents and services of libraries and other information resources, combining an on-site collection of current and heavily used materials in both print and electronic form, with an electronic network which provides access to, and delivery from, external worldwide library and commercial information and knowledge sources.

Additional terms for the virtual library include the "digital library", the "electronic library", and the "library without walls". Many libraries are hybrids, providing virtual access to electronic resources and services, while maintaining and supporting use of a physical collection housed in a library building.

With the tremendous growth of the Internet, e-learners have access to an overwhelming range of information sources available at the click of a mouse: library resources; government information; news sites; advertising; even whole Web sites devoted to Elvis sightings, crop circles, and JFK conspiracy theories. Librarians have traditionally selected and organised resources with great care. In building virtual libraries, librarians have the opportunity to provide e-learners with direction and to rescue them from information overload. A virtual library can link e-learners to library catalogues, licensed journal databases, electronic book collections, selected Internet resources, electronic course reserves, and tutorials, and to forums for communication and interaction with librarians. The virtual library permits e-learners to access library and networked resources and services anytime and anywhere that an Internet connection and computing equipment are available.

THE LANDSCAPE OF LIBRARY RESOURCES

Technology offers opportunities to be innovative, as the following discussion of electronic resources and services demonstrates, but it is important to bear in mind that not all e-learners are equal when it comes to access to computing equipment; the availability, speed, and stability of Internet connections; or the information skills that are needed to make optimum use of virtual libraries. Access to print-based library materials continues to be important, because not all of the information resources that elearners need are available in electronic format: many of our most valuable research materials are still print-based.

The Digital Library Federation and the Council on Library and Information Resources commissioned a survey of the use of print and electronic scholarly information resources at institutions of higher education across the United States. The survey found that, although almost half of undergraduates report using electronic resources all or most of the time for their coursework, this was the case for only 35.2% of graduate students. Only 34.7% of faculty indicated that they use electronic resources all or most of the time for their research, and just 22.7% said this of their teaching. Although there has been a shift away from purchasing print materials to be housed in a physical building and towards providing access to licensed digital resources made available over a computer network, librarians continue to work to resolve issues pertaining to distance delivery of resources that are unavailable in digital format.

Online catalogues and indexing and abstracting systems provide elearners with convenient access to bibliographic information about valuable scholarly documents. When those documents are not available in full-text form online, a demand is generated for delivery from a library's print collection or from the collections of other libraries through interlibrary loans.Typical solutions for delivery of non-digital formats include the use of mail and courier services, the establishment of collections at designated sites, and the negotiation of agreements with other libraries through consortia. Given that a growing number of learners are accessing library collections online, librarians are working to develop an integrated approach to providing access to electronic resources that facilitates retrieval and reduces confusion.

A library Web site can function as an information gateway, an entry point to a range of online resources, with key components being the library catalogue and journal databases. Most online catalogues permit the integration of electronic books and electronic journals, enabling learners to locate items from digital and physical collections with one search. User services—such as the ability to check due dates, renew materials, and request materials online—are also provided. Gateways may also organise collections and incorporate directories like that provided by Athabasca University's Journal Databases: List Databases by Subject page. Librarians have become increasingly creative in enhancing their Web sites. Because not all e-learners have physical access to reference tools—the quick fact-finding tools that are the staple of library collections—libraries can perform a valuable service by providing pointers to online versions. Athabasca University Library's Digital Reference Centre, for example, offers a digital version of an academic library's reference collection, including almanacs and directories, atlases and maps, data and statistics, and dictionaries and encyclopaedias. Librarians select quality Internet resources to help e-learners navigate the Web. For example, the British Open University Library's ROUTES database contains quality-assessed, courserelated Internet resources "selected by course teams and the Library's

Information Specialists". As libraries work to enhance their presence on the Web, a growing number are investigating the potential of electronic course reserves. The traditional course reserves desk of an academic library, with its limited copies, short loan periods, and high late fines, can be a considerable source of frustration for students.

In the e-reserves model, the library makes available, through the World Wide Web, items that faculty have selected and "placed on reserve" for students in a particular course. San Diego State University (SDSU) pioneered e-reserves in the early 1990s. SDSU uses Docutek's ERes, a system that provides access to course readings, chat rooms, and bulletin boards. Many other libraries have initiated their own projects. Electronic delivery of course reserve material has become a hot topic in the library literature.

The Association of Research Libraries (ARL) maintains the Electronic Reserves Listserv, and an archive of the discussion can be accessed on the Web. Most e-reserves operate on a password-protected model: one must be affiliated with the institution, or even registered in the course, to view course reserves. A typical e-reserve solution is to employ an electronic course reserve module that permits full integration with the library's online catalogue.

Content in ereserves databases varies. Scanning and mounting readings in portable document format (PDF) is time-consuming and requires copyright clearance. Other options for content include incorporating institution-produced materials (*e.g.*, lecture notes and video or audio clips), using licensed digital resources through direct linking to items by means of a persistent URL, and including selected resources freely available through the World Wide Web. Librarians can take a creative, pro-active approach to e-reserves. Athabasca University Library has developed a platform for ereserves that operates on a somewhat different model than do other e-reserves systems. The Digital Reading Room offers a digital solution for course readings and supplementary materials.

An in-house storage and retrieval system was developed for the DRR using open source software. The model operates along the principle of open access to collection creation tools, thus permitting course content creators, educational media developers, and librarians to develop a multidisciplinary knowledge database.

Each course in the Digital Reading Room has a Digital Reading File (DRF). The licensed contents, such as journal database articles, require authentication through the Library's proxy server, permitting only the Athabasca University community of users to access them; non-licensed resources, such as Web sites, are freely available to the public. A search engine permits e-learners to search across the DRFs, providing a multidisciplinary aspect to course reserves that is not typically encountered.

By encouraging the inclusion of resources in a variety of formats, including text, graphics, video, audio, simulations, and games, the DRR supports a wide range of learning objectives and styles. The DRR accommodates the inclusion of non-digital resources by providing e-learners with a means to request them from the Library.

The DRR is being developed using metatags that conform to the IEEE LOM standards and use the CanCore implementation guidelines to insure consistency and search capability across database collections such as MERLOT. Managing the remote access and authentication issues involved in making digital resources available has become a significant area of support to users of the electronic library.

Librarians may be called upon to respond to questions concerning log-in and password information, browser configuration, software installation, and a range of troubleshooting needs. Access problems are hugely frustrating for e-learners, and must be resolved quickly. Ensuring that front-line library staff are adequately trained, providing clear instructions on the library's Web site, and coordinating support activities with computing services personnel can contribute to effective technical support.

E-learners also benefit from having a variety of means of contacting the library, including e-mail, Web forms, and a toll-free telephone number.

LIBRARY SERVICES: CHALLENGES AND OPPORTUNITIES

REFERENCE

E-learners require more than access to e-resources. Traditionally, a reference librarian acts as an additional type of resource, one who can be counted upon to provide expertise in making sense of library systems and research tools, and to offer a helping hand along that often slippery path known as the research process. Virtual library users face additional challenges in mining relevant information out of a computer system that "obstinately" returns zero hits in response to a query that does not match the character strings in its database files. The most common means of providing electronic reference services to remote users has been e-mail, the advantages and disadvantages of which have been well documented in the literature.

The around-the-clock and around-the-world accessibility of e-mail allows users to connect with librarians beyond the walls of library buildings and outside the usual hours of operation. E-mail provides a written record of requests and responses, permits the electronic transmission of search results, and allows librarians time to reflect on requests. One of the most serious concerns about e-mail reference services is their impact on the traditional face-to-face reference interview, particularly the absence of the verbal and non-verbal cues that typically assist a librarian in effectively responding to a question. Hulshof identifies three issues related to the use of electronic communication in serving virtual patrons: immediacy, intricacy, and interaction. Because it is so easy for a learner to send a request electronically and have it arrive at the library instantly, there is a perception that the librarian's response will be as immediate.

The learner may become frustrated, not realising that the process of locating information and developing a response takes the librarian just as long when the request is made electronically as when it is made in person or in any other way. The more intricate or complex the request, the longer it will take for the librarian to clarify it and respond appropriately: a series of e-mail messages may be required, which will further reduce the immediacy of the e-mail request.

Immediacy and intricacy relate to the lack of interaction: the opportunity to discuss and clarify enquiries that occurs in person or over the telephone is not so easily accommodated by e-mail. There are ways to deal with some of these issues. A welldesigned reference Web form, such as that provided on the Ask AU Library: Ask about a Research Topic Web page, which encourages elearners to include full identifying and course information, to describe clearly their research problem and search terminology, and to state the parameters of the assignment, can clarify requests for librarians and reduce the need to e-mail back and forth.

Automated replies, which are sent out by the e-mail programme in response to the receipt of a message, can be used to reassure e-learners that their messages are being received, and can let them know what to expect in terms of service. E-mail reference service can be enhanced and supplemented with additional technologies that raise the level of interaction with realtime or live communication.Chat technology allows e-learners and librarians to send text messages back and forth instantly, using a form of communication that is familiar to most Internet users. There have been a number of library experiments with Web contact center software, which is modeled on the private sector's online solution to providing customer support. Web contact center software provides a higher level of interaction than does basic chat software, allowing for queuing and routing of messages, as well as enabling librarians to "push" Web pages to users. Providing e-learners with a toll-free telephone number remains an effective and convenient reference services strategy, particularly for intricate enquiries. The telephone reference interview works best when both librarian and e-learner are working in front of computers connected to the Internet.

INSTRUCTION

E-learners are frequently silent and invisible as they search and explore a library's online resources, and they do not have the same access that on-campus learners have to formal library instruction sessions. With the array of digital resources available to them, the multiplicity of interfaces and search tools, and the need for evaluation and critical thinking when using the Internet for research, "information literacy" skills are a must-have for e-learners. Information literacy refers to competencies with information sources in a variety of formats. According to the Association of College and Research Libraries, an information literate individual is able to:

* Determine the extent of information needed
* Access the needed information effectively and efficiently
* Evaluate information and its sources critically
* Incorporate selected information into one's knowledge base
* Use information effectively to accomplish a specific purpose
* Understand the economic, legal, and social issues surrounding the use of information, and access and use information ethically and legally

Supporting the integration of information literacy skills training into the core curriculum has become an important issue for libraries. As an extension of their traditional role of providing library instruction sessions and developing instructional materials, librarians are designing online tutorials and courses that promote information literacy and encourage active learning.

Particularly fine examples are the University of Texas System Digital Library's *TILT—Texas Information Literacy Tutorial;* and Utah Academic Library Consortium's *Internet Navigator,* a multi-institutional online course developed by a team of librarians and Web developers. The British Open University Library has developed *SAFARI,* a freely available interactive tutorial, as well as an information literacy course called *MOSAIC (Making Sense of Information in the Connected Age).*

Many libraries provide instruction to e-learners by making information available on their Web pages, including frequently asked questions, library glossaries, research guides, and "how-to" pages. Athabasca University Library's Digital Reference Centre integrates resources with contextual instruction and provides links to instructional resources, including a detailed guide to Internet searching that encourages e-learners to think critically about Internet resources, and library research guides such as the *AU Library Guide to Researching Topics in Women's Studies*. Online tutorials usually operate on a model in which the e-learner interacts in isolation with a computer.

Their effectiveness can be enhanced by the addition of more interactive forms of instruction. The librarians at the Florida Distance Learning Reference and Referral Center, for example, have experimented with chat software to simulate a virtual classroom and open up "live" group instruction to e-learners. Librarians can also work with faculty to develop a library thread in a course discussion area, or to open a discussion forum on the library Web pages.

THE SUCCESSFUL VIRTUAL LIBRARY: PARTNERSHIP AND COLLABORATION

In reviewing definitions of the virtual library, Sloan identifies an emphasis on the technological and informational building blocks, and a neglect of human components, such as the service tradition and human interaction. The continuing changes in technology have been truly astonishing, and the scope for building new information services and new ways of representing content seem unlimited. However, it is very important to remember that investment in human capital is also a strategic investment, especially when introducing new technologies, procedures, and processes. Although technology is the key infrastructure of the virtual library—a tool used to support library goals—human factors are the most important determinants of the success of the virtual library.

The digital library serves mainly as a facilitator in organising and providing knowledge and resources to its users. Sharing knowledge and information among library staff, researchers, faculty, students, and other departments within the institution encourages them to work together, develop their skills, and form strong and trusting relationships. A focus on collaboration between the library and the faculty promotes a responsive approach to course design and supports teaching and learning objectives, particularly when this collaboration incorporates student contributions and feedback. All parties must have a common vision in which each one participates actively by contributing their skills and perspectives to the building of a genuine partnership.

This new approach considers the library as an active partner of the learning community, helping learners to become "information literates" by integrating information literacy skills into the curriculum. For example, the library can help learners to evaluate critically the authority and authenticity of the resources they find, and to enhance their critical thinking skills. The library can also offer support to learners, and can mentor their work by offering one-to-one communication and interaction, and by achieving a deeper level of understanding of what learners need. From a research perspective, a number of models can be involved in creating an environment that is responsive to the scholarly information needs of a diverse group of e-learners.

Librarians locate, select and describe quality Internet resources, and provide access to journal databases and electronic book collections, providing e-learners with full-text content from a wide range of online resources and publications, including peer-reviewed journals. Within this framework, the library works with faculty, researchers, scholarly societies, and publishers in developing and managing a collection of enriched online scholarly resources. Such a partnership enables researchers to interact with others, exchange experiences, and publish their works online.

The library role is thus transformed from simply being a provider of library resources, into meeting the ongoing support needs of the parties involved. The library also serves to foster research skills by encouraging students and other learners to search, investigate, discover, and take advantage of these valuable online resources.

Management support is as much a key to success in developing the virtual library as in any other project. Athabasca University's strategic plan incorporates a distinct section related to library strategies and projects, and explains how these strategies are aligned with the overall mission of the University.

A virtual library should have a high profile leader, a key person who can work to obtain the support of the institution's management and promote a climate of change. In addition, the leader must work with different groups within the institution to ensure that the project responds to their specific needs and goals. For example, when Athabasca University Library initiated the Digital Reading Room project as an enhanced electronic course reserves system, the Library entered into partnership with the Educational Media Development unit to ensure a best practices approach to Web- and visual-design aspects. Consultation with faculty has been an ongoing element of the project, with faculty selecting content and acting as consultants in evaluating the design and functionality of the DRR in relation to their course development and delivery needs.

All staff involved in providing library support to e-learners must be included in the partnership. Technological changes have been the dominant force reshaping library services. Instilling a culture of sharing, motivation, equity, and active partnering encourages library staff to respond positively to the changing roles, responsibilities, and skills that the integration and use of technology requires. A well-designed, ongoing training programme enables library staff to upgrade their skills to their new assignments, and helps them to understand and control fear of change. External partnerships, collaborative efforts, and consortia form another important bridge to the effective support of e-learners.

Within Canada, university libraries extend in-person borrowing privileges to students, faculty, and staff from across the country through the Canadian University Reciprocal Borrowing Agreement. There are also initiatives to share virtual reference desks, such as the National Library of Canada's Virtual Reference Canada, which allow learners to benefit from the range of information resources and staff expertise available at a variety of participating institutions. Consortial approaches to database subscriptions enable libraries to expand the scope of the electronic resources they are able to offer their learners in a time of shrinking budgets and escalating journal costs. The Canadian National Site Licensing Project negotiates licensing agreements that permit participating universities across Canada to access a suite of research databases in the science, engineering, health and environmental disciplines.

CONCLUSION

In summary, library services are an essential component of a quality online learning system. As access to Internet-based courses grows, an increasing number of e-learners are dispersed around the globe, often in parts of the world where physical access to the collections of large academic and research libraries is impossible. These learners are largely dependent on the quality and academic usefulness of services that the library can offer electronically. The strength of virtual libraries and digital collections depends on the relationships libraries develop and maintain with the creators, publishers, and aggregators of e-resources, as well as with those who use, learn from, and evaluate these resources. Providing ongoing technical, reference, and instructional support to elearners requires that libraries redefine their values and services, collaborate with their users, and approach their tasks creatively.

14

Supporting the Online Learner

INTRODUCTION

The ability and potential of online learning to enhance access to education, particularly higher education, is largely determined by the potential learner's circumstances, which in many ways define the learning environment. Not surprisingly, online learning's evolutionary predecessor, distance learning, has been applied to two situations in which access to education is problematic. The first occurs when a very large population has access to a limited number of "seats" in conventional educational institutions. This situation gives rise to what Daniel refers to as "megauniversities"— distance teaching universities with 100,000 students or more.

Indira Gandhi National Open University (IGNOU), with an estimated 500,000 students, is one example, and the Open University of Hong Kong (OUHK), with over 400,000 students, is another. The second situation is one of sparse population— one in which the community of learners is spread over a wide geographical area. The fledgling University of the Arctic is an example of a response to this situation. In both of these cases, the learner's physical environment presented a need that online learning could address. A third situation is emerging. Learners who wish to use technology to structure their learning environment are seeking out the means by which they can do so. In a sense, their preferred learning environment presents the access issue that online learning can address. In all three situations, the challenge is to provide access to higher learning, determining what the learner brings to the environment, and what they need in terms of support. These factors can vary—after all, the first two situations are artifacts of geography, whereas the third has more to do with personal learning preference.

That is why designing learner supports requires an understanding of the learners' circumstances. This chapter discusses the importance of setting up a supportive learning environment for online learners, and provides some practical advice. Underlying this advice is a philosophy that encourages an environment that aims to develop the learner's independence, while ensuring that supports are readily available when needed. Student supports that are flexible, clear, and continuously available are described, and best practices outlined.

KNOWING THE LEARNER

It is a good idea to remind ourselves that the learning enterprise is not about us as educators: the focus should be placed on the learning, not the teaching. Similarly, in providing learner supports, we should focus on what the learner needs, not on what we want to or are able to supply, but it is surprising how easily this emphasis can be lost in our wish to help. We identify real needs best if we know our learners. Therefore, we must ask questions about the learner's readiness for online learning, access to and familiarity with the technology required, proficiency in the language of instruction, individual learning style, and educational goals, as well as about how aspects of the individual's culture can affect learning.

These are some of the things that we need to understand about the learners; they are also things that the learners need to know about themselves in order to benefit from the learning experience. Once the institution has this information, it must determine what supports are most critical for learners, and must establish priorities to ensure that resources, which are always limited, are directed to the most useful supports. In doing so, the institution must keep in mind that some learners will require more support than others, and that any learner may need more help at one point in their educational career than at others. So the institution must find a balance between "just-in-case resources" and "just-in-time resources" that recognises that an online learner is often an adult with responsibilities other than their educational goals.

Flexible, continuously available, easily accessible learner support systems are required, but such systems must be genuinely useful. Learners have been clear that they need to see the value added by a resource, or they will not use it; they have also let us know that supports should be available but not intrusive.

LEARNER READINESS FOR ONLINE LEARNING

The learner brings a set of skills, experiences, and expectations to the learning environment. This section outlines the resources necessary, first, to assist potential online learners to make informed decisions about their readiness for this form of learning experience, and then, to provide advice for making specific programme decisions.

To encourage independence in the learner, the focus should be on self-assessment, although counseling backup should be available when needed. The list below presents a series of questions that learners who are thinking about post-secondary study online should ask themselves, and identifies the kinds of assessment tools that are available to answer them.

* Am I ready for university?—This type of online resource provides the opportunity for the prospective learner to determine their readiness from academic, financial, family support, and time perspectives. Such a self-assessment, which is Web-based and easily completed by the student, serves to highlight areas that might need special attention. It guides the learner through a series of questions in which they examine their own expectations and readiness. Once the assessment is complete, follow-up e-mail counseling complements the process.

* Am I ready for studies in the English language (or other language of instruction)?—This type of online resource assists the learner to decide if their command of the language is sufficient to allow for success, and places the learner in specific language course levels. The learner may be directed to online remedial resources, and should always have the option of contacting an advisor.
* Am I ready for online learning? This type of online resource assists potential learners to determine if they have the necessary hardware and networking capabilities, and should help them to explore whether this learning environment is comfortable. Short sample experiences should be available to assist with the process.
* What is my preferred learning style?—As does any form of learning, online learning makes demands on the learner. The institution can make many resources available in a variety of formats, to suit different learning styles and preferences. However, a learner may not have identified the format they find most useful, and it can be helpful if the institution assists the learner to examine their own learning style. Interactive tools are available on the Web to help the learner to do so; however, these tools vary in quality, and the institution can assist by providing an annotated evaluation of these resources.
* Am I ready for university-level mathematics?—Proficiency in mathematics, as well as in language of instruction, has proven to be a significant success factor, particularly for adult learners returning to the educational environment after some time away. However, mathematics can also be a significant stressor. Assisting the prospective learner to identify their strengths and weaknesses in mathematics, and making remediation available, can reduce this stress. An online self-assessment can be designed to help the learner to determine their readiness for particular mathematics courses, to recommend a mathematics course

appropriate to the learner's level, and to identify remediation resources.

* Do I have the skills to be successful in my chosen programme?— This type of online resource outlines what skills are needed for particular areas of study. The resource should be programspecific and should refer the student to online tutorials if needed.

MATCHING EDUCATIONAL PROGRAMMES TO CAREER INTERESTS

Often, potential learners will seek out online learning opportunities to create or enhance career goals. As educators, we may want to view the educational experience outside the context of career development, the learning experience is not about us. The fact is that learners bring that context to their educational decisions, and we need to understand that they do so. Online resources designed to assist learners to determine their own interests and skills, and then provide a career map aligned with educational programmes, is a reasonable expectation. After all, most of these learners will experience several career changes—some of them quite significant—throughout their working lives.

The United Kingdom's Open University focuses on the learner's need to contemplate the future in making educational choices. "Mapping Your Future" on the Athabasca University Services to Students Web site provides the learner with a means of exploring career clusters and the credentials required to pursue them. After an initial exploration, the learner may wish to communicate online with a counselor to refine their career goals. Once this is achieved, electronic "programme plans" are designed by an advisor, taking the career goals as well as prior learning into account. It is important to have the learner explore first, and then have counselors provide assistance as needed.

SUPPORTING THE LEARNER

Well-designed course materials and strong academic and tutorial support are necessary in all educational enterprises, and the special considerations in the case of online learning are the subject of a separate chapter. This chapter deals with non-academic supports for the learner. Having assisted the potential learner to make an informed decision to pursue online learning, we have enhanced their chances for success, but quite different support is now required. Once again, the balance between being available and being intrusive is important. Learners require support in different areas, and as providers, we must anticipate the array of needs, and then work with individual learners to clarify what is needed at a given time. Learners need to know exactly what they can expect in support, how to interact with the institution, what is expected of them, and how to determine when they need assistance.

EXPECTATIONS

Learners need to know both what is expected of them, and what services they can expect to receive from the institution. Online learning may be a new experience for the learner, and it is important that service standards be clear and easily available: How long should it take to receive confirmation of my registration? How much time does it take to receive my examination grade? How quickly should I expect a response to e-mail? Who should I contact for library assistance? These standards should be published for all students to see, and can serve as benchmarks for service units within the institution.

INFORMATION AND ADMINISTRATIVE SUPPORT

Daniel points out that a key component of supported open learning is "effective administration and logistics." Institutions engaged in distance and online education know that smooth administrative processes can be as much a factor in learner success as the design of learning resources.

The learners themselves report that flexibility of access and smooth administrative support are important to the learning environment. One would expect that learners who have chosen an online learning environment prefer to perform administrative functions (such as registration) online as well, and this is proving to be the case. Institutions that provide online learning report that students express a preference for having the control that online administrative processes afford. Providing online administrative access is not without challenges, and improved technology, carefully designed Web pages and helpdesk support are crucial. Constant monitoring and updating of procedures is required, to find smoother interactions and to tease out administrative frustrations. Designing Web pages and then forgetting them is simply not acceptable.

The following list outlines a process for the continuous improvement required:

* Design the administrative Web page;
* Test the technology and revise as necessary;
* Observe the learners using the Web page and ask for feedback, then revise;
* Monitor the use of the Web page regularly;
* Look for enhancements and improvements, and incorporate them; and
* Always have helpdesk attendants available to troubleshoot.

At the institutional level, regular learner satisfaction surveys can ensure that administrative interactions are not barriers to learning. Portals designed to individualise and personalise interactions enhance the learner's experience. Portal software is growing in popularity as more institutions become involved in online learning.

TECHNOLOGICAL SUPPORT

The learner must know what technology is needed for the online environment, before they decide to register. A person engaged in online learning requires technological support that is clear and readily available. Drawing the line between technological support on the one hand and academic support on the other is often a challenge, and these types of support must be coordinated carefully. There are three common support formats: an information center provides institutional and programme information; computing helpdesks troubleshoot technological issues; and call centers are frequently used to support a particular programme area. All three must work together to support the whole learning process.

Successful information centers, helpdesks, and call centers have the following characteristics:

* Reliable networks;
* Asynchronous access "24/7";
* Synchronous access at clearly identified times;
* Quick response, with acknowledgment and follow-up;
* Follow-through to resolution of the issue;
* Simple, clear instructions;
* Access by attendants to all critical databases and expertise; and
* The ability to identify problems with policies, procedures, or systems, and to suggest change.

STUDY SKILLS ASSISTANCE

The online learner may be returning to learning after some time away, may be new to post-secondary study itself, or may not have experienced online learning before. Assisting the learner to identify particular needs in the area of study skills can reduce stress and enhance the experience. For example, it is critical to understand that "life happens" and the learning experience may be just one of the demands that the learner faces. This is particularly true for adult learners. Some resources that may help online learners who was facing challenges to their study skills include

* Web pages designed to assist in the development of time management and study schedules;
* Resources to help students learn to balance educational pursuits with other life demands;
* Tools for facilitating "study buddy" connections for peer assistance;
* Online strategies and exercises to reduce "exam anxiety";
* Resources to assist in reading for comprehension;
* Assistance in annotating online resources such as e-books;
* Resources to assist in writing papers;
* Clarification of rules for citation and avoiding plagiarism;
* Assistance in searching library resources on line; and

* Assistance in making critical analyses of information from online resources.

ONLINE EDUCATIONAL COUNSELING

Well-prepared Web resources can be provided online, but asynchronous counseling assistance is required as well, particularly for learners who are experiencing difficulty. The online environment is one in which learners can "fall through the cracks" if assistance is not readily available. From time to time a learner may need someone to assist in keeping a positive outlook and determining if an intervention is needed. Learners need to know that help is there if they need it. The institution should provide this resource and all institutional staff should be trained to identify when a learner might benefit from a session with a counselor. It is important to remember, however, that while referrals can be made, the decision to pursue them belongs to the learner. The work of the counselor in an online learning environment has three aspects. The first is to work with Web designers to develop online resources to help learners to identify and address barriers to reaching their educational goals. The second is to interact with the learners when an intervention is required. The third is to work with other institutional staff to ensure that processes and procedures enhance learning. Educational and career counseling are well suited to the online environment, but personal counseling is less so. Personal counseling should be limited to immediate crisis resolution and referral. Counseling units need information about community resources to which they can refer clients.

ONGOING PROGRAMME ADVISING

Distance and online learners are often adults and they frequently spread their learning over a number of years. They report that they need programme planning that will help them achieve educational goals in an expeditious manner. Moreover, learners often transfer between institutions and jurisdictions, increasingly so in a global learning environment. Learners need to plan their coursework based on particular programmes, while remaining aware of course transferability. The role of advisors is to assist learners to understand programme requirements, match courses they may be transferring into a programme, and then plan the remainder of their programme accordingly. Since, the adult learner may change career and educational goals at any time during the process of completing a programme, advisors need to be readily available and to have access to all programme and transfer information. Software products are available to allow advisor and learner to navigate this process. Academics, counselors, and others within the institution need to know when to refer learners to an advisor.

THE DIGITAL LIBRARY

In the early years of distance education, providing library support to learners was a challenge. Courses were developed in print format, and comprehensive course packages were sent to each learner. The library typically developed a collection that was made available, by mail or fax, to the learner on request. Distance educators worried that learners were not gaining the library search experience that would enhance their studies and their research skills.

Online sources of information have transformed libraries in distance education: where in the past libraries focused on holdings, they can now focus on access; where they used to be information repositories, they can now be gateways to information. This transformation has allowed the library experience to be more profound for the learner and more integrated within the learning process.

From a learner support perspective, a welldesigned online library

* Is easily found among other institutional Web pages;
* Provides an up-front tutorial for the new learner;
* Is integrated with the institution's online courses;
* Provides tools to assist with online searches; and
* Provides access to personal assistance, if needed.

The transformation of libraries in distance education has posed some interesting fiscal issues for institutions. In the past, acquisitions budgets provided for purchasing holdings that became part of the collection, part of the assets of the institution.

Annual funding was provided for collection development and updating. Even subscriptions to periodicals, an annual expense, resulted in a "holding." Subscriptions to online resources are another matter entirely. As libraries move towards becoming gateways rather than repositories, a new way of viewing funding is needed.

ACCESS FOR STUDENTS WITH DISABILITIES

Online learning can enhance access for people with disabilities. New assistive technologies can allow access to learning opportunities previously denied to this population. Increasingly, the legal requirements to provide accommodations that allow access are being defined by the courts, and institutions are required to ensure that necessary accommodations are provided, without compromising academic rigour. In an online environment, the following services are expected:

* Administrative accommodation with respect to timed assignments and examinations;
* Alternative formats for learning materials;
* Advocacy within the institution;
* Advice about assistive technologies;
* Advice about funding sources;
* Referral for specific needs; and
* "Reasonable accommodation" as outlined in law.

STUDENT RIGHTS AND ACCESS TO OMBUDS SERVICES

Online learners have as much need of clearly articulated rights as do learners in traditional educational settings. An advocacy process designed for online learners is one in which the learner is made aware of student rights and responsibilities. An institution can fulfill its basic legal responsibility by making a student code of conduct available on the Web and in print on request. However, a prudent institution will go well beyond this demonstration of due diligence. Web sites that clearly outline intellectual honesty expectations should be readily available on the Web and should be referred to frequently. Reminders just prior to assignment preparation reduce the chance that the learner will fail to provide proper scholarly acknowledgment.

Traditions regarding what constitutes intellectual property and what is generally accepted common knowledge are not universal concepts, nor are they always understood. Cultural views about ownership of knowledge vary, and if the rules that are to apply within the institution are to be understood, then the institution must ensure that they are properly explained. For example, although many educators do not accept the idea, the reality is that students do not always understand the concept of plagiarism, much less how to avoid it.

To address this problem, the University of Puget Sound has designed an excellent Web page that provides learners with exercises to enhance their understanding of the concept of plagiarism and to assist them in avoiding it. All efforts to provide smooth interactions between the learner and the institution notwithstanding, there will be situations in which the learner becomes ensnared and does not know where to turn. A highly visible ombuds office should be available. Moreover, from the institutional perspective, the ombuds office can assist in identifying policy and procedure problems that require attention within the institution.

THE ONLINE LEARNER'S ROLE IN GOVERNANCE

Online learners have valuable contributions to make to an educational institution. Institutions that specialise in distance and online learning can provide opportunities for students to participate in institutional governance. Student government is possible in such an institution as well, but administration must make special arrangements to facilitate the process. In many ways, the student union has the same issues in keeping in touch with its constituency as does the institution itself. Both are vying for the attention of a learner who may be juggling learning with other life demands. It is in the institution's best interests to have a healthy student union and to work with that union to meet the needs of the learners.

Some means by which to achieve these goals include

* Making networks available to the student union;
* Providing one main institutional contact with whom student union representatives can interact;

* Assisting in collecting student union fees;
* Making information available, within the confidentiality guidelines;
* Having student representatives on all decision-making bodies;
* Having decision-making bodies meet through electronic means (video-conference, online conference, etc.) to maximize participation;
* Keeping the student representatives and the student union apprised of significant events, initiatives, etc. (*e.g.*, strategic planning, budgeting, tuition fee increases);
* Engaging in shared initiatives with the student union (include them in convocation, copublish newsletters, etc.);
* Seeking advice from the student union on important issues; and
* Demonstrating appreciation for the work of the student union.

LEARNER SATISFACTION MONITORING AND ENVIRONMENTAL SCANNING

Regular monitoring of the learners' satisfaction levels and scanning of the student services environment assist the institution to make continuous improvements. Year-over-year comparisons are possible if the survey instruments are carefully designed. In this way, trends and areas in need of attention will become apparent. Focus groups are being successfully conducted online by institutions that are at a distance from their constituents. Such groups can be used, for example, to test out the efficacy of a new course, programme, or service.

UNIVERSITY OF THE ARCTIC—STRETCHING THE LIMITS

University of the Arctic is a virtual university in the real sense of the word. It is a consortium of universities and colleges from the northern countries known as the "Arctic Eight" (Canada, Finland, Greenland, Iceland, Norway, Russia, Sweden, and the United States). It was formed because there was a sense that these northern countries represented a community that transcended national boundaries by virtue of their "circumpolarity." There was also a sense that the northerly parts of these nations shared cultural, environmental, and learning issues with one another that the more southerly parts did not necessarily experience. The founding principles were based on notions of development "in the north, by the north, for the north." This university would develop an issues-based curriculum culminating in a Bachelor of Circumpolar Studies. At the time of writing, five courses have been developed.

The first, *Introduction to the Circumpolar World,* has been pilot tested in classroom format in one location, and as a Web-based offering involving learners from institutions from four of the Arctic Eight countries. The Web-based offering stretched the limits of online learning, and serves as an example of the potential of online learning to acknowledge a community of learning based, not simply on geography, but on shared realities.

SOME EARLY DECISIONS

Language of instruction was one of the first decisions taken. It was decided to develop the courses in English and translate them at a later date. Subject matter experts from Russia, Greenland, Finland, Canada, Norway, and the United States wrote the curriculum in English, and the material was edited into fourteen modules. Another early decision was that the online delivery would take place within a portal environment that would foster a community of learning.

WebCT was used for delivery, largely because this platform was well recognised throughout the circumpolar world. The portal was designed to provide a supportive learning environment, and at the same time, an uncomplicated technical environment. The realities of the variability of technical resources across the Arctic became apparent, and the motto became "as inclusive as we must be, striving to become as innovative as we can be." It was important that no group be excluded from the project. Reliability of networks was seen to be important, as was the need for a "Plan B." The course was housed on the server of the institution that was thought to have the most reliable server arrangement. In addition, learners were provided with print materials should any technological mishaps occur. The pilot of the introductory course began in mid-February 2002, and lasted for fourteen weeks. Learners from Russia, Greenland, Finland, and Canada all worked with their local university or college. There was a site coordinator at each location, and the instructor was located in Canada.

THE COMMUNITY OF LEARNING

Largely because of the instructor's skill, but also because the learners shared so many issues, a community of learning soon developed. Asynchronous discussions formed the basis for exchange, with informal study groups (often conducted in the local language) arranged by on-site coordinators. Because of the time zone issues, chat rooms were not initially designed into the portal, but the students asked that this utility be added. This was done, and a few hardy souls spent the wee hours of the morning communicating with colleagues across the North Pole. Learners shared resources via the Web, and each institution was expected to provide library and other student support resources.

LESSONS LEARNED

The decision to keep the technology simple was a wise one. The simple portal and WebCT worked quite well, but a more comprehensive orientation to WebCT and online learning will be designed for the next offering. The best approach to the orientation is to have a training session with the site coordinators first, and have them, in turn, conduct an orientation with the learners.

This strategy allows first-language assistance with the technology. Because of the variation in institutional resources, subsequent online offerings will include computing helpdesk access, which will be provided by the institution that is most experienced in online delivery of services. Although it was expected that the up-front preparation by the curriculum developers, Web designers, and the instructor would be substantial, the workload for the instructor was excessive. This was partly because the volume of the learner postings was larger than expected. In addition, more of the learner activities could have been built into the course materials themselves.

A surprising outcome was the extent to which learners for whom English was not the first language felt quite comfortable participating. The concern that the sessions would be dominated by learners for whom English was a first language, was not borne out. The participating institutions had ensured that the learners had a sufficient command of the English language before registering them. Attempts to incorporate traditional knowledge into the course materials were a challenge because of the large number of Aboriginal groups around the circumpolar world. In the end, this issue was best addressed by having students share information with colleagues.

The result was somewhat serendipitous, but this strategy may be preferable to something more structured. Attempts to ensure that all of the students had broad access to online library resources across all institutions were not successful, largely because of the language issue. It may be that in cases where such geographically and linguistically diverse groups are brought together, the provision of learner support in areas such as library, counseling, and so forth are best left to the "home" institution. This suggestion assumes that learners will inevitably be tied to an institutional setting. More investigation is required as these kinds of initiatives develop.

CONCLUSION

As the learning environment becomes a global community of learning, the cognitive sciences are merging with computing and telecommunications technologies to form what distance educators refer to as "knowledge media". The Organisation of Economic Cooperation and Development (OECD) recognises that these trends can provide more equitable access to higher education, and hence, more social equity, as campus-bound and distance-education paradigms merge and complement each other. There is an ongoing discussion about new terminology that should replace "distance education," but at the same time be more inclusive than "online education." Terms such as "distributed learning," "technology mediated learning," and "telematics" are often used in North America. Elsewhere, other terms are being used, such as "resource based learning" and "flexible learning". This discussion exemplifies the role that technology can play in placing the focus on making resources available for the individual learner. Whatever we call it, however, online learning only enhances a focus on the learner as an individual within a community of learning if individual differences are acknowledged and addressed in the design of learner support services.

15

The Quality Dilemma in Online Education

INTRODUCTION

With the proliferation of online learning providers and the challenges presented by the distance education sector to state regulators and accrediting bodies, it is not surprising that "buyer beware" is the watchword for students, institutions, and public agencies alike. In the current environment, it is incumbent on organisations to demonstrate the quality of their services in ways that are intelligible to potential students and their employers, faculty and staff, regulators, and government agencies.

The admirable attempts to define quality standards and best practices for online education have done little to assuage the skepticism of representatives in the academy, who are more accustomed to face-to-face delivery directed to bounded communities. Fully addressing the roots of such skepticism is beyond the scope of this paper; however, its presence informs much of the technical discussion around quality assurance frameworks in higher education in general, and in online delivery in particular.

Purveyors of online learning programmes maybe inclined to attribute a lack of broad acceptance among their colleagues to the paradigm shift that higher education has been undergoing in the past 15 years. In many cases, however, it must be admitted that potential of electronic delivery modes has not been fully realised in the execution of online courses. Some have suggested that these shortcomings are the result of trying to replicate the classroom environment, instead of maximising the new configurations of knowing and community formation possible in an interactive online environment. Moreover, finding appropriate comparators for the efficacy of any particular mode of delivery is difficult when the broader questions of quality assurance in higher education are far from settled. An examination of definitional issues points to a long-standing conflict in values between business modeling and public services. It is important to acknowledge these tensions fully before turning to the more technical, but admittedly value laden, exercise of reviewing the standards proposed by different quality assurance agencies.

After a discussion of the contexts of quality assurance activities in higher education in general, and of the competing paradigms highlighted by online learning, this chapter examines quality standards that have been proposed for the delivery of online instruction in four jurisdictions. The full range of state licensing, voluntary accreditation, and market driven seals of approval reveals tensions between externally driven compliance and internally driven improvements.

Although the regulatory frameworks for quality assurance vary dramatically in Australia, the United Kingdom, Canada, and the United States, there is still enough common ground to establish some general characteristics for a scholarly approach to online teaching and learning. At a basic level, the characteristics of quality educational delivery demonstrated in these frameworks include

* Providing clear statements of educational goals;
* Sustaining the institutional commitment to support learners;

Engaging in a collaborative process of discovery, which ontributes to

proving the teaching and learning environment. her area of commonality is the fact that, while self- v can be a key component for any of the rks, to a large degree they are being driven by emands.

One area of contention, the degree to which quality assurance activities can or should be targeted to outcomes as opposed to internal processes, is addressed in a separate section. On a wider level, each of the projects seeking to establish quality standards for online education appears to aim towards inculcating a set of values that prizes management by measurement. Recognising that the terms "quality" and "online education" are so burdened with assumptions as to create their own problematic is a necessary prelude to what follows.

DEFINITIONAL ISSUES

The greatest challenge for trying to define quality in any product or service is that quality remains a relative experience, realised in large part through an individual's level of expectation. Since, quality necessarily rests in the eye of the beholder, at first glance, systems developed around the concept must necessarily be exercises in systematic subjectivity. In higher education, quality is a construct relative to the unique perspectives and interpretations of different stakeholder groups (students, alumni, faculty, administrators, parents, oversight boards, employers, state legislatures, local governing bodies, accrediting associations, transfer institutions, and the general public).

It follows, therefore, that the effectiveness of any quality improvement activities will be as much a function of the ability to foster agreement around common goals as of any substantive input or process adjustments attempted by an institution. Fostering agreement, however, is much more difficult when the term "quality" is burdened with the legacy of failed management fads.

In many circles, the term "quality" is understood as shorthand for Total Quality Management (TQM), or its close cousin, Continuous Quality Improvement (CQI). Some may believe that these fads peaked and retreated in the last century; however, recent modeling, and examples of the pursuit, by individual institutions, of the Malcolm Baldridge Awards or ISO9000 recognition in distance education suggest that TQM still has a foothold in higher education, in spite of the problems posed by the fact that its language carries a corporate flavour. The International Standards Organisation makes the central principle of the pursuit of quality clear—to establish processes that will maximize service to customers.

The pressure to apply management techniques to higher education came from a perceived crisis in confidence with post-secondary systems, and from the growth of state-sponsored accountability systems. For supporters it "has long been understood in organisations that when you want to improve something, you first must measure it". But measurement systems are about much more than the technical specifications of various indicators—they are about control.

The first iteration of TQM/CGI provoked a debate about its social as well as technical implications, and demonstrated the "disconnect between the philosophy of the management process and the purposes of the institution[s] for which it was being proposed". The engineering (or re-engineering) of systems designed to guarantee that manufacturing processes would meet technical specification might seem to imply a uniformity that may not be possible, or even desirable, in the dynamic and heterogeneous environment of higher education.

The annual race past the post in national press or government scorings, while clearly suspect, still draws a surprising amount of attention from audiences within the academy and government. This is a bitter pill for academics, who are accustomed to casting their institution's function as being nothing less than to maintain the foundations of the civil state. From that perspective, the vision of customer satisfaction is a pale substitute for contributions to knowledge and community formation. It also suggests an ideological congruence with the reduction of "citisens" to "taxpayers," and as the focus moves to "value added" activities, the terrain of the debate is being narrowed to shorter and shorter transactional terms. To many within the academy, the "learner as consumer/information as commodity" world presupposed by the business model of higher education remains antithetical to independent scholarship in pursuit of the advancement of knowledge. If these observations hold true, then it is fair to ask why one would engage in a discussion of quality in relation to any form of education. Why not just stand on the self-evident virtues of the "sacred spaces" of the classroom, library, and laboratory? The answer to that question resides in how contested meanings can be both signals of power relations and tools of resistance.

Traditionally, universities achieved quality in intellectual endeavors through the professionalism of academics, the principles of scholarship, and the rigors of peer review; and they gained standing in society by communicating those standards to political and social elites. More recently, massification, diversity, and cuts to funding, along with a wider political movement to demonstrate efficiency and responsiveness, have spawned different conceptions of accountability. The attempt to lift the meaning of quality education to something beyond short-term fiscal efficiencies and taxpayer benefits is a matter of trying to regain some of the ground lost in previous decades.

It is also an encounter with what has been represented as a paradigm shift in higher education that has been highlighted by the advent of online education. It must also be admitted at the outset that, with the shift to wireless technologies, "online" education may well appear to be an outmoded shorthand for computer or Web-enabled activities. The term has appeal, however, since, it carries the sense of a linked community of learners. It still resonates of bounded communities with the possibilities of transformative experiences, rather than the sporadic or strictly utilitarian viewing of information on screens.This feature distinguishes online teaching and learning systems from Web-based publishing. It also presumes a qualitative difference from the convergence of distance and face-to-face delivery techniques being experienced on many campuses. With the proliferation of easily accessed Web tools, mounting a course's syllabus on its own home page, directing students to relevant electronic journals or Web-sites, and accepting assignment submissions by e-mail are no longer enough to allow one to lay claim to providing a distinct online teaching and learning environment. Textbook publishers are adapting, providing an increasing range of electronically delivered content systems and customised companion Web sites to supplant traditional student guides. When these resources are coupled with course management systems, the online environment begins to take shape.

Until students and instructors engage, however, it is still just a shell. It has been suggested that online learning is best conceptualised as "an environment that integrates collaboration, communication, and engaging content with specific group and independent learning activities and tasks". More particularly, the ability of students to engage in "asynchronous interactive learning activities" has been described as the "signature characteristic of this technology".

The importance of the flexibility inherent in asynchronous activities challenges the assumption that emulating the classroom constitutes best practice in online teaching and learning environments. However, the degree to which technology has driven, or simply enabled, the paradigm shift in higher education, is debatable. Whether their adherents have overstated the changes that have taken place as a result of Web-enabled learning technologies is another question worthy of consideration.

PARADIGM SHIFT

Although there had been many examples of applications of computer technology in classrooms for at least a decade before 1995, Michael Dolence and Donald Norris have been credited with issuing a "wake up call" for higher education administrators. In *Transforming Higher Education,* they purported to offer ways for colleges and universities to survive the transition from the Industrial Age to the Age of Information. Even though their vision for the future has not be realised on a wide scale, it is clear that many of the conceptual juxtapositions they offered have gained currency in higher education.

These juxtapositions include a shift from episodic access, to clusters of instructional resources, to integrated perpetual learning, with a separation of teaching and certification of mastery, and a reconceptualised role for faculty— from deliverers of content to mentors and facilitators of learning. The most pervasive of these changes is the shift from a "provider focus" to a "learner focus," with its attendent mass customisation through individualised learning systems. More recent elaborations on this theme have indicated that the capabilities of the Internet have overturned "the traditional roles of the college or university as the leading

* Research source and knowledge creator,
* Archivist and gateway to knowledge,
* Disseminator of advanced knowledge, and
* Referee and evaluator of truth".

If the production and dissemination of knowledge are no longer the restricted purview of higher education, the roles of postsecondary institutions in the worldwide network are increasingly vulnerable. The need to be more open and to promote capacities to analyse, interrelate and communicate about facts gleaned from network-based knowledge will become essential for students and faculty alike. The traditional quality measures associated with accreditation or state administered quality assurance frameworks do not match this new climate of teaching and learning.One of the most common measures, and a unit of analysis for costing, is "seattime," which does not translate to an online environment. Yet Lawrence N. Gold, higher-education director for the American Federation of Teachers, claims that the amount of time a student spends in class is still an important measure of quality.

Even when adapted to an online environment, other common measures rely on inputs (averages of entering students, number of students, qualifications of instructors, systems development) or outputs (numbers completing courses; satisfaction ratings by students and alumni; revenue generated from tuition, intellectual property, or commercial partnerships), but lack in measures to address the fundamental integrity of the online learning environment.

Wallace Pond summarised some of the old and new paradigms for accreditation and quality assurance as follows. According to Pond the old paradigm measures could be characterised by the following words and phrases: teacherinstitution centred, centralised, hegemonistic, "one-size-fits-all," closed, "us versus them," quantitative, prescriptive, time as constant with learning as variable, teacher credentials, consolidated experience, regional/national, static, single delivery mode, process, infrastructure. In contrast, the new paradigm measures can be seen as learner centred, local, deferential, tailored, open, collaborative, qualitative, flexible, learning as constant/time as variable, teacher skills, aggregated experience, international/global, dynamic, distributed delivery model, outcomes, services.

They do not address some of the other questions generated by the entry into online course delivery. The first questions must relate to the degree to which online learning environments have delivered or can deliver on their promises. The greater access afford through Web-based delivery systems has been one of the key advantages cited by observers of the technological transformation in higher education.

Whether depicted as an advantage in developing greater economies of scale for delivery systems or in ameliorating social inequalities, broader access has been lauded as a key feature of the new paradigm. However, electronic learning systems are not always as billed. From the perspective of Thomas Booth, president of the Canadian Association of University Teachers (CAUT), the access argument carries very little weight, because people who have less education to begin with are less likely to have access to the tools and services they would need to study online. He also suggests that "Students traditionally excluded from post-secondary education are the most dependent on face-to-face interaction and least able to deal with the frustration and isolation of Web-based distance education".

Another caution rests in the comparative completion rates between online and classroom delivery. If intended economic and social transformations are to be realised, access must be examined at more than just the point of entry. The promise that economies of scale will make education more affordable is perhaps even less persuasive to most academics. That "proprietary institutions are likely to enter the market by contracting with the best professors to provide video-based courses with exclusive rights to their distribution and use" was a vision of higher education in the 1990s. It is painfully obvious that the proponents of such models have missed the significance of interactive technologies. Providing more efficient delivery of "lectures by famous faculty" would recreate in cyberspace the "world of the passive listener and single speaker that has marked much of what passes for higher education". Making the doubtful system of mass lectures more efficient does not appear to be much of an advancement over the correspondence school's traditional coursein- a-box.

Another tension emanates from the fact that the bulk of what is delivered in the online environment consists of discrete training modules directed to particular job skills or competencies. While there seems to be slippage between what is being articulated in the realm of learning outcomes (the skills we expect graduates to demonstrate) and expectations around the values associated with the liberal arts, it is fair to say that higher education aims should be broader than the goals of the corporate training sector.

Critics such as David Noble have presented almost apocalyptic views on the incursion of educational technologies into the classroom. The Web's "dark side" has been depicted as the "rapidly growing trend of university corporatism" and the exploitation of knowledge workers. Challenges from the for-profit sector, the influence of corporate training agendas, and "the 'rush to serve' different clienteles" have been described as jeopardising the position of the post-secondary sector as the "source of objective analysis of the society in which it exists".Acting as the conscience of civil society speaks to a much broader purpose than meeting the immediate training needs of corporations. If this ideal is taken seriously, then one should expect that faculty would lead the debate from a perspective broader than their own protectionist instincts. An alternative vision of democratic ideals in the digital age would have education enabling "people to learn about, with, and beyond technology" to open the "doors of economic, educational, and personal empowerment". The reconceptualisation of higher education should be done by the academy. Establishing the terms through which online education should be assessed should not be left to the marketplace or to self-perpetuating bureaucracies. Taking back some of the momentum will be a challenge, however, since, attempts to establish standards and best practices are well under way.

STANDARDS FROM FOUR JURISDICTIONS

The formulation of quality assurance systems for online education, while most frequently regulated at a regional or national level, has in recent years been driven by international developments. The global reach of the Internet and the lack of ways to regulate transnational commercial activities allow fraudulent operators to spring up. One response has been the promotion of consumer education by sites such as AboutEducation; another possibility is free-lance course reviews from former students, similar to the book reviews found on the sites of online booksellers such as Amazon.com. Not surprisingly, the appetite for allowing the marketplace to determine the outcomes in a wide-open, for-profit model is not large. Simply stated, it does not seem either ethical or efficient to leave students to bear the full risks for the product testing of online education ventures.Alternative responses have involved trying to develop quality assurance and accreditation systems, or regionally harmonised systems, such as those proposed under the Bologna Declaration. Responses from national and local quality assurance interests have varied. Some of the differences rest in the degree to which state- sponsored quality auditing procedures have become entrenched in the past decade; others reflect the suspicions or traditions associated with distance education in general.

Australia has a national instrument, in the form of its Qualifications Framework, for protecting the quality of its educational and training programmes. Even the use of the term "university" is restricted by State or Territorial legislation, and universities must demonstrate that they have appropriate quality assurance procedures in place. Within this framework, "universities are expected to engage in a pro-active, rigorous and ongoing process of planning and self-assessment which will enable them to ensure the quality outcomes expected by their students and the wider community". The Australian government policy framework has been presented as a marketing tool to address the advantages that global competitors enjoy by having "centralised, separate, and highly visible" bodies responsible for quality assurance.

The rationale for the development of the national system was explicitly framed in terms of competitive challenges, domestic and international, and of policies that have encouraged the universities to "align themselves more closely with industry needs". Under the revised regime, creditable quality assurance systems providing evidence of the quality of service and skills of graduates were explicitly intended to make the universities more attractive to business investors.

The systems include national qualification schemes that communicate expected standards for each level of post-secondary achievement. Quality assurance for online offerings by Australian universities are within the self-accrediting models that include peer assessment processes. Registered training organisations (RTOs) have also been affected by quality audits, and draft guidelines have been developed for auditing online learning. The standards include statements on organisational commitment, learner support systems, learning designs, learning outcomes and assessments, and technology plans. Other features relate to managing risks by arranging for the stability of Web sites, and to cross-jurisdictional regulations.

A key principle in this framework is that online delivery standards are incorporated within comprehensive criteria, and do not operate as stand-alone schemas. A general institutional standard can easily encompass online learning; for example, having written policies and procedures to ensure that educational offerings and assessment processes are consistent with the scope of the institution. The full ramifications of these elements for post-secondary institutions will depend on how the audit processes and guidelines are implemented in Australia over the next three years. The examples of quality assurance frameworks from the United Kingdom are all centered around open and distance learning, with e-learning issues being acknowledged variables within a spectrum of delivery mechanisms.

Three different external approaches to assessing the offerings by individual institutions include licensing procedures under the auspices of a government agency, a voluntary accreditation association, and a scheme for certification through quality marks. Again, much of the drive to enhance quality assurance schemes has been presented in the context of potential regional and global competition. Each of these examples also demonstrates ongoing tensions between external regulatory approaches and internal aspirations for improvement. It has been suggested that the Quality Assurance Framework in the United Kingdom is not just comprehensive, it is "the most complex anywhere in the world". The Quality Assurance Agency for Higher Education (QAA) was incorporated in 1997, with the aim of reducing some of the reporting burdens created by a combination of external assessments by funding agencies, and quality assurance processes driven by peer review. Its mission is to "promote public confidence that the quality of provision and standards of awards in higher education are being safeguarded and enhanced".

The QAA has developed codes of practice for ten areas: postgraduate research programmes; collaborative provision; students with disabilities; external examining; assessment of students; programme approval, monitoring and review; career education, information and guidance; placement learning; recruitment; and admissions. Further regulation has developed in the form of benchmark information for different subject areas, linked to the national frameworks for higher education qualifications.

These are the explicit learning outcomes meant to communicate to the public and to potential employers the attainments to be expected from programme graduates. The main thrust of the QAA guidelines for distance learning is integration between distance delivery and the general quality standards for teaching and learning activities expressed in the other codes of practice. While not addressing online education directly, the six sections of the guidelines (system design, programme design, programme delivery, student development and support, student communication and representation, and student assessment), include examples of questions that address electronic delivery systems.

The guidelines are notable in that, whereas the codes of practice for higher education apply equally in distance education, the guidelines are intended to deal with aspects of quality assurance that are "likely to require attention in a particular way" when study is undertaken at a distance. The elaborate state licensing approach has been depicted as excessive and a sign of the erosion of the autonomy of higher education. To some, these measures have demonstrated the drive to "harness the universities to perceived economic priorities". In that light, it is interesting that the criteria of the state licensing agency have largely subsumed standards that had been developed for a peer review model of accreditation. The QAA distance learning guidelines reference the work of the voluntary association in the United Kingdom's distance education sector, citing the Open and Distance Learning Quality Council standards.

These accreditation standards, revised in 2000, are organised into the following discrete operational areas:

* Course objectives and outcomes (providing clear statements of what will be achieved on successful completion; having objectives that are compatible with the method of delivery);
* Course contents (providing sufficient content to enable the target group of learners to meet the course objectives);
* Publicity and recruitment (providing accurate materials and direct communication to give potential learners the best basis for deciding to take the course);
* Admission procedures (communicating the terms of the course, including its scope and the requirements needed to realise the intended outcomes, and providing applicants with enough information to assess their own needs and level of preparation);
* Learning support (monitoring student progress, providing appropriate supports, including supplementary material, and facilitating peer group interactions);
* Open learning centers (identifying groups of users and ensuring that sufficient resources are available to serve them);

* Learner welfare (maintaining accurate records, providing appropriate guidance, demonstrating learner satisfaction and appropriate completion rates);
* Providers (having appropriate plans and resources to meet their mission, adopting good business and employment practice, adhering to relevant legal requirements, ensuring that staff have appropriate qualifications, monitoring performance);
* Joint provision (specifying respective rights and responsibilities, including procedures to meet standards); and
* Accreditation (having procedures for application, limitation, and review).

The operational recommendations around learning support resonate with the models developed by the Open University, and technical supports appear almost incidental in the entire scheme. This model demonstrates an integrated understanding of the practice of distance learning, in contrast with the market model for applying quality marks, which draws on more generic business process analyses.

The British Association for Open Learning (BAOL) is an external marketing agency that applies self-assessment and external review processes. Of all the frameworks summarised here, it is the one most explicitly tied to TQM precepts.

Using the Business Excellence Model developed by the European Foundation for Quality Management, BAOL has developed five "enabler" criteria that cover how an organisation is managed: leadership, people, policy and strategy, partnerships and resources, and processes. BAOL had also developed four "results" criteria: people, customer, society, and key performance results.

Together, these nine generic aspects of an organisation "contribute to and enable" the achievement of quality. BAOL has developed quality marks to cover materials development, advice and guidance, learner support, and learning centers. It is claimed that earning these quality marks provides a market advantage for e-learning providers, especially as they face the prospects of competing internationally.

BAOL targets a broader range of education providers than does the university sector, and so its criteria have points in common with the suggestions for the registered training organisations in Australia. The existence of BAOL is an explicit acknowledgement that the market sector can be a powerful external influence on attempts to inculcate internal quality assurance values.

With such an array of quality assurance prospects, it is noteworthy that, in their study of "borderless education," the higher education agencies in the United Kingdom have acknowledged that public accountability arrangements and elements of the credentialing or qualification schemes have been challenged by developments in for-profit, virtual, and corporate providers in the domestic and international higher education market. They have proposed that the quality frameworks addressing these developments would include

* Currency and security of qualifications; audit of the system for design and approval of curricula or appropriate learning contracts; an internationally recognised system of educational credit; licensing of staff; security of assessment; adequate and accurate public information about learning opportunities; approved guidance and complaints systems for learners; transparent quality management processes for each agent in the educational supply chain; access to learning resources assured by the provider; and publication of guidance relevant to different modes of provision.

It has also been suggested that the thinking on quality assurance will have to shift dramatically, from external "compliance-based approaches" towards "comparative benchmarking" and mutual recognition arrangements for international quality standards. Attempts to integrate an array of international standards have been made in other jurisdictions. In Canada, the responsibility for education rests at the provincial, not the national, level. Each province has its own quality assurance framework or approach to determining whether post-secondary programmes are eligible for student funding or to receive public money. The degree to which a province might regulate or even provide subsidies to private or for-profit educational institutions varies widely. It is fitting, then, that the Canadian example of quality guidelines originates with a private corporation sponsored by community and government-funded agencies. The *Canadian Recommended e-Learning Guidelines* bill themselves as "consumer-oriented, consensus-based, comprehensive, futuristic, distinctively Canadian, adaptable, and flexible." The last feature admits that "not all guidelines will apply to all circumstances".

This qualification is only realistic, as the list is exhaustive. The 138 items are organised into three distinct sections: "Quality Outcomes from e-Learning Products and Services" includes 15 items related to how students acquire content skills, knowledge, and learning skills; "Quality Processes and Practices" includes 20 items on the management of students, and the delivery and management of learning, using appropriate technologies; and "Quality Inputs and Resources" includes the remaining 103 items, which range through intended learning outcomes, curriculum content, teaching and learning materials, product and service information, learning technologies, technical design, personnel, learning resources, comprehensive courses packages, routine evaluation, programme plans and budgets, and advertising, recruitment, and admissions information. A more succinct adaptation issued under the same initiative was the *Consumer's Guide to e-Learning,* which structured 34 questions into basic, discerning, and detailed levels. The instructions to consumers provided with the *Consumer's Guide* are more telling.

Before you sign up of an e-learning course or programme ask yourself:

* What is my purpose for taking this course? Do I know what I want or need to learn?
* Do I need a credit or certificate when I finish or do I just want to know more?
* How much can I afford to spend? How much time can I invest?
* What hardware and software do I have, and is it enough?

* Where will I access the Internet, what will it cost, and how convenient will it be?
* Are my computer and Internet skills good enough for the course I have in mind? Will I need technical help?

Institutions intending to adapt their offerings to the online teaching and learning environment would be well advised to rephrase these questions along the following lines:

* What is our purpose for offering this course?
* Do we know what we expect students to learn?
* Do we have the technological infrastructure to support our students? Is it up-to-date?
* How skilled are our course developers and instructors in the online environment?
* What technical assistance do we have available?

Such questions are at the heart of the two models proposed in the United States. In an analysis of the impact of electronically delivered distance education, undertaken for the American Council of Education, Judith Eaton suggested that the emergence of electronically delivered degrees, programmes, courses, and services, has the potential to undo the delicate balance between "accreditation to assure quality in higher education, the self-regulation of higher education institutions, and the availability of federal money to colleges and universities".

Although higher education institutions are subject to state funding and regulatory bodies, and although the systems of accountability may vary from state to state, the federal government relies on accredited status to signal that institutions and programmes are of sufficient quality to allow the release of federal funds in the forms of student grants and loans, research grants, and other federal programme funds. Under traditional approaches to accreditation, the focus was on the verification of site-based resources contributing to a learning environment. To address some of the concerns raised by electronic delivery, the eight regional accrediting commissions in the United States developed the *Statement of Commitment for the Evaluation of Electronically Offered Degree and Certificate Programmes,* which declares the resolve of the commissions to sustain the following values:

* That education is best experienced within a community of learning where competent professionals are actively and cooperatively involved with creating, providing, and improving the instructional programme;
* That learning is dynamic and interactive, regardless of the setting in which it occurs;
* That instructional programmes leading to degrees having integrity are organised around substantive and coherent curricula which define expected learning outcomes;
* That institutions accept the obligation to address student needs related to, and to provide the resources necessary for, their academic success;
* That institutions are responsible for the education provided in their name;
* That institutions undertake the assessment and improvement of their quality, giving particular emphasis to student learning;
* That institutions voluntarily subject themselves to peer review.

The regional commissions also committed themselves to a common statement titled *Best Practices for Electronically Offered Degree and Certificate Programmes,* developed by the Western Cooperative for Educational Telecommunications (WCET). The statement was organised into five discrete sections:

* Institutional context and commitment;
* Curriculum and instruction;
* Faculty support;
* Student support;
* Evaluation and assessment.

Taken together, the *Statement of Commitment* and the *Best Practices* propose a consistent framework for developing quality standards. How those standards might translate into benchmarks was the subject of as study prepared by the Institute of Higher Education Policy. In Quality on the Line, Phipps and Merisotis surveyed the literature to compile a list of 45 possible benchmarks. They then determined whether those benchmarks were recognised at various institutions delivering online courses, and examined the importance of each benchmark to administrators, staff, faculty, and students at those institutions. The result was a list of 24 benchmarks that should be considered "essential to ensure the quality in Internetbased distance education". The elements include institutional support, course development, teaching and learning, course structure, student support, faculty support, and evaluation and assessment benchmarks.

The similarities between these benchmarks and the proposals from the accrediting agencies clearly demonstrate a common conceptualisation of distance education in the United States. Where they diverge is in the degree to which the actual curriculum elements are prescribed, and in the relative weights given to institutional structures. It is also apparent that both sets of standards are designed more for traditional face-to-face institutions introducing distance education programmes than for distance education providers updating their mode of delivery. The provider focus remains a strong orientation under both U.S., schemes, and unlike the accreditation standard for open and distance learning in the United Kingdom, neither U.S., scheme speaks to the importance of encouraging learners to take responsibility for their own learning.

PROCESS VERSUS OUTCOMES

One of the first principles in all of the quality assurance schemes considered here is guaranteeing consistency in the product's results. In the view of TQM advocates "many quality management initiatives, especially in service industries, die because we fail in measurement of the outcomes". The dangers of presenting higher education outcomes as strictly utilitarian competencies are familiar features in the debate about quality assurance activities. However, even if outcomes could be framed in wider terms, there is also a hazard of sliding into what has been aptly described as a variation on the "naming fallacy"; that is, assuming that "explicitness about standards" somehow provides assurance that the standards have been or can be achieved. Major efforts have been directed to identifying "quality in undergraduate education," but according to Ernest Pascarella, some of these efforts are "based on a naive understanding of just how difficult it is to accomplish in a valid manner".

Most notably, he argues that institutional reputation and resources, and student or alumni outcomes are "potentially quite misleading," and that results based on either of these common approaches are more likely to be driven by inputs than by effective educational practices. The solution to this problem should rest in careful measures that address the integrity of the teaching and learning processes within institutions. The seemingly insatiable appetite for comparable measures, regardless of their validity, is a dimension of the operating environments of most post-secondary institutions. While it is clear that the rhetoric of accountability and the bureaucratic systems it has spawned are not likely to disappear, it may be possible to present a framework for quality online teaching and learning that attends to more than short-term transactional or monetary values.

RESHAPING THE DEBATE

Whether or not the demands of stakeholder groups, the threat of fraud, or the intensification of competition from local or international providers are behind the current impulses for elaborating quality assurance mechanisms, a dual challenge is being presented to the providers of online teaching and learning. The common thread across quality assurance schemes in the four jurisdictions is the need to address the concerns from both inside and outside the academy. Even if online and distance delivery institutions have been made the scapegoats for a wide range of changes, not the least of which being the erosion of the power of institutions of higher education to regulate themselves, there may still be an opportunity to address some of the concerns presented by colleagues in more traditional institutions.

It follows that an overarching principle of any proposal to address quality assurance in online teaching and learning environments must be to recognise the integrity of higher education—no matter how it is delivered. The rhetoric of both the Australian and British qualification frameworks suggests just such an integrated approach, but the regulatory burdens they have spawned do little to reassure those who value the independence of higher education. In the process of taking back some of the momentum in the debate, the academy must provide clear statements of educational goals. Such goals need not be restricted to technical mastery in specific subjects; the opportunity to pursue ideas beyond the needs of corporate sponsors should not be ignored.The measure of the effectiveness of the articulation of the educational goals should be the ways a course, programme, and institution's goals align with one another. The demonstration of a consistency of purpose should be persuasive to internal and external stakeholders alike, but should not presuppose that students are responsible for seeking their own learning outcomes. This suggestion returns to the essential need for quality to be constructed through consensus building among a range of institutional stakeholders, who must, at the same time, not promise, or be promised, more than can be delivered.

A second theme running through all of the frameworks presented here is the need for sustained institutional commitment to support distance learners. The precise nature of that support would be determined by the nature of the programmes and by what students need in order to have a reasonable chance of attaining their aspirations in a given programme. All too often, online delivery of courses and programmes has been presented in an experimental mode, without long-term, planned infrastructure development. Whether it involves investing in technical systems, or in training for support and instructional staff, the process of developing robust online teaching and learning environments should not be attempted as "one-offs." Some observers have gone so far as to suggest that digital technology may hamper rather than promote educational change, because the focus of investment becomes the short lifecycle technologies, rather than the longer view needed for effective education.

An institutional commitment to supporting learners will go a long way to satisfying other stakeholders, without displacing the fundamental project of scholarship. This can only be true, however, if students and educators are engaging in a collaborative process of discovery; that is, if academics are not simply dispensers or interpreters of content for passive students. Learning technologies can promote powerful connections to content, context, and community. Unfortunately, they can also offer broad access to poorly designed and executed courseware.There are deliberate choices to be made in how to accommodate a generation of students who expect independent investigation, collaboration, and peer contacts to be facilitated in an online environment. The threats to traditional delivery, and most especially the disaggregation of tasks associated with teaching in higher education, are providing new opportunities for exploring the constructions of community and knowledge, teaching and learning.

In the generation of documentary evidence of interactions with content and with others, the structure of the online environment lends itself new kinds of exploration. Eventually, the goal of such enquiries should be to point to ways to improve the teaching and learning environment. Ultimately, the online programmes should be able to mobilise recent theory and research into how people learn, and to enhance learning by "enabling the identified characteristics of effective learning environments and ensuring that they are present and accessible" From that perspective, the pursuit of quality online teaching and learning environments may become as much an exercise in scholarship as it has been in market or state control.

Bibliography

Aghatise, E.: *Libraries, Community and Technology,* Maharashtra: Pune Publications, 2004.

Agrawal, A.: *Public Library Service in India,* New Delhi: Long Life Publications, 2003.

Alexander, John M.: *Information: The Last Variable,* Finland: United Nations University, Helsinki, 2003.

Balagopal, K.: *The Library and Information Sector,* Hyderabad: Perspectives Publishers, 1998.

Balkus, R.: *Writing Abstracts for Free-text Searching,* Washington: Social Security Administration, 2009.

Bandyopadhyay, N.: *History and Development of Libraries in India,* Hyderabad: Economic and Political Weekly Press, 2005.

Chamala: *Microcomputer Circulation Control Systems: An Assessment,* Brisbane: Australian Academic Press, 2003.

Chambers, R.: *The New Alexandria: CD-ROM in the Library,* London: Intermediate Technology Publications, 2004.

Chattopadhyay, K.: *Accreditation Instrument,* Kolkata: ICSP Publication, 2006.

Dahlman, C.: *Library Management in India: Strengths and Opportunitie,* London and New York: Longman, 2000.

Dasgupta, A.K.: *Insuring and Protecting Your Library's Collections,* London: Yale University Press, 2008.

Dearden, L.: *Training and Corporate Productivity in a Panel of Indian Libraries*, London: University College London, 2004.

Harris, J. L.: *Training for Change: New Skills for the Electronic Library, New Technology, New Librarians?*, London and New York: Longman, 2005.

Hey, A.: *Issues of Libraries in the Digital Era*, Chicago: University of Chicago Press, 2006.

Hunt, M.: *Electronic Journals: Promises and Challenges in Indian Academic Libraries*, Amritsar: Guru Nanak Dev University, 2006.

John, V.: *Putting Content onto the Internet: The Library's Role as Creator of Electronic Information*, Aisawl: Mizo History Association, 1995.

Kapil: *Library Classification and Browsing*, New Delhi: Sege Publications India, 2001.

Kapoor, Bupesh.: *The Library and the Accreditation Process in Design Disciplines: Best Practices*, India: Cambridge University Press, 2003.

Lee, S.: *Library Acquisitions: Practice and Theory*, Minnesota: Univesity of Minnesota, 2003.

Lewis, D.: *Cataloging Architectural Drawings*, India: Open University Press, 2006.

Mahalingam, T.V.: *Faculty Use of Subject Searching in Card and Online Catalogs*, Madras: University of Madras, 2004.

Marion, J.: *An Online Library Catalog Offering Menu and Keyword User Interfaces*, New Haven: Yall University Press, 2001.

Index

M

O

P

R